Charles Edward Curtis

Estate Management

A practical handbook for landlords, stewards, and pupils. With a legal supplement by a barrister. Also tenant right from a landlord's point of view

Charles Edward Curtis

Estate Management

A practical handbook for landlords, stewards, and pupils. With a legal supplement by a barrister. Also tenant right from a landlord's point of view

ISBN/EAN: 9783337311964

Printed in Europe, USA, Canada, Australia, Japan

Cover: Foto ©Lupo / pixelio.de

More available books at **www.hansebooks.com**

ESTATE MANAGEMENT.

A PRACTICAL HANDBOOK FOR

LANDLORDS, STEWARDS, AND PUPILS.

With a Legal Supplement by a Barrister.

ALSO

TENANT RIGHT

FROM A

LANDLORD'S POINT OF VIEW.

BY

CHARLES E. CURTIS.

LONDON:
"THE FIELD" OFFICE, 346, STRAND, W.C.

1879.

LONDON:
PRINTED BY HORACE COX, 346, STRAND, W.C.

TO

GEORGE ARTHUR JERVOISE SCOTT, Esq.,

OF

ROTHERFIELD PARK, HAMPSHIRE,

THIS WORK IS MOST RESPECTFULLY DEDICATED BY

THE AUTHOR.

PREFACE.

In order to obtain the necessary knowledge for the good conduct of an estate, it is now generally admitted that a thorough and complete course of study must be undertaken. During an experience of several years of the requirements of those engaged in such study, I have found the want of a practical handbook which should place before them an outline of the various branches of estate management. The following pages are an attempt to supply that want.

Whilst endeavouring to treat of every important branch of work connected with the management of an estate in an agricultural district, I have not aimed at exhaustive and elaborate discussion. Such a mode of treatment would have tended to repel, instead of attracting the persons to whom the book is primarily addressed. If I have succeeded in putting before the pupil such an outline of the matters with which he must be acquainted as shall induce him to take a more intelligent interest in his work and to study other treatises upon the different branches of it, my object will have been attained. He who intends to qualify himself for such interesting and responsible work as the care and oversight of landed property must, in these days of keen competition, give up the idea that he need only abandon himself to the pleasures of a country life, and that all needful information will be picked up by the way. An out-of-door life he can, and should have; but it must be a life of practical observation, and of observation directed to its object by such a knowledge of principles as is only to be obtained by a study of books.

But although my principal object has been the one thus indicated, I trust that the work may be found to be of a sufficiently practical character as to make it of some service to the profession generally.

In conclusion, I have to express my thanks to my friend and brother-in-law, Mr. Frederick Green, M.A., of the Chancery Bar, who, during a leisure enforced by ill-health, has kindly prepared for me some chapters upon the law relating to estates and estate agents. I have also to thank my father, William Curtis, of Alton, for the section relating to Geology.

C. E. C.

"*Deanyers*,"
Farringdon, Alton, Hants,
1879.

TABLE OF CONTENTS.

CHAPTER I.
LETTING AND LEASES.

Section 1.
Introductory Remarks.

	Page
Landlords and farmers	1
General duties of land steward in selecting a tenant	2
Fixing the rent	2
Fictitious rents	3
Making terms with the tenant	4

Section 2.
The Form of the Lease.

Example A.: Agricultural lease by deed for a term of years from Michaelmas	5
Leases when a deed is not necessary	14
Example B.: Agricultural lease by memo. of agreement from year to year from Lady-day	14
Agreements to grant or accept leases	21

Section 3.
The Subject Matter of the Lease.

Analysis of contents of lease	22
Name and description of farm	25
Trees and underwood	25
Game	25
Minerals	27
Payment of rent	28
Rates and taxes	28
Tithe rentcharge	30
Repairs	34
Insurance	35

	Page
Cultivation	37
Consumption of hay, straw, &c.	38
Compensation and rights of lessee at expiration of term	39
Lessee's power of re-entry	41

SECTION 4.
Compensation for Unexhausted Improvement.

Agricultural Holdings Act, 1875	42
Erection of buildings	44
Laying down of permanent pasture	45
Making and planting osier beds	46
Planting hops	47
Reclaiming waste land	47
Chalking land	48
Claying land	48
Clay burning	48
Boning land	49
Liming land	51
Consumption of cake and other purchased food	53
Application of artificial manures	54
Advice to land stewards	55

CHAPTER II.
FARM VALUATIONS.
SECTION 1.
Valuation Generally.

Valuation from outgoing to incoming tenant	56
Valuers, their appointment and procedure	57
Valuation of tillages	59
Allowance of rent, rates, and taxes	61
Michaelmas valuations	62
Growing corn	62
Root crops	63
Preparation for wheat :	
Fallows	63
Clover leys	64
Clover and grass seeds	64
Straw and hay	65
Farm yard dung	66
Lady-day valuations	66
Half tillages	67
Wheat crop	68
Seeds	68
Sainfoin roots	69
Survey of dilapidations	70
Fixtures	71

CONTENTS. xi

Section 2.

Page

Rules for ascertaining weights of hay and cattle and contents of ash heaps 71

Section 3.

Forms of valuation 76

CHAPTER III.
FORESTRY.
Section 1.
Timber and Timber-like Trees, their Propagation, Treatment and Uses.

Oak..................	83
Elm..................	87
Wych elm..................	88
Ash..................	89
Beech..................	91
Horse chestnut..................	94
Spanish chestnut..................	95
Walnut..................	96
Poplar..................	97
Birch..................	99
Alder..................	100
Lime..................	101
Sycamore..................	103
Plane..................	103
Willow..................	104
Osier..................	105
Elder..................	106
Trees grown principally for ornament..................	107

Section 2.
The Coniferæ, or Cone-bearing Trees, their Propagation, Treatment, and Uses.

Larch..................	109
Scotch fir..................	114
Common or Norwegian spruce..................	117
Common silver fir..................	118

Section 3.
Timber Measurement.

Measurement of standing timber..................	120
Measurement of sawn timber..................	122
Summary of rules with examples..................	123
Instruments used in timber measurement..................	125
Sliding rule, its description and use..................	127

Section 4.
Sale of Timber.

	Page
Sale by public auction	129
Sale by bill of exchange	131
Sale by tender	134
Private sale	136

CHAPTER IV.
UNDERWOOD.

Section 1.
Underwood and its Management.

Underwood as a source of income	137
Sale of underwood	138
Cutting and sorting underwood	139
Time for cutting underwood	139
Underwood in the hands of a tenant	139
The planting and protection of underwood	140
Tables for calculating number of plants required for planting different areas	141

Section 2.
Plants Suitable for Underwood.

Hazel	143
Sweet Chestnut	144
Ash	145
Oak	146
Maple	146
Willow	146
Beech	146
Birch	146
Other varieties	147

CHAPTER V.
FENCES.

Section 1.
Fences, their Varieties and General Management.

Economy of good fences	148
Planting of new hedges, preparation of bed	149
Time and mode of planting	150
Management of old quick hedges	151
Grubbing hedges	152
Trimming hedges	152

	Page
Practical hints as to hedges generally	152
Dead fences of different kinds	153
Post and rails	153
Park paling	154
Scotch fence	154
Other kinds of wooden fence	155
Wire fencing	155
Continuous iron fencing	156
Walls	156
Tables for calculating the number of plants requisite for planting	158

SECTION 2.
Plants Suitable for Fences.

Common thorn	159
Beech	161
Hornbeam	162
Holly	162
Furze	163

CHAPTER VI.
GRASSES SUITABLE FOR WOODS AND PLANTATIONS.

Selection of seeds	165
List of useful grasses	165
Mode of sowing	166
Treatment of rides in woods	167

CHAPTER VII.
THE HOME FARM.

Land steward's relation to the home farm	168
Experiments on the home farm	169
The bailiff and his duties	170
Labourers	172
Annual valuation	173
Supply of produce to the house	174
Live stock	174
Dairy cows	174
Fat stock	175
Store and young stock	177
Sheep	177
Lambing	179
Sheep feed	180
Horses	181
Pigs	184
Poultry	184

	Page
Farm yard manure	185
Seeds	189
Hay	190
Harvest	192
Implements	193
Ear-marking cattle for purposes of registration	194
Top-dressing experiments upon grass land	195

CHAPTER VIII.
REPAIRS AND MATERIAL.

Repairs generally, clerk of the works	198
New erections, farm buildings, tanks, cottages	199
Material, timber and mineral substances	204
Utility of geological knowledge	204
Granite	208
Slates	209
Trap or greenstone	209
Sandstone	210
Limestone	211
Malm rock	214
Chalk and lime	214
Sand	217
Mortar	218
Cement	218
Concrete	219
Bricks and brickmaking	220
Tiles	224

CHAPTER IX.
REPAIRS AND MATERIAL (*continued.*)
RULES FOR ESTIMATING AREAS AND CAPACITIES.

Area of barge roof	225
Hipped roof	225
Circular roof	226
Area of brickwork	226
Capacities of tanks	226
Examples	227

CHAPTER X.
THE BLIGHTS OF WHEAT AND OTHER CERELS.

Vibrio tritici, " burnt corn," or " earcockles "	229
Cecidomyia tritici," wheat midge "	230
Uredo segetum, " black head "	230

Uredo caries, " smut " 231
Uredo rubigo, " red gum ".. 231
Puccinia graminis, " mildew " 231
Secale cornutum, " ergot of rye ".. 234

CHAPTER XI.
ACCOUNTS.

Section 1.
Farm Accounts.

Accounts kept by bailiff 235
    Journal.. 235
    Cash book 235
    Labour book 236
Inspection by steward 236
Steward's ledger... 236
Farm balance sheet 237

Section 2.
Estate Accounts.

Clerk of works accounts 239
Forester's accounts... 239
Steward's estate accounts... 240

CHAPTER XII.
USEFUL RULES OF ARITHMETIC AND MENSURATION, 242

ESTATE MANAGEMENT.

CHAPTER I.
LETTING AND LEASES.

SECTION I.
Introductory Remarks.

LANDLORDS AND FARMERS — GENERAL DUTIES OF LAND STEWARD IN SELECTING A TENANT — FIXING THE RENT — FICTITIOUS RENTS — MAKING TERMS WITH THE TENANT.

ONE of the striking characteristics of our English social system is the distinction, so generally prevalent that it is frequently regarded as a part of the natural order of things, between landlords and farmers. The owner of the land scarcely ever farms it, which is the same thing as saying that the person who does farm it is scarcely ever the owner. Whether this fact is due to the inevitable operation of the land laws, or of some special tendency or economical force which prevents the same person from being at once the owner of the soil and the possessor of the skill and capital necessary to develope it, we need not now inquire, although it may be observed, in passing, that the latter cause is the more probable. For the person possessing the requisite skill to conduct successful farming operations, requires, and

Landlords and farmers.

CHAP. I.
Sect. 1.
Introductory Remarks.

ought to have, a large return on his capital and industry which he is obliged to employ and to risk. Assuming that he has such a return, he will probably decrease it by investing part of that capital in the purchase of the soil, because the soil is generally bought up by persons in a position which enables them to give such a price for it that it will, as an investment, yield only a very small return; consequently, their competition will prevent the farmer from obtaining it at a price which will make it for him a remunerative purchase. And, if it is thus clear that there are obstacles in the way of the farmer becoming a proprietor, it is equally clear that there are causes which prevent the proprietor from becoming a farmer.

In the first place, his education does not specially fit him for the work, and, in the second place, the amount of ready money required is often beyond his reach, in spite of the position of apparent wealth which he occupies. The natural course for him to adopt is to insure the proper cultivation of his land by letting or "leasing" it to another—in other words, by parting temporarily with the possession, reserving to himself a "rent," or sum of money for the privilege granted.

General duties of land steward in selecting a tenant.

The "letting" of land, then, forms the most important and responsible of all acts of the land steward. It is, in fact, what answers to the investment of an employer's capital, and it is as necessary to the proprietor that his land should be let at a full rental to responsible persons, who will make the most of it, as that his money should be invested at good interest and on good security.

It is the part of the land steward to obtain a person capable of fulfilling the duties requisite to the full development of the land; and he must select a man with a thorough knowledge of agriculture, with sufficient capital, and also a man of sound moral character. These qualities are absolutely necessary to bring about a satisfactory arrangement between the parties.

Fixing the rent.

It will also be the duty of the land steward to advise his

employer with reference to the amount of the rent which is to be asked for the land. Rent is the annual sum made payable to the landlord by the terms of the lease or agreement. Correctly speaking, a fair rent is that amount of money which the tenant should have in his hands after deducting from the receipts of the farm the expenditure—such expenditure including a fair interest upon the tenant's capital, and a reasonable remuneration for his skill and labour. Rent, however, is subject to be modified by many important circumstances. The demand for farms constitutes the principal of these; there are also the sporting rights connected with the land or the district, the proximity to railways, and other means of transit, to towns or schools, and many other circumstances of this character.

CHAP. I.
Sect. 1.
Introductory Remarks.

When these modifications are pressed too far, to the disadvantage of the tenant, the rent becomes "fictitious," and it is such a pressure which a wise land steward will endeavour to avoid. "Rack" rent is the full rent, *i.e.*, the highest rent which the land will yield, after allowing the tenant a fair return, taking seasons into consideration. A rent beyond this is "fictitious." When fictitious rents are obtained, the landlord's property is as unsafely dealt with as is the property of a capitalist invested on risky securities. Not only does he run the risk of non-payment of his rent, but he also must be prepared to see his property depreciate, the land becoming less productive by over and injudicious cropping. These fictitious rents are, however, very tempting to needy landlords, and are often willingly asked, when the farm in question presents some unusual attraction. As a rule, however, they lead to disappointment, and ultimate loss. Consequently, the influence of the land steward should be used in favour of asking such a rent as the land will fairly produce, taking into consideration adverse seasons and losses. If this is done, the rent may be looked upon as a permanent income; and to secure this permanence of his income, a landlord may well be satisfied with a somewhat lower rent.

"Fictitious" rents.

Chap. I.
Sect. 1.
Introductory Remarks.

Making terms with the tenant.

The novice in his profession, who has found a tenant willing to give the required rent, and fulfilling the conditions already referred to, may perhaps think that his work is done, and that he can leave the preparation of the necessary formalities in the hands of the solicitor. But no mistake can be greater. For the steward should be able, not merely to criticise and to amend, by his suggestions, the draft agreement or lease submitted to him by the solicitor, but he should possess such a knowledge of the form and usual contents of an agricultural lease as to be himself able to draw up, out of his own head, a memorandum which shall express all the material part of the stipulations and covenants which are to be inserted in the lease. We would be the last to advise him to dispense with legal assistance in the granting of leases, or to commit himself or his employer unnecessarily by the signature of informal agreements. But it may be often necessary to bind the intending tenant by obtaining his signature to a memorandum containing the heads of the proposed lease when there is neither the opportunity nor the desire to refer to a solicitor; and in any case, unless he has the matter so thoroughly at his fingers' ends that he can discuss in the first instance with the applicant the leading provisions which he intends to have inserted in the lease, he may probably experience the annoyance of finding, when the negotiation is far advanced, that there is such a material difference between the views of the parties as to necessitate concession on his part or the breaking off the arrangement. The student who thoroughly familiarises himself with such simple legal principles affecting this matter as are contained in the supplement will be at a great advantage; for such a knowledge will materially assist him in informing him how far he may rely upon the law of tenancy, and how far it is necessary to protect the landlord by contract.

SECTION II.

THE FORM OF THE LEASE.

EXAMPLE A. (AGRICULTURAL LEASE BY DEED FOR A TERM OF YEARS FROM MICHAELMAS)—LEASES WHEN A DEED IS NOT NECESSARY—EXAMPLE B. (AGRICULTURAL LEASE BY MEMORANDUM OF AGREEMEENT FROM YEAR TO YEAR FROM LADY-DAY)—SUPPLEMENTAL AGREEMENT FOR COMPENSATION OF OUTGOING BY INCOMING TENANT—AGREEMENTS TO GRANT OR ACCEPT LEASES.

BEFORE making any observations upon the different subjects to which the lease relates, we would ask the student's attention to at least one of the examples of leases given in this section. Familiarity with the form and substance of a single good example will do more to enlighten him than any amount of general observation. We shall proceed in the first place to give *in extenso* the lease of a farm which was carefully considered, and which after it was settled for us by counsel, appeared to be a clear and useful form.

CHAP. I.
Sect. 2.
The Form of the Lease.

In the books upon the subject shorter forms may be found, but for the purposes of study it seems better to select an example in which may be read a plain and full expression of a farming agreement; and to give in the form of marginal notes an outline of its terms. This outline will serve as a basis for such general remarks upon the subject matter of leases as will be made in the next section.

EXAMPLE A.

AGRICULTURAL LEASE BY DEED FOR A TERM OF YEARS FROM MICHAELMAS.

THIS INDENTURE, made the   day of   18   between   1. Date and parties.
Abraham Broadacres, of   in the parish of   in the
city of   , Esquire (hereinafter called the "Lessor") of the one
part, and Charles Diggins, of   in the parish of

CHAP. I.
Sect. 2.
The Form of the Lease.

2. Demise of described farm.

3. Exception of trees and underwood, with liberty to lessor to enter and fell.

4. Exception of game, with liberty to lessor to sport.

5. *Habendum* defining the length of the term.

6. *Reddendum* or reservation of certain annual rent.

7. And of penal rent for breaking up pasture.

in the city of   , Farmer (hereinafter called "the Lessee") of the other part, WITNESSETH that in consideration of the rents hereinafter reserved, and the covenants by the lessee hereinafter contained, THE LESSOR doth by these presents GRANT AND DEMISE, unto the lessee, his executors, administrators, and assigns, ALL that messuage or farmhouse, and the several lands and hereditaments specified in the first schedule hereto situate in the parish of   in the county of   containing in the whole 500 acres or thereabouts, known as Blackacre Farm, together with all rights, easements, and appurtenances thereto belonging, or usually held and enjoyed therewith, EXCEPT AND RESERVING unto the lessor, his heirs and assigns, all timber and other trees, and wood, and (save as to the underwood mentioned in the second schedule hereto) all underwood which are, or is, or during the term hereby granted, shall be, upon the said premises, with liberty for the lessor, his heirs and assigns, and all persons authorised by him or them, at all seasonable times during the term hereby granted, with or without horses, carts, and carriages, to enter upon the said premises, and every part thereof, and dig, cut, fell, top, stub up, convert, and carry away the said timber trees, wood, and underwood, and to do all acts necessary or convenient for any of those purposes, and in particular, to have sufficient and convenient ground and room for laying down and stacking such timber trees, wood, and underwood, AND ALSO EXCEPT AND RESERVING unto the lessor, his heirs and assigns all the game, woodcock, snipe, quail, landrail, rabbits, wild fowl, and fish, upon the said premises with exclusive liberty for him and them, and all persons authorised by him and them, at all times during the term hereby granted, to enter and be upon the said premises for the purpose of hunting, sporting, and killing, or taking such creatures as aforesaid, and for all other reasonable purposes in connection therewith TO HAVE AND TO HOLD the premises hereinbefore expressed to be hereby demised unto the lessee, his executors, administrators and assigns for the term of seven years from the 29th day of September 1876, YIELDING AND PAYING therefor during the said term the yearly rent of 500*l.* by equal quarterly payments, on the 25th day of December, the 25th day of March, the 24th day of June, and the 29th day of September, in every year, the first payment to be made on the 25th day of December, 1876, and the last payment to be made in advance on the 24th day of June next preceding the determination of the term; AND ALSO YIELDING AND PAYING by like quarterly payments the additional yearly rent of 50*l.* for every acre (and so in proportion for a less quantity) of land which being now meadow or pasture, shall, without the previous consent in writing of the lessor, his heirs or assigns, be broken up or converted into tillage, the said additional rent to be computed from such one of the said quarterly days of payment as shall immediately precede the period when such breaking up or conversion shall occur, and so that the first payment thereof shall be made on such of the said quarterly days of payment as shall next follow the same period, and to continue payable during the residue of the said term, and the last payment thereof to be made in advance on the said 24th day of June next preceding the determination of the term; AND ALSO YIELDING AND PAYING, in the event of and immediately upon the said term being determined by re-entry under the proviso hereinafter contained a proportionate part of the said several rents for the fraction of the current quarter up to the day of such re-entry, the said several rents to be paid clear of all deduction except land tax and property tax. AND THE LESSEE DOTH hereby, for himself, his heirs, executors, administrators, and assigns, COVENANT with the lessor, his heirs and assigns, that he the lessee, his executors, administrators, and assigns, will pay unto the lessor, his heirs and assigns, the said yearly rent of 500*l.*, and also, if the same shall become payable, the said additional yearly rent and the aforesaid proportionate parts of the same rents at the times and in the manner hereinbefore appointed for payment thereof respectively, clear of all deductions except as aforesaid; AND ALSO will during the said term pay all existing and future taxes, rates, assessments, and outgoings of every description (except land tax and property tax) for the time being payable either by landlord or tenant in respect of the said premises (including tithes or the proportionate amount of the rentcharge, or commutation rent in lieu of tithes); AND ALSO will, throughout the said term, at his or their own expense, and without being thereunto required by notice, well and sufficiently repair, maintain, scour, cleanse, and keep in good and tenantable repair the said messuage or farmhouse, and all stables, drains, sheds, cottages, and other buildings hereby demised, and all fences (live or dead), walls, rails, gates, stiles, drains, ditches, banks, bridges, watercourses and appurtenances for the time being upon or belonging to the same premises; AND particularly will, at or before the expiration of the third and sixth years of the said term, in a workmanlike manner limewash all such parts of the interior of the said premises as have before been limewashed; AND will at or before the expiration of the third and sixth years of the said term, in like manner paint with two coats of good oil paint all the external wood, iron, and other work of or connected with the said premises previously or usually painted, or which ought to be painted, and will once at least during the said term in like manner paint with two coats of good oil paint all the internal wood, iron, and other work of or connected with the said premises previously or usually painted, or which ought to be painted; AND will once at least during the said term tar over in a workmanlike manner with good tar all the external woodwork of or connected with the said premises previously or usually tarred; AND ALSO shall and will permit the lessor, his heirs and assigns, and his and their agents, servants, and workmen, twice or oftener in every year, during the said term to enter into and upon

CHAP. I.
Sect. 2.
The Form of the Lease.

8. And of proportionate part of rents in case the lease is determined between two quarter days.

9. Lessee covenants to pay rent.

10. And to pay rates and taxes (and tithe rentcharge).

11. And to repair.

12. And particularly to limewash,

13. Paint externally and internally,

14. And tar necessary woodwork.

15. And to permit lessor to enter to view and give notice of repairs

ESTATE MANAGEMENT.

Chap. I.
Sect. 2.
The Form of the Lease.

needed, which repairs may be executed by the lessor at the lessee's expense if the notice is not complied with within three calendar months.

16. Liability of lessee in respect of repairs to be conditional on lessor supplying materials specified.

17. Liability of lessee in respect of repairs not to extend to cases of damage by fire or tempest exceeding 2l.

18. Lessee further covenants not to assign or underlet without licence.
19. And to cultivate in a husbandlike manner according to the custom of the country.
20. And not to break up pasture.
21. And to lay out hay and straw moneys in purchase of cake and manure, and produce accounts.

the said premises or any part thereof to view the condition of the same, and of all defects and wants of repair then and there found, to give or leave notice in writing at or upon the said premises or some part thereof for the lessee, his executors, administrators, or assigns, to repair the same within three calendar months from the day of such notice, within which said time the lessee, his executors, administrators, or assigns, will repair the same accordingly; AND ALSO shall and will, in case of non-compliance with such notice within the said three calendar months permit the lessor, his heirs and assigns, and his and their agents, servants, and workmen, to enter upon the said premises and execute the required repairs; AND ALSO shall and will pay the amount of the expenses of such last mentioned repairs on the quarterly day of payment of rent next after the same shall have been completed; and in default thereof the amount of the said expenses may be recovered by the lessor, his heirs and assigns, by distress in the same manner as rent in arrear is recoverable; BUT SO THAT the liability of the lessee, his executors, administrators, and assigns, under the aforesaid covenants to repair, maintain, limewash, paint and tar, shall, if he or they shall give reasonable and timely notice in writing to the lessor, his heirs or assigns, of the materials requisite to enable him or them to perform the same, be conditional on the lessor, his heirs and assigns, providing and allowing at the expense of the lessor, his heirs or assigns, at any place upon the said premises, or within a distance of seven miles therefrom, all such converted timber, bricks, slates, tiles, lime, paint and tar, as may be sufficient for the purposes aforesaid, all such timber and other materials as aforesaid to be cut and carried to such place at the expense of the lessor, his heirs and assigns; AND SO THAT the lessee, his executors, administrators, and assigns, shall not be liable, under the aforesaid covenants, to repair, to make good any damage by fire or tempest when the cost of such repair and making good shall (exclusive of the cost of materials) exceed the amount of 40s.; AND ALSO shall not, nor will, assign, underlet, or otherwise part with the possession of any part of the said premises without the previous licence in writing of the said lessor, his heirs or assigns. AND ALSO shall, and will, throughout the said term, manage and cultivate the said farm and lands in a good and husbandlike manner according to the custom of the country in reference to farms of a like nature, except so far as hereby varied, and not impoverish any part thereof; AND ALSO shall not, nor will, during the said term, without the previous consent in writing of the lessor, his heirs, or assigns, break up or convert into tillage any land which is now meadow or pasture; AND ALSO shall, and will, lay out in the purchase of oil or cotton cake, or artificial manure, all sums of money to be received by him or them from the sale of hay or straw produced on the said premises, and will produce on each of the said quarter days, or so soon thereafter as thereunto required, a properly vouched account of all moneys expended in purchase of oil or cotton cake, or artificial manure, and an account of all moneys received from the sale of hay or straw during the then preceding quarter ; AND ALSO shall not, nor will, sell any part of the hay or straw of the last crop preceding the expiration of the said term ; AND ALSO shall, and will, spend and consume on the said premises all oil and cotton cake and artificial manure so purchased, and also all hay and straw produced on the said premises, which shall not be sold, including a sufficient part of the hay and straw of the last crop preceding the expiration of the said term, and also all roots and green crops or fodder produced thereon ; AND ALSO shall, and will, at all proper times, and in a husbandlike manner, lay and spend upon the lands hereby demised all the dung, muck, and compost produced on the said premises ; AND ALSO shall and will preserve all timber and other trees, woods, and saplings, and all underwood (save and except the underwood mentioned in the second schedule hereto) from being cut, injured, or destroyed ; AND ALSO shall and will, cut open and spread all the anthills which shall be upon the same premises, and destroy the rats, mice, and moles thereon ; AND ALSO shall and will every year during the said term mow and destroy the rushes, nettles, and other weeds growing upon the pasture lands or any other part of the said premises; and also weed the fences belonging thereto, to prevent the weeds seeding or growing thereon ; AND ALSO shall and will keep properly clean all the water courses, ditches, underdrains, and outfalls on the said premises ; AND ALSO shall and will permit the lessor, his heirs and assigns, and his and their agents and stewards, at all reasonable times during the said term, to enter upon the said premises to examine the state and condition thereof, and to exercise the rights, liberties, and privileges hereinbefore expressed to be reserved. AND ALSO shall and will warn off all persons who, during the said term, shall hunt, hawk, shoot, fish, or sport upon the said premises without the licence of the lessor, his heirs or assigns, and give to the lessor, his heirs and assigns, notice of any person who shall hunt, hawk, shoot, fish, or sport upon the said premises ; AND ALSO shall and will permit the lessor, his heirs, and assigns, in case any person or persons shall, during the said term, hunt, hawk, shoot, fish, or sport upon the said premises, to bring and prosecute any action or other proceeding against such person or persons in the name or names of the lessee, his executors, administrators, or assigns, and will not release or discharge any such action or proceeding if he or they are indemnified from the costs thereof without the written consent of the lessor, his heirs, or assigns ; AND ALSO shall and will, at the expiration or other determination of the said term, deliver up the said premises and all additions thereto, together with all fixtures, fences, walls, rails, gates, stiles, drains, ditches, banks, bridges, and water courses for the time being upon or belonging to the said premises, except such fixtures and buildings as the lessee, his executors, administrators, or assigns shall

CHAP. I.
Sect. 2.
The Form of the Lease.

22. And not to sell hay or straw of last crop.
23. And to consume all also all unsold hay and straw, and also all other fodder on the premises.
24. And to expend on the premises all the dung there produced.
25. And to preserve all trees and underwood.
26. And to destroy ant hills and rats.
27. And to destroy weeds, &c., in pasture and fences.
28. And to cleanse ditches.
29. And to permit lessor to enter to view condition of premises.

30. And to warn off poachers.

31. And to permit lessor to sue poachers in name of lessee.

32. And to deliver up the premises at the end of the term in good repair.

Chap. I.
Sect. 2.
The Form of the Lease.

33. And to leave on the premises at the end of the term unconsumed straw of last crop (if already thrashed), and unconsumed hay, to be paid for by lessor or incoming tenant, at a valuation.

34. And to thrash out the whole of the last crop by the 6th May next after the expiration of the term, having accommodation allowed him for the purpose, straw to be paid for in like manner.

35. And leave dung upon premises without compensation.

36. Lessor covenants for quiet enjoyment during term, and to allow use of messuage, barns, and stack yards up to succeeding 6th May.

37. And to rebuild in case of fire.

be entitled to remove under or by virtue of any Act of Parliament applicable to these presents, and which the lessor, his heirs or assigns, shall not have elected to purchase, in such good and tenantable repair as aforesaid, and in all respects in such state and condition as shall be consistent with the due performance of the several covenants hereinbefore contained; AND ALSO shall and will leave upon the said premises at the expiration of the said term carefully stacked and thatched all unconsumed straw of the last preceding crop of corn, grain, or pulse that shall have been thrashed out prior to the expiration thereof, and also all unconsumed hay of the last preceding crop, such straw or hay to be paid for by the lessor, his heirs or assigns, or by the incoming tenant, by valuation to be made by two valuers or their umpires in the usual way; AND ALSO shall and will as to so much of the said last preceding crop of corn, grain, or pulse as shall not have been thrashed out prior to the expiration of the said term, thrash out the same in the said barns before the 6th of May next ensuing after the expiration of the said term, having accommodation allowed to him or them for that purpose in accordance with the covenant in that behalf hereinafter contained, and will permit the lessor, his heirs or assigns, or the incoming tenant to stack and take the straw hulls, chaff, and other litter and fodder therefrom, the same to be paid for by valuation as hereinbefore mentioned; AND ALSO shall and will leave upon the said premises all the muck, dung, and compost produced upon the said premises and then unconsumed, without receiving any compensation for the same. AND THE LESSOR for himself, his heirs, and executors, and administrators, doth hereby covenant with the lessee, his executors, administrators, and assigns, that the lessee, his executors, administrators, and assigns, paying the said yearly rents and performing all the covenants and agreements by the lessee herein contained, may quietly hold the said premises during the said term, and may also hold the barns and stackyards for the laying, thrashing, and dressing of his or their last crops, and the said messuage or farmhouse, and also stabling or standing room for four horses until the 6th day of May next ensuing after the expiration of the said term without paying any rent for the same; AND ALSO that if the said messuage, farmhouse, stables, barns, sheds, cottages, and buildings, or any of them, or any new buildings or erections which shall be built or erected in lieu thereof, shall at any time during the said term be destroyed or damaged by fire, except by the wilful act, neglect, or default of the lessee, his executors, administrators, or assigns, then and so often as the same shall happen and within a reasonable time not exceeding one year thereafter, the lessor, his heirs or assigns, will at his or their own cost sufficiently rebuild, restore, or repair and complete the premises which shall be so destroyed or damaged except as aforesaid, or except the damage be of such small amount that the lessee, his executors, administrators, or assigns, is or are bound to make good the same in accordance with the covenants by the lessee hereinbefore contained; AND ALSO that the lessor, his heirs, and assigns, shall and will throughout the said term, on the receipt of reasonable and timely notice in writing of the materials requisite for the performance of any repairing, lime washing, painting, or tarring, in accordance with the covenants by the lessee hereinbefore contained, provide and allow on any part of the said premises or within a distance of seven miles therefrom, all such converted timber, bricks, slates, tiles, lime, paint, and tar, as may be sufficient for the purposes aforesaid; AND ALSO that at the expiration of the said term the lessor, his heirs or assigns, or the incoming tenant, shall and will pay to the lessee, his executors, administrators, or assigns, for the straw, hay hulls, chaff, and other fodder grown upon the said premises, and then being properly unconsumed or not threshed out thereon, such sum of money to be ascertained by valuation as hereinbefore mentioned, such valuation to be made as to the said straw at fodder price, and as to the said hay and other materials at market price; AND ALSO shall and will take away and remove all straw to be thrashed out by the lessee, his executors, administrators, or assigns, after the expiration of the said term, as it comes from the machine; AND ALSO shall and will pay to the lessee, his executors, administrators, or assigns, such sum of money as shall be determined by valuation as hereinbefore mentioned as compensation for all such of the following matters as the lessor, his heirs or assigns, or the incoming tenant, shall have the benefit of, viz.: For all grass and clover seeds, and the cost of sowing the same; For all tillage operations, seeds, and manure expended on the root crops; For all ploughings and all preparations for wheat; For all tillage operations upon fallows; For all labour upon farm-yard manure, and for all land in sainfoin not exceeding three years lay; AND ALSO shall and will pay to the lessee, his executors, administrators, or assigns, one equal third part of all moneys (exclusive of the moneys produced from the sale of hay or straw of any previous year or years) expended during the last year of the said term in the purchase of oil or cotton cake which shall have been consumed on the said premises, provided that the total amount (exclusive of the moneys produced from the sale of hay and straw as aforesaid) expended during the said last year does not exceed the average amount (exclusive as aforesaid) expended for the like purpose during the three years immediately preceding, and provided that such oil and cotton cake be submitted to the inspection and approved by the lessor, his heirs or assigns, or his or their agents or agent; but so that the amount payable in respect of oil and cotton cake under this covenant shall be subject to a proportionate reduction in respect of so much (if any) of such oil or cotton cake as shall have been consumed on land which the lessee shall during the season immediately preceding the expiration of the term have cultivated in corn; AND ALSO that the lessor, his heirs, or assigns shall and will permit the lessee, his executors,

CHAP. I.
Sect. 2.
The Form of the Lease.

38. And to supply lessee with specified materials when required for repairs.

39. And to pay for unconsumed straw, hay, and other produce at the expiration of the term.

40. And to remove straw as it comes from the machine.

41. And to pay compensation for the unexhausted tillages specified.

42. And to pay a share of the moneys expended during the last year of the term in cake.

43. And to permit lessor to destroy rabbits in February and March.

CHAP. I.
Sect. 2.
The Form of the Lease.

44. Power to lessor to re-enter in case of non-payment of rent or breach of covenant.

45. Power to lessor to resume parts for planting, he allowing reduction of rent.

46. Arbitration clause.

47. Agricultural Holdings Act, 1875, not to apply.
48. Renewal clause.

administrators, or assigns, to kill and destroy and appropriate the rabbits on the said premises during the months of February and March in every year during the said term, but nevertheless not by shooting the same. PROVIDED ALWAYS that if and whenever any part of the said several rents hereinbefore reserved shall be in arrear for twenty-one days, whether the same shall have been legally demanded or not, or if and wherever there shall be a breach of any of the covenants by the lessee herein contained, the lessor, his heirs, and assigns, may re-enter upon any part of the said premises in the name of the whole, and thereupon the said term shall absolutely determine. PROVIDED ALSO that the lessee, his heirs or assigns, may, at any time during the said term resume the possession of the whole or of any part or parts of so much of the said premises as are referred to in the said schedule by the Nos. 35, 36, and 37, for the purpose of planting the same; BUT SO THAT he or they shall give to the lessee, his executors, administrators, or assigns, or leave upon the demised premises, one year's previous notice in writing of his or their desire so to do, and shall from the time of the expiration of the notice allow a reduction of rent to an amount not exceeding twenty shillings for every acre so taken, and so in proportion for any less quantity than an acre, and shall also pay such gross sum by way of compensation as would be payable under the covenants hereinbefore contained (exclusive of the covenants relating to the repayment of moneys expended in oil or cotton cake) in respect of the lands so taken if the time of the expiration of the said notice were the time of the expiration of the said term, the amount of the said reduction of rent, as well as the amount of the said compensation, to be determined in case of difference by arbitration in manner hereinafter provided; AND ALSO so that in case possession of any part or parts of the said premises shall be resumed by the lessor, his heirs or assigns, as aforesaid, the covenants, provisions, conditions, and agreements herein contained with reference to the whole of the said premises shall, so far as the same may be applicable, continue in force, and apply to such part of the same as shall be left in the possession of the lessee, his executors, administrators, or assigns, in the same manner as if such part only had been originally included in these presents. AND IT IS HEREBY AGREED AND DECLARED that every valuation or arbitration under this lease shall be made by two indifferent, &c. &c. [Proceed by copying clause 31, on p. 19.] AND IT IS HEREBY ALSO AGREED AND DECLARED that no part of the Agricultural Holdings Act, 1875, shall be applicable to these presents. AND IT IS HEREBY FURTHER AGREED AND DECLARED that if the lessee, his executors, administrators, or assigns shall be desirous of taking a renewed lease of the said premises for the term hereinafter mentioned, and of such desire shall, prior to the expiration of the term hereby granted, give to the lessor, his heirs or assigns, or leave at his or their last known place of abode in England, two years' previous notice in writing, and shall pay the said rent hereby reserved, and observe and perform the several covenants and agreements herein contained, and on the part of the lessee, his executors, administrators, or assigns, to be observed and performed up to the expiration of the term hereby granted, then and in such case the lessor, his heirs or assigns will, at the expense and at the request of the lessee, his executors, administrators, or assigns, and upon the execution and delivery by him or them of a counterpart, execute a renewed lease of the said premises for a further term of seven years from the expiration of the term hereby granted at the rents and subject to the provisions, covenants, agreements, and conditions contained in these presents, save and except this present covenant. IN WITNESS whereof the said parties to these presents have hereunto set their hands and seals the day and year first above written.

FIRST SCHEDULE (referring to Ordnance Maps).

No. on Map. (Map 43.7)	Description.	Cultivation.	Quantity. A. R. P.
No. 101	House and garden		0 2 10
No. 105	Lower Mead	Meadow	10 3 0
No. 35	Long Bottom	Underwood	5 0 4
	&c.	&c.	

SECOND SCHEDULE.

[This schedule comprises the underwood which is not excepted and reserved by the lease.]

Seal.

ABRAHAM BROADACRES.

Signed, sealed, and delivered by the within-named Abraham Broadacres, in the presence of Jonathan Crowquill, of   , in the county of   , Gentleman.

A document of the above nature is executed (*i.e.*, signed and sealed) by the landlord, and handed to the tenant hiring a large farm for a term of years, the terms being, of course, varied according to the agreement come to between the parties. The tenant will himself execute a copy of the lease which is called a " counter-part," and the latter will be held by the landlord.

It will be found in the supplement that a formal deed of this kind is not in every case necessary; and that tenancies

CHAP. I.
Sect. 2.
The Form of the Lease.

from year to year, or even for short terms of years not exceeding three, may be made without the execution of any deed at all. In these cases it is usual to have a writing embodying the terms of the letting, and this writing is in fact a lease though it is generally from its terms called an agreement. It is wanting in that formality and prolixity which we are accustomed to associate with deeds; but the words which it should use to express the substantial part of the arrangement will not differ materially from the like expressions in a deed. When the tenancy is of this nature, the provisions of the lease will naturally be less elaborate and precise than in a letting for a long term of years.

EXAMPLE B.

AGRICULTURAL LEASE BY MEMORANDUM OF AGREEMENT FROM YEAR TO YEAR FROM LADY-DAY.

N.B.—In order to facilitate comparison between the provisions of the two leases given as examples, we have appended in brackets to the marginal notes of this lease the number appended to that clause of Example A., which relates to the same subject-matter. When no number is appended, Example A. contains no corresponding clause.

1. Date and parties (cl. 1).

1. Memorandum of Agreement made the   day of   1879, between Sir Alfred Bareacres, of Bareacres, in the parish of   in the county of   Baronet (hereinafter called "the landlord,") of the one part, and Christopher Drinkwater, of   in the parish of   in the county of   Farmer (hereinafter called "the tenant"), of the other part.

2. Words of demise (cl. 2).

2. The landlord agrees to let, and the tenant agrees to take the farm and lands situate in the parish of   in the county of   hereinafter described, with the exceptions or reservations, for the period, at the rent or rents, and subject to the obligations by the tenant, and upon the terms and conditions set forth in the several parts of this agreement hereinafter contained.

Part I.
The Farm and Lands the Subject of this Demise.

3. All that farm and lands situate in the parish of   in the county of   known as "   Farm," and consisting of the following particulars, namely:

Chap. I. Sect. 2. The Form of the Lease.

3. Description of farms (cl. 2).

No. on Parish or Ordinance Map.	Description.	Cultivation.	Quantity.

Part II.
Exceptions and Reservations.

4. Excepting and reserving all timber and timber-like trees, tellers, pollards, and saplings, and also all chalk, gravel, sand, and stone standing, lying, and being upon or under the said lands, with liberty of ingress, egress, and regress for the landlord and his agents, servants and workmen at all reasonable times, to mark, fell, work, dig, take, and carry away the same; paying reasonable compensation for all damage (if any) done thereby.

4. Exception of timber, and timber-like trees and saplings: and also of chalk, gravel, sand and stone, with liberty to landlord to enter and cut or work (cl. 3).

5. Excepting and reserving also all game, woodcock, snipe, quail, landrail, rabbits, wild fowl, or fish in or upon the said lands, with liberty for the landlord and his friends, companions, gamekeepers, and servants at all reasonable times of the year, to hunt, shoot, fish, and sport over the said lands.

5. Exception of game, with liberty to landlord to sport (cl. 4).

Part III.
Duration of Tenancy.

6. A term of one year certain commencing on the 25th day of March, 1879, and continuing from year to year, until the tenancy shall be determined by either party by one year's notice to quit, expiring at the end of a year of tenancy.

6. Duration of tenancy (cl. 5).

Part IV.
The Rents to be paid by the Tenant.

7. The yearly rent of £   to be paid by equal quarterly payments without any deduction (except for land tax and the landlord's property tax) on the 24th day of June, the 29th day of September, the 25th day of December and the 25th day of March in every year; the first payment thereof to be made on the 24th day of June next.

7. Annual rent (cl. 6).

8. The further yearly rent of 50*l*. for every acre, and so in proportion for any less quantity than an acre of meadow or grass land (parcel of the said farm) which the tenant shall at any time plough and break up or convert into tillage or garden ground without the landlord's consent, the first payment to be made on such of the said quarterly days as

8. Penal rent for breaking up pasture (cl. 7).

CHAP. I.
Sect. 2.
The Form of the Lease.

9. Additional rent in respect of improvements executed by landlord.

shall first happen after such ploughing, breaking up, or converting into tillage as aforesaid, and to continue payable during the remainder of the tenancy.

9. A further yearly rent equivalent to interest at the rate of 5*l.* per cent. per annum on any money which may be hereafter expended by the landlord on drainage or other improvements on the premises with the tenant's consent. The said rent to run from the date of such expenditure, and the first proportionate payment thereof to be made on such of the said quarterly days as shall first happen after such expenditure.

PART V.

Tenants' Obligations.

10. Tenant's agreement to pay rent (cl. 9).

10. The tenant shall pay the said yearly rent of £   , and also the additional rents above reserved, if the same shall become payable at the times hereby appointed for payment thereof.

11. And rates and taxes, and tithe rent charge (cl. 10).

11. The tenant shall also pay the tithe, rent-charge, and all rates, taxes, and assessments (except the land tax and the landlords' property tax.)

12. And to repair, landlord finding materials (cl. 11. and see also cl. 15, 16, 17, 26, 27, 28 & 29).

12. The tenant shall keep in good and tenantable repair the interior of the houses and other buildings, and the glass in the windows thereof, and in such repair leave the same at the end of the tenancy. He shall also, at the proper season, well and sufficiently lay, cut, repair, and keep repaired all hedges, mounds, rails, gates and fences, and stoned and other roads; and open, scour, and cleanse, all ditches, water-courses, and drains, and so leave the same at the end of the tenancy. But the tenant's obligation to repair shall be conditional on the landlord's providing such of the requisite materials as are specified in the agreement by the landlord, hereinafter contained.

·13. And particularly to paint (cl. 12, 13 & 14).

13. In particular the tenant shall paint with two coats of oil paint once in every three years (if the tenancy shall so long last), all the outside wood and iron work previously or usually painted, and once in every seven years (if the tenancy shall so long last) all the inside wood work previously or usually painted, the landlord providing paint as aforesaid.

14. And to haul materials for repairs (cl. 16).

14. The tenant shall haul, without charge, all materials for repairs or improvements, whether to be done by the landlord or tenant, provided that such materials be not brought from a distance exceeding seven miles from the said farmhouse.

15. And not to assign without licence (cl. 18).

15. The tenant shall not assign or underlet or part with the possession of any part of the premises (except cottages to labourers), without the licence in writing of the landlord or his agent.

16. And to cultivate in husbandlike manner according to best mode of husbandry (cl. 19).
17. And not to break up pasture (cl. 20).

16. The tenant shall stock, manage, cultivate, and farm the premises in a good, clean and husbandlike manner, according to the best and most approved mode of husbandry, in reference to farms of a like nature; and shall keep and leave the same in good heart and condition.

17. The tenant shall not at any time pare off the turf, or destroy or burn the herbage of any meadow or pasture-ground, or break up the

same, or convert it into tillage or garden ground without the written consent of the landlord or his agent.

18. The tenant shall consume upon the premises all roots and green fodder grown or brought thereon, and shall convert into manure, at the homestead, all hay, straw, haulm, and other fodder grown, made, or brought upon the premises, in a husbandlike manner; and shall spread, use, and expend thereon all manure made or brought on the premises in a husbandlike manner at the proper seasons. Provided that he shall be at liberty until notice to quit be given by either party to sell and remove hay and straw, on condition of bringing back and bestowing on the land the market value of the quantity sold, in oil or cotton cake, rags, fur-waste, or guano, or any other artificial manure which may be approved by the landlord or his agent, and giving when required to the landlord or his agent satisfactory proof of the value of the hay and straw so sold or removed; and also of the cake, rags, fur-waste, guano, or manure so brought back and bestowed. *[margin: 18. And to consume hay and straw and other fodder, and all dung on the premises, but with liberty to sell hay and straw, on bringing back equivalent in cake or manure (cl. 21, 22, 23 & 24).]*

19. The tenant shall not cause or permit any timber or other trees to be lopped or topped, or any such tree or any pollard to be felled, cut down, injured, or destroyed, without the written consent of the landlord or his agent, but shall to the utmost of his power preserve the same, and also all fruit trees, from any spoil or damage either by cattle or otherwise. The tenant shall also at his own expense plant, fence and protect all fruit trees supplied by the landlord. *[margin: 19. And to preserve trees (cl. 25).]*

20. The tenant shall allow no person to sport without the landlord's permission, and shall sign all notices against trespass required by the landlord or his agent, and shall permit the landlord to bring any action or other proceeding in the tenant's name against poachers or trespassers on the premises, and shall preserve all game and fish or other animals excepted out of this demise: Provided that the tenant may destroy rabbits, but by purse nets and ferrets only. *[margin: 20. And to do necessary acts for preservation of game, except rabbits (cl. 30 & 31).]*

21. The tenant shall to the utmost of his power prevent any new footpaths from being made over the premises. *[margin: 21. And to prevent making of new foot paths.]*

22. The tenant shall, in the last year of the tenancy, prepare in good condition and sow in good season with wheat such proportion of the arable land as shall then be in due course for the same, and shall sow good grass seeds with the last year's Lent crops. *[margin: 22. And in the last year of the tenancy to prepare for wheat crop, and to sow with grass seeds.]*

23. The tenant shall give up possession of the whole of the premises on the day of the expiration of the tenancy, notwithstanding any custom of the country to the contrary, and the repair and condition at the time of giving up possession shall be such as is required by a due performance of his obligation herein contained. *[margin: 23. And to give up possession of premises at expiration of tenancy in good condition (cl. 32).]*

24. The tenant at the end of the tenancy shall leave all the hay, straw, and roots remaining unconsumed by him, being paid for the same by the landlord or incoming tenant, as hereinafter provided, and shall leave all dung, compost, and manure without compensation. *[margin: 24. And at end of tenancy to leave hay, straw, and roots on compensation, and dung without compensation (cl. 33, 34 & 35).]*

CHAP. I.
Sect. 2.
The Form of the Lease.

25. Landlord's agreement to do substantial repairs.
26. And to supply specified materials for tenant's repairs (cl. 38).

27. And to insure (cl. 37).

28. And that landlord or incoming tenant will allow compensation for matters specified (cl. 41 & 42).

PART VI.

The Landlord's Obligations.

25. The landlord shall keep in good and tenantable repair the main walls, main timbers, floors and roofs of the houses and other buildings upon receiving notice from the tenant that any such repairs are, and upon such repairs being in fact, wanted.

26. The landlord shall on the receipt of notice in writing of any converted timber, posts, rails, paint, bricks, tiles, slates, or lime, or of any quicks for hedges being required by the tenant for the purpose of putting or keeping the premises in a proper condition, supply such of the said materials as may be necessary, at some place within seven miles from the said farmhouse.

27. The landlord shall keep the farmhouse and farm buildings insured against loss or damage by fire, in a sum sufficient to cover the value thereof, and the money received under such insurance shall be forthwith laid out in rebuilding and reinstating the premises in respect of which the same shall be received.

28. The landlord or the incoming tenant shall pay or allow to the tenant at the end of the tenancy, according to valuation, for the following matters and things:—

(*a*) For the wheat sown as before provided.
(*b*) For the grass seeds sown with the last year's Lent crops and the cost of harrowing the same.
(*c*) For every acre of the last crop of roots fed off an amount not exceeding 40*s*. per acre, and so in proportion for a less quantity than an acre.
(*d*) For the unconsumed hay, straw and roots, at a consuming price.
(*e*) For one-third of the oil and cotton cake consumed on the premises during the last year of the tenancy, but cake purchased with hay or straw money, or cake (beyond the amount of the cake last aforesaid) consumed on land from which a corn or other crop shall have been taken since consumption shall not be taken into account in calculating the third.

PART VII.

General Provisions.

29. Power to landlord to re-enter for non-payment of rent, breach of agreement, or bankruptcy (cl. 44).

29. If a quarter's rent shall be in arrear for forty days, whether the same shall have been legally demanded or not, or if there shall be any breach of the obligations by the tenant or the conditions herein contained, or if the tenant shall become a bankrupt, or a liquidating or compounding debtor, the landlord may forthwith re-enter and eject the tenant.

30. Account to be taken at the end of the tenancy.

30. At the end of the tenancy an account shall be taken between the landlord and tenant as follows, namely:—

1st. A valuation shall be made of the several matters and things which are hereinbefore agreed to be paid or allowed for by the landlord or his incoming tenant, and the amount of such valuation shall be debited to the landlord; and, secondly, the valuers shall determine whether any and (if so) what sum of money ought to be paid or allowed by the tenant to the landlord for any breach by the tenant of the terms and conditions of the tenancy or in respect of the condition in which he has left the farm, and the same, together with any arrear of rent or of rates and taxes which may be owing from the tenant, shall be debited to the tenant: And the balance which upon such account shall appear due from one party to the other shall be forthwith paid with interest thereon after the rate of 4 per cent. per annum computed from the end of the tenancy.

The Form of the Lease.

31. Every valuation under this agreement shall be made by two indifferent persons, one to be named by each party interested, and in case of their disagreement, then by an umpire to be chosen by the valuers previously to entering upon the consideration of the matters referred to therein, and in case either of the parties shall neglect to name a valuer for the space of seven days after a notice in writing so to do shall have been given to him by the other party, or shall name a valuer who shall refuse to act, then the valuation may be made by the valuer named by the other party alone. The valuers or their umpire shall have power to decide any questions which may arise in the course of their valuation, and in particular any questions as to what matters or things are proper subjects of valuation or allowance according to the true intent and meaning of this agreement. Every reference to valuers under this agreement shall be deemed a reference to arbitration within the provisions of the Common Law Procedure Act 1854, and shall have all the incidents and consequences of an arbitration under that Act.

31. Arbitration clause (cl. 46).

32. No part of the Agricultural Holdings Act, 1875, shall apply to this contract of tenancy,

32. Agricultural Holdings Act not to apply (cl. 47).

As witness the hands of the said parties.

ARTHUR BAREACRES.

Witness: JONATHAN CROWQUILL,
Solicitor,
Newtown, Hampshire.

CHRISTOPHER DRINKWATER,

Witness, &c.

It will be observed that the above agreement, and this observation applies also to the other lease (Example A.), makes no provision for the payments which the tenant may properly be called upon to make to the outgoer in respect of operations by the latter of which he will take the benefit. These

Supplemental agreement for compensation of outgoing by incoming tenant.

c 2

CHAP. I.
Sect. 2.
The Form of the Lease.

payments should be the subject of a subsidiary agreement between the landlord and tenant at the time that the letting is agreed upon; and the terms of that agreement must depend upon the compensation which the outgoer is entitled to under the terms of his holding. Assuming that he is holding on the same terms as those agreed to by the incomer, and that those terms are the terms expressed in Example B., the subsidiary or supplemental agreement will be in the form set out below. The important point for the landlord or his agent to attend to in any case is that the incoming tenant shall definitely undertake to liquidate the legitimate claims, whatever they may be, of the outgoer.

Supplemental Agreement.

Whereas the said farm is at present in the occupation of X. Y. (hereinafter called the outgoing tenant), under an agreement dated   day of   18   , and he has received notice to quit, which will expire on the   day of   next, and by the said agreement it is provided (in clause No.   of Part VI. thereof) that the landlord, or his incoming tenant, shall, at the end of the said tenancy, pay or allow to the outgoing tenant according to valuation for the following matters and things, namely (specifying them). And it is provided (in Clause No.   ) that at the end of the tenancy an account shall be taken between the landlord and outgoing tenant as follows:—1st, that a valuation shall be made of the several matters and things which are thereinbefore agreed to be paid or allowed for by the landlord or his incoming tenant, and the amount of such valuation shall be debited to the landlord, and secondly, that the valuers shall determine whether any and (if so) what sum of money ought to be paid or allowed by the outgoing tenant to the landlord, for any breach by the tenant of the terms and conditions of the tenancy, or in respect of the condition in which he has left the farm, and the same together with any arrear of rent, or of rates and taxes owing from the tenant, shall be debited to the outgoing tenant; and that the balance which upon such account shall appear due from one party to the other shall be forthwith paid with interest thereon, at the rate of 4*l.* per cent. per annum, computed from the end of the tenancy NOW IT IS HEREBY AGREED between the landlord and tenant under this agreement (hereinafter called the incoming tenant), that whatever sum of money shall, under the said recited agreement, become payable to or from the outgoing tenant, shall be paid or received (as the case may be) by the incoming tenant, and the valuations to be made under the said agreement shall be binding on the incoming tenant. AND IT IS ALSO AGREED that if any sum of money shall, by the valuation to be made as aforesaid, be awarded to be paid or allowed by the outgoing tenant to the landlord, or the incoming tenant, for any breach by the outgoing tenant of the terms and conditions of the tenancy, or for the state of the farm, and which sum of money shall accordingly be brought into the account, and paid or allowed for as aforesaid, the incoming tenant shall lay out an equal sum on the farm forthwith, or so soon as the same can profitably be laid out thereon. AND whatever sum of money (if any) shall be found owing by the outgoing tenant for arrears of rent, or of rates and taxes as aforesaid, and which shall accordingly be brought into the account, and allowed for as aforesaid, shall be forthwith applied by the incoming tenant in the payment of such arrears.

CHAP. I.
Sect. 2.
The Form of the Lease.

As witness the hands of the parties, &c.

An agreement such as Example B., which is in fact a lease (see Supplement), is to be distinguished from a mere preliminary memorandum, such as the parties often sign with a view to bind one another to the granting or acceptance of a lease. For the signature of a party or his authorised agent is essential in order to bind him to accept or to grant a lease; therefore, when the bargain is to be actually struck before the necessary lease can be prepared, the heads of the arrangement are frequently reduced into writing. A., for instance, agreeing to grant, and B. to accept, a lease of the premises in question, the lease to provide that the term shall be so many years from such a date, the rent to be £   payable on usual quarter days, the tenant to pay rates and taxes except as specified, and to repair, or lessor to repair at lessee's expense if latter fails to do so after notice, lessor to provide material gratis and carriage free on premises, and so on, particular care being taken to express what are to be the general terms of the compensation clauses, unless each party is familiar with a generally prevailing local custom on the subject, and they intend to abide by it.

Agreement to grant or accept leases.

Although these preliminary writings are absolutely essential where either party proposes to take any important steps on the faith that a lease will be executed, it is evidently much better, and less likely to produce complications, for the matter to remain entirely open until a draft

Chap. I.
Sect. 2.
The Form of the Lease.

of the proposed lease can be read and discussed, and so all possibility of misunderstanding avoided. Where the steward is reletting a farm on the terms of the last tenancy, or with only very slight variations, difficulty may, however, be avoided by giving the intended tenant an opportunity of reading the old lease, and then binding him by a memorandum to accept a lease on similar terms.

Agreements to grant or accept leases, when clearly and precisely drawn, are frequently deemed sufficient by the parties without the lease being drawn and executed. The stamp upon them is the same as would be the stamp upon the lease itself, and in the event of a lease being executed within a certain period a second *ad valorem* stamp is not required.

SECTION III.
The Subject-Matter of the Lease.

ANALYSIS OF CONTENTS OF LEASE—NAME AND DESCRIPTION OF FARM—TREES AND UNDERWOOD—GAME—MINERALS—PAYMENT OF RENT—RATES AND TAXES—TITHE RENT-CHARGE—REPAIRS—INSURANCE—CULTIVATION—CONSUMPTION OF HAY, STRAW, ETC.—COMPENSATION AND RIGHTS OF LESSEE AT EXPIRATION OF THE TERM—LESSOR'S POWER OF RE-ENTRY.

Analysis of contents of lease.

If we revert now to the contents of the lease by deed (Example A.) above set out, we find that its contents naturally divide themselves into four leading divisions. After the date and parties, there is, *firstly*, that part of the document which constitutes the actual grant of the lease, defining the property granted, the rights which the landlord reserves over it, the length of the term, and the amount of the rent. This part ends with clause 8. Then come, *secondly*, the lessee's covenants contained in clauses 9 to 35. *Thirdly*, we have the lessor's covenants (clauses 36 to 43.) And, *lastly*, come the miscellaneous clauses, viz., the power of re-entry, together in this case with another less usual clause, and certain provisions, as to arbitration, the application of the Agricultural Holdings Act, and renewal; but of these clauses, the power of re-entry and the arbitration clause, are the only ones which are always, under every circumstance, to be inserted. The order of arrangement of the several clauses may, of course, vary, but the outline of classification above described and followed in this lease appears to be one easy to understand and remember.

CHAP. I. Sect. 3. *The Subject-Matter of the Lease.*

So much for the general form of the document. It may be worth while now to indicate the several leading points which the student will find by careful study of the example are raised by it, and to which he will have to direct his attention on making terms with a tenant. We shall number these points, as nearly as may be, in the order in which they occur in this lease.

The first part of the lease (clauses 1—8) suggests that he must be ready, in the first place, with

(1.) The description and acreage of the farm (clause 2).

In the next place he must know his intention with reference to the rights to be retained over the soil by the landlord, so as to make his bargain with reference to

(2.) Trees and underwood (clause 3; see also clause 25);

(3.) Game (clause 4; see also clauses 30, 31, and 43); and

(4.) Minerals (as to which the lease is silent).

The other points raised by this first part of the lease are less likely to escape his attention; they are

(5.) The commencement and length of the term (clause 5).

(6.) The annual rent and time of payment (clause 6).

(7.) Penal rents for prohibited acts, if it is desired to reserve any (clause 7).

When we come to the second and third parts of the lease, containing the lessee's and the lessor's covenants, it is to be observed that the form of the document makes it necessary for the whole of the obligations undertaken by the lessee to be kept separate from those undertaken by the lessor, although their respective obligations may relate to the same subject-matter. This difficulty may be avoided in a lease made without a deed, but by memorandum of agreement, because in that case each paragraph may be, and is often, drawn so as to express an agreement between the parties, and to imply a number of promises or undertakings by both of them. But a study of the covenants will be found to raise (expressly or by implication) the following leading points:

(8.) Payment of rates and taxes and tithe rentcharge (clause 10);

(9.) Repairs (clauses 11—17 and 38);

(10.) Insurance (as to which the lease is intentionally silent, but see clause 37);

(11.) Assignment, or parting with possession (clause 18).

(12.) Cultivation (clauses 19 and 20).

(13.) Consumption of hay and straw, or of cake, or purchased manure in lieu thereof (clauses 21—23), and of dung (clause 24);

(14.) Compensation and rights of lessee at expiration of term (clauses 33—36, and 39—42).

Finally, what we called the third part of the lease brings us to the important clauses as to

(15.) Lessor's power of re-entry;

(16.) Valuation and arbitration;

(17.) Provisions for renewing the lease, or for determining it on notice.

All these seventeen points will, in every case of an agricultural lease, require attention; and, although every letting will probably need some covenants and provisions special to its own peculiar circumstances (*e.g.*, clause 45 in this lease, giving lessor a power to resume parts for planting), the above enumeration comprises the material part of the subject-matter of every lease. As to some of the parts enumerated, the mere mention of them is sufficient, but there are others upon which some observations may be made with a view to the assistance or information of the beginner.

But he may here be again reminded of the desirability of understanding, at least, so much of the legal aspect of the matter as is put before him at the end of the book.

Chap. I. Sect. 3. The Subject-Matter of the Lease.

It seems usual in the body of the lease to call the farm by its ordinary name, and state the total acreage; and, then, in a schedule to give the full particulars. This is done by giving the number of each field, either on the Tithe or Ordnance map, followed by its name, cultivation, and acreage. The sum total of the quantities must, of course, agree with the acreage specified in the beginning of the lease. It is to be observed that mistakes in these schedules are easily made, either in the drafting or copying, and it is always worth while to see that the schedule is correct on the engrossed lease.

Description and acreage of farm.

The landlord, in all cases, has the sole right to the timber; but, so long as it is standing, it is a part of the land, just as much as a house or building upon the land. Therefore, if it is demised, the landlord has no power over it during the term; he can no more go and cut it down than he can knock down the homestead. If he desires to fell it, it is necessary to except the timber from the demise, to reserve the right to enter, and to fell and draw it away at all seasonable times. The word "seasonable" or "convenient" is usually attached to the covenant, as it would not be right to conduct this operation at a season when the doing so would injure the crops of the tenant. It is also desirable to except underwood. The tenant's rights in respect of this are larger than they are with regard to timber-trees. As to the latter, he may only use them as they stand; that is, his cattle may benefit by their shade, and he may have the fruit or mast from them. But as to underwood, or at least as to such part of it as can never become timber, the tenant may, in the absence of agreement to the contrary, have a right to cut it.

Trees and underwood.

The exception or reservation of game is absolutely necessary, whenever the landlord desires the right of shooting; as, by the law, the game belongs to the tenant. To what

Game.

CHAP. I.
Sect. 3.
The Subject-Matter of the Lease.

extent this reservation is to be made, and whether it should include rabbits, is a matter of arrangement which need not be discussed. It is more important to allude to the question of game damage, as a clause on this subject is often required by the tenant (although no allusion to it is contained in our example), and will then need the most careful consideration of the land-steward. To allow a clause providing compensation without limit for damage by game is, perhaps, one of the most fatal errors into which he can fall; for he may thereby involve his employer in most costly damages. Such a clause opens to an unscrupulous tenant a door of deceit beyond his power to close. Netting or wiring the centre of fields surrounded by woods, sowing the headlands late, applying ammoniacal dressings here, withholding the same there, neglecting cultivation, and attributing the result to game, are all schemes resorted to by a certain class of men when detection is difficult or impossible. Nevertheless, damage done by game is within limits, and under certain circumstances, a fair subject for compensation. We, however, desire strongly to impress upon all those connected with land management the necessity of granting only "limited damage." The following clause was carefully drawn up and submitted to counsel for insertion in another lease, and may serve as an example:—The lessor "shall and will, in the event of any damage being caused to the extent hereinafter mentioned, but not further or otherwise, to the crops on the demised premises during the said term by the rabbits hereinbefore excepted or reserved, pay to the said   , his executors, administrators, and assigns, the sums of money following, that is to say, in every year (each year being regarded as commencing on the 25th day of March) in which the damage shall exceed the amount of Ten Pounds, but shall not exceed the amount of Thirty Pounds, a sum equal to half the amount of the damage, and in every year commencing as aforesaid in which the damage shall exceed the amount of Thirty Pounds, a sum equal to the whole amount of such damage as shall exceed the amount of Ten Pounds, so long as the sum payable hereunder shall not in any one year exceed Sixty Pounds, and the amount of damage caused in each year shall be ascertained by valuation or arbitration in accordance with the provisions hereinafter contained."

CHAP. I.
Sect. 3.
The Subject-Matter of the Lease.

It is sometimes thought better to require from the lessee an express covenant to the effect that he will not injure, but do his utmost to preserve and protect, the nests, and eggs, and young birds; but, as will be observed in our example, the exception and reservation were considered sufficient. The other clauses on this subject—those usual as to prevention of poaching, and the tenant's right to kill rabbits during certain seasons—sufficiently explain themselves.

The term "Minerals" applies, of course, to all substances below the surface, whether they may be used for building or for any other purposes. As a rule, a tenant can work no substance of this kind. But this rule does not seem to apply where there are pits or mines in actual working at the time of the letting, and forming a regular item in the profit of the property. It is, therefore, generally best for the landlord to claim the whole right to the minerals; and if there is any probability of his needing to work them, he should also reserve a right to enter and work them, and use such part of the surface as he may need. But he must, in the event of occupying surface, either by the withdrawal of material or the formation of roads, give fair compensation to the tenant. This may be done by allowing a reduction of rent, in accordance with the surface occupied. In the lease before us nothing was said about minerals; but in that case there were no open pits which the tenant could possibly have claimed to work, so there was no need of a clause to protect the minerals from him. And the property was of such a nature that there was no kind of likelihood of the landlord needing to resort to it for the purpose of digging any minerals whatever. The above observations as to the tenant's right are to be read with this very important qualification, that as to such substances

Minerals.

CHAP. I.
Sect. 3.
The Subject-Matter of the Lease.

as chalk, gravel, clay, or the like, which he may need for the purpose of fulfilling his covenant to repair, &c., or for application to the soil, he is always at liberty to dig a necessary quantity unless they are expressly excepted out of the demise.

Payment of rent.

It will be observed that the rent is made payable quarterly, the quarter days being December 24 (Christmas), March 25 (Lady-day), June 24 (Midsummer-day), and September 29 (Michaelmas-day). It is customary, however, to collect half-yearly, and when the half-years fall upon September 29 (Michaelmas), and March 25 (Lady-day), it is a good practice to give some certain period say, three or four months credit, and for the following reasons. At "Michaelmas" the farmer has just passed through the heavy expense of harvesting his crops, and has not had time to realise. It is in fact the end of his financial year, when his funds are naturally at a low ebb. At "Lady-day" the corn-stacks have not recovered from the winter; if threshed, the grain will be cold, and will fetch but a low figure. The fattening of cattle and sheep also will have been a heavy expense for some months, and the prices of meat are often low at this time of the year.

It is wise in collecting the rent to remember those matters and assist the tenant as far as is compatible with the interest of the landlord.

Rates and taxes.

Rates are generally paid by the tenant. It is, however, a matter of arrangement. If the landlord pays them, as is sometimes the case, in order to avoid disturbing the arrangement of the rate-book, the amount is reckoned and added to the rent, so that it is really paid by the tenant directly or indirectly. It may here be mentioned that all rates are collected in advance; therefore, if an out-going tenant has paid a rate, and a portion of the time for which it is collected is unexpired when he quits his farm, he is fairly entitled to recovery from the landlord or the in-coming tenant for that portion. Rates are collected from every parish for the purposes of the poor, the highway, and the county. They are collected by the "overseers" when demanded by the "Board of Guardians." The rate levied is upon the value of the property in the parish (a value being ascertained for the purpose and called the rateable value), and is generally a shilling or two in the pound. The collection takes place two or three times a year, as may be required. The rate-book, every time a rate is levied, must be made out and signed by two justices before collection. The amount required, being duly notified by the clerk of the board to the overseers, must be paid in to the credit of the "guardians" punctually to the day; it is therefore necessary to collect with all dispatch, and also right that those who can pay should do so promptly, as it otherwise throws upon an unpaid official a great deal of undeserved anxiety. When the office of overseer is too heavy, the ratepayers in vestry can appoint a clerk or assistant overseer to make out and collect the rate, levying a special rate to defray the expense. The appointment, however, must be submitted to the approval of the "board," and does not relieve the "overseers" from any responsibility of office.

With regard to the taxes, the "Property Tax," or schedule A. Income Tax (called Property Tax when levied upon land), is collected from the occupier or tenant, and must be paid by him. He, however, when he pays his rent carries the receipt with him, and demands deduction. This the landlord is compelled to allow him, as any agreement to put the charge upon the tenant will be void. It is intended to be a tax upon the landlord's income as opposed to Schedule B. Income Tax, which is levied upon farmers' incomes, and which, unlike other incomes derived from ordinary trade, is reckoned at one half of the amount of the rent they pay.

The Land Tax is collected from the tenant at the same time as the Property Tax, and is repaid him by the landlord, unless the latter has, as he may do, contracted himself out of his liability to repay it. The important point to notice with regard to it is, that before any considerable improvement in the estate it ought to be redeemed; although, in the

CHAP. I.
Sect. 3.
The Subject-Matter of the Lease.

absence of an intention to materially improve, there is little reason for doing so. Full information with regard to the redemption of Land Tax can be obtained on application to the clerk of the Land Tax Commissioners in the division in which the property is situate, or directly from the Commissioners in London. The redemption is allowed upon the payment of such a sum of money as if invested in the funds will produce a similar amount to that of the tax levied in the year upon which the application is made. Therefore, if the landowner is in possession of money in the funds, he may clear his estate of the tax without altering his income; if, however, his money is better invested, it will hardly be worth his while to do so except in the event above mentioned, in which case he will be wise to recollect that the tax is levied in accordance with the value of the estate.

It is not necessary that the person redeeming should be the absolute owner of the estate. For instance, if a tenant for life thinks proper to buy up the land tax upon his estate as an investment he can do so, and leave the sum so invested to his younger children; for the estate will then be charged in his favour with the amount he paid for redemption, with interest thereon equivalent to the land tax redeemed. And if he wishes to benefit his successors, he can have the charge merged in the estate.

It may interest the student to know that this tax, which had been imposed under different forms from very early periods of our history, was levied under its present name in the reign of William and Mary. It was made perpetual by Mr. Pitt in the reign of Geo. III., and it was he who introduced the plan for its redemption.

Tithe rent-charge.

Tithe rent-charge, though not a tax in the correct sense of the word, is nevertheless a charge upon the land, and may be considered under this head.

Tithe, as its name denotes, is the tenth portion of the produce of the land set aside for the purposes of the Church. Previous to the year 1836, when the Act was passed for the commutation of these tithes to a money payment, entitled

Act for Commutation of Tithes (6 & 7 Will. 4, c. 71), the amount was collected in kind. At harvest time parties duly authorised entered the various fields and placed an arrow in every tenth shock of corn, thus appropriating it to the use of the rector of the parish. When the corn was carried by the farmer these shocks were left in the field, and were then carted away to tithe barns, and threshed and sold by the rector. This arrangement was attended with much annoyance and occasioned much ill-feeling, as of course the rectors benefited directly by the diligence and exertion of the farmer, or *vice versâ*.

The farmer felt aggrieved from the fact that the better he farmed and the heavier his crop, the more he had to pay his rector; and the rector laboured under the disadvantage of having to thresh and market his crop before he could reap the benefit of his income. This, therefore, brought about the Act, as already named. Tithes were converted into corn-rent charges, equal portions of the amount to consist of wheat, barley, and oats, valued in the commutation at 7s. 0¼d. for wheat, 3s. 11½d. for barley, and 2s. 9d. for oats per imperial bushel.

These prices were fixed upon as the standard, and by the Act it was enacted, "That immediately after the passing of the Act, and also in the month of January in every year, the Comptroller of Corn Returns for the time being, or such other persons as may from time to time be in that behalf authorised by the Privy Council, shall cause an advertisement to be inserted in the *London Gazette* stating what has been, during seven years ending on the *Thursday* next before Christmas-day then next preceding, the average price of an Imperial bushel of British wheat, barley, and oats, computed from the weekly averages of the Corn Returns."

Having thus fixed a standard of value, it was necessary to arrive at the quantity which the land was capable of producing. For this purpose the whole country was valued, a map called the "tithe map" and "award" being supplied

CHAP. I.
Sect. 3.
The Subject-Matter of the Lease.

to every parish based upon this valuation. Upon this map every field shows a number which corresponds with the award, which contains every information as to acreage, description, ownership, name of occupier, and the amount of commuted tithe. This amount represents the *commuted sum*, and it is upon this that the septennial average is brought to bear. For example: Suppose the corn rent-charges upon a farm are commuted at 100*l*., what is the present value of this amount according to the average prices of corn for the seven years preceding Christmas, 1877? Also what is the method of arriving at this value?

Rule.—Divide the several prices per imperial bushels, in farthings increased one hundredfold, by 1011 that of wheat, by 570 that of barley, and by 396 that of oats; then add the several quotients together, and the sum will be the value of 100*l*. apportioned tithe rent-charge in pounds and decimals of pounds.

EXAMPLE.

Average price of wheat to Christmas, 1877 6s. 8½d.
,, ,, barley ,, ,, 4s. 10¼d.
,, ,, oats ,, ,, 3s. 3¼d.

6s. 8½d. = 322 Farthings.
4s. 10¼d. = 233 ,,
3s. 3¼d. = 157 ,,

Therefore—

$$\text{Wheat } \frac{322 \times 100}{1011} = 31{\cdot}849$$

$$\text{Barley } \frac{233 \times 100}{570} = 40{\cdot}877$$

$$\text{Oats } \frac{157 \times 100}{396} = 39{\cdot}646$$

Value of £100 tithe rent £112·362

This method of arriving at these yearly charges should be understood, but the actual working of these figures is rendered unnecessary in practice on account of the valuable "Supplement to Willich's Tithe Commutation Tables," compiled by Montague Marriott, barrister-at-law, and published yearly by Messrs. Longmans for the sum of one shilling, and which can be purchased through any bookseller. It is, in fact, a ready reckoner, giving the present value of the commuted sum from 3d. to 2000l.

CHAP. I.
Sect. 3.
The Subject-Matter of the Lease.

Having thus given briefly the history of tithe, and the way in which it is calculated, we will proceed to discuss it in a landlord's and tenant's point of view.

Though a charge upon land, it is, nevertheless, a direct charge upon the crops, and as such is payable by the tenant. It is not in any sense a landlord's charge, and can only be exacted from him when every means to obtain payment from the tenant has failed—*i.e.*, if no agreement has been entered into relieving the tenant of the charge.

Tithe from a landlord's and tenant's point of view.

Collection is made half-yearly, viz., on the first day of April and the first day of October, and represents the amount due from the crop of the same year. This is important to bear in mind, for this reason: if a change of tenancy takes place between Michaelmas and Lady-day, and the growing crop is valued to the incomer at the cost of cultivation, the payment of the charge due on the 1st of April will fall upon the incomer, and, in the event of the outgoer having paid the amount, he is entitled to recovery in the valuation. If, however, on the other hand, the outgoer retains the crops and reaps them for his own benefit, he pays both the April and October amount.

Collection of tithe.

Farms may be let tithe free under certain circumstances; when, for instance, the charge is the property of the landlord, or when the charge has been merged in the freehold, or when the farm forms a portion of the estate, and has not been separated for tithe purposes. These circumstances, however, do not in any way affect the case, as the rent will, of course, be increased in proportion.

When farms may be let tithe free.

From the foregoing, then, we have shown that the rent-charge is purely a tenant's charge; nevertheless, to prevent error or misconception, it will be better to provide for the payment of it in the lease.

D

**Chap. I.
Sect. 3.
The Subject-Matter of the Lease.**

Repairs.

Repairs are always a difficult subject, and, as some observation upon it will be made in the legal supplement, it is perhaps not advisable to dwell upon it here. But it may be noticed that the basis of the contract should always be that the premises are in good and tenantable repair at the time of entry by the tenant, and the liability undertaken by him should be worded in accordance with this assumption. If at the time the lease is signed it is agreed by the parties that work remains to be done by the landlord in order to put them in tenantable condition, this work should be clearly and specifically defined in the lease, and care should be taken to execute it forthwith, and to obtain from the tenant an admission that it is executed, as otherwise the tenant may attempt to get rid of the liability on his own covenant by alleging neglect by the landlord to do what he had undertaken. Assuming the premises to be in repair, the tenant for a term of years will always be willing to execute all repairs during the term of his lease, provided his landlord supplies him with the necessary material.

Haulage of material.

The material may be found, either in the rough or converted, on or within a reasonable distance of the farm, say ten miles; but the tenant should generally haul it a reasonable distance at his own expense. Where the estate employs a saw-mill the timber may with propriety be converted for the use of the tenant; a small charge being made for this if deemed advisable.

Power of steward to inspect buildings.

A clause should also be inserted which will enable the steward to inspect the buildings at all reasonable times; and providing that in the event of repairs being needed, or in the event of any wilful neglect, he should be able to give notice in writing that the specified matter needs attention; and should the same not be performed in a workmanlike manner within a reasonable time (the time being specified), he should be at liberty to perform the same, and charge the tenant with the amount.

At a change of tenancy the state of repair needs particular attention, as, in the event of these repairs not having been duly executed by the outgoing tenant, he must be called upon either to do them, or allow a deduction from the amount of the valuation, to the extent of the amount required for such purpose; such amount being arranged by qualified surveyors.

<small>Chap. I. Sect. 3. *The Subject-Matter of the Lease.*

Outgoing tenant's liability to repair.</small>

Although the matter is primarily one between landlord and tenant, it is in practice essential to the incoming tenant to see to it, as he may otherwise, when he enters finally upon his holding, find that he has incurred unintentional liability.

Insurance is a matter upon which different opinions exist. Some consider that the insurance of the buildings should fall upon the tenant, he producing his vouchers for payment of premiums at each audit, and either providing for the payment of the sum assured in the event of fire to the landlord (who on his part should enter into a covenant to immediately rebuild); or else undertaking to expend the money himself in rebuilding. Others consider that the landlord should insure all his own buildings, wheresoever situated, and covenant to immediately rebuild. We agree with the latter opinion, and strongly recommend the subject to the attention of landlords. Let them insure their buildings in some first-class office, and authorise their bankers to pay the annual premiums, and so prevent the lapse of insurances by forgetfulness or neglect. In the event of fire, they will then, of course, immediately commence rebuilding, and, if the tenant suffers much loss or inconvenience beyond what he himself ought to have provided against by means of a private insurance, a reasonable reduction of rent may be allowed during the progress of the building.

<small>Insurance.</small>

But, as a rule, we object to any *covenant* by the landlord to allow a reduction of rent during rebuilding. The property is in the hands of the tenant, and it is his duty, and not the landlord's, to take all reasonable precautions against it being burnt down. If such a covenant is admitted the whole burden of the disaster falls upon the landlord. There is a

<small>Reduction rent during rebuilding.</small>

D 2

CHAP. I.
Sect. 3.
The Subject-Matter of the Lease.

twofold loss to be guarded against. Firstly, there is the loss of the buildings of which we have spoken, and which the landlord is sure to see covered by an insurance, either by himself or the tenant. Secondly, there is the tenant's oss in business or convenience, a loss represented by the amount of rent which he has to pay for a non-existing thing; this loss he should provide against by an insurance on his own account. For the tenant to insure the payment to himself of a year's rent, in the event of destruction by fire, is really the reasonable course.

Plan for purposes of insurance.

COPY OF PLAN FOR PURPOSES OF INSURANCE.

Home Farm. *Parish.*

Eight hundred pounds on the following, viz. :—

On farm-house, brick and tile, lettered A.	300
,, cart-shed near, timber, stone, and slate, lettered B.	50
,, piggeries, timber, stone, and slate, lettered C.	25
,, stable and cowhouses, stone and slate, lettered D.	150
,, barn and stables, timber and slate, lettered E.	150
,, granary, timber, stone, and slate, lettered F.	25
,, range of sheds, stone and slate, lettered G.	100
	£800

No. of policy, 147,866

The above plan and statement illustrates a method of arranging the matter, which was recommended to the writer by a gentleman of great experience, and which has been found very useful.

This plan is made upon the estate, and then forwarded to the insurance office, and the policy, based upon it, is made out. Copies of these plans should be kept by the steward for reference, as more handy for casual purposes than the policies themselves. Mistakes also are rendered almost impossible, provided care is exercised in the execution of the plan.

*Chap. I.
Sect. 3.
The Subject-Matter of the Lease.*

It was at one time necessary to insert in leases restrictive clauses as to cropping; the object of this was to prevent the too constant repetition of exhaustive crops. Artificial manures and oil cake were unknown articles, and it was difficult to give back to the soil what was taken from it. The raising of two corn crops in succession was looked upon as a flagrant act, and one which brought down upon the offending tenant the weight of the landlord's family solicitor's just wrath and displeasure. The growth of potatoes was also strictly forbidden, on account of it being a crop taken from the land, and not fed on the farm like the ordinary root crop. The course generally laid down was the Norfolk or four-corner rotation, *i.e.*, barley, clover, or pulse, wheat, and roots. In those days this plan was a wise and just one, and necessary to secure a balance of plant food.

Cultivation. Restrictive clauses.

Two corn crops in succession.

Four course rotation.

Times have changed, however; men of science have shown us not only what the various plants require, but where and how to procure the necessary ingredients. The use of oil and cotton cake and artificial fertilisers have entirely revolutionised agriculture, and enabled us to omit from our leases these now objectionable clauses. To bind an agriculturist at the present day to any strict course of husbandry is not only unwise, but almost impossible. Barley after wheat (for example) is now a recognised mode of culture, and will probably become more and more the practice. The reason of this is so evident as to show the unreasonableness of disallowing two corn crops in succession. Barley grown after swedes fed off the land is often sown late, and necessarily upon a new furrow; the result is

Restrictive clauses no longer required.

Barley after wheat.

a flaggy crop, with a thin grain; and, from the amount of straw, more time is necessary to fit it for stacking, thus exposing the grain and causing discoloration. When grown after wheat, all these evils are avoided. The seed can be sown early on a furrow that has been exposed to the winter frosts, and the roots take a firm hold by the time the genial warmth of spring exerts its influence upon the young blades, thus giving vigour to the plant, a firm straw that will stand up and bear a heavy head, an early maturity, and a plump grain. Under this course, too, the sowing of clover seeds with the barley is avoided, often a source of difficulty at harvest time, rendering as it does the rapid carting of the barley a matter of impossibility.

These cropping clauses must therefore vanish from our leases, and we must secure the fertility of the soil by a careful selection of tenants, and by watching the course of their farming, to see that nothing is done which is clearly bad husbandry.

The fact of occupation alone will imply in law an obligation to follow the rules of *good husbandry;* the landlord therefore is secure to ascertain extent when no written contract exists at all.

It is possible, without injuring the interest of the tenant, to provide for a return to the four-course shift during the last few years of the lease. This is a matter open to the judgment of the steward. But the compensation clauses, to which we shall presently allude, are the most to be relied upon for securing good farming up to the end of the term.

Up to a recent date, and to a very great extent even now, the sale of hay and straw has been strictly forbidden, either by the covenants of the lease, or the custom of the country. For distant outlying farms, surrounded by bad roads, the restriction is a wise one, often, however, unnecessary on account of the impossibility of drawing such heavy produce away. But where farms are situated near towns or railways, the restriction is certainly unwise. For example: Suppose a farmer is able to sell straw for 2*l.* 10*s.*

or 3*l.* a ton, delivered at a railway station within one or two miles of his farm. A railway truck will hold, perhaps, two tons, or 6*l.* worth of straw; this 6*l.* will bring back to the farm fifteen tons of good town stable dung, or nearly three times the quantity the two tons of straw would make in the farmer's own yard.

CHAP. I.
Sect. 3.
The Subject-Matter of the Lease.

Again, with regard to hay. Two tons of hay at 4*l.* 10*s.* per ton, will nearly equal a ton of oilcake, which will yield 3*l.* of manurial value, more by far than the hay would produce if fed at home.

It is clear, however, that if the sale of hay and straw is permitted, it can only be upon the terms of an equivalent being returned in purchased food or manure; otherwise the productive power of the land will soon depreciate. The provisions which we have adopted will be found in clauses 21-23 of the lease, and amount simply to this, that the money (or not less than two-thirds of the amount) obtained from sale of hay and straw shall be expended in purchasing oil or cotton cake, or artificial or other manures, proof of such purchases being given by the production of vouchers, and a statement of the various sales being made, at every audit if so demanded.

Equivalent of hay and straw sold.

The removal from the premises of the dung produced upon them would be so clearly against the rules of good husbandry, that it is unnecessary to do more than allude to it.

One of the most important questions for consideration in letting land is the adoption of some provisions which will secure such a cropping and treatment of the land as that it will at the termination of the lease revert to the landlord in an improved, instead of in an exhausted condition, so as to fit it for re-letting at an advanced figure. Whilst a tenant feels that his capital is insecure, he will naturally, towards the end of his lease, put as little into the land, and extract as much out of it, as he can. He will at least try and recover from it the value of all the manure that he has put in. In other words, he will "whip" the

Compensation at the expiration of the term.

CHAP. I.
Sect. 3.
The Subject-Matter of the Lease.

land, to recoup himself for his unexhausted capital lying in it, if he knows he will be unable to obtain that capital from his landlord. To guard against this, the lease or agreement must provide such "compensation clauses" as will induce the tenant to farm well up to the last day of his term.

The question of compensating the lessee for what are commonly called "unexhausted improvements," or, in other words, for the expenditure of capital out of the ordinary and necessary course of husbandry, will be discussed in the next section. Our lease (Example A.) makes no provision for any such matters, except in so far as the application of purchased manures or the consumption of purchased foods may come within that category.

For, as a rule, the compensation clauses need only touch the question of purchased food, unconsumed straw, hay, and dung, and the ordinary acts of husbandry of which the tenant cannot reap the full benefit, either because the benefit of them extends beyond one year, and his lease expires in the meantime, or because, although they may be called annual operations, his lease expires between the season for performing them and the season for profiting by them. Of these acts of husbandry, the application of purchased manure may fairly be considered a part. It is to be noted that the custom of the country usually, or often, entitles the tenant to compensation for all these matters, except purchased foods, in the absence of any agreement at all. And the custom of the country in all agricultural matters may be insisted upon by either party, if not varied by written agreement, just in the same way as though it were a part of the law of the land; subject to this important qualification, that the party insisting upon it must prove its existence. But custom will not generally touch the question of purchased food; and as to the ordinary acts of husbandry (of which the application of purchased manure is treated in the lease as a part), the tenant may fairly object to relying upon his chance of getting payment from an

Rule of custom of country.

Custom, as it affects purchased food.

incoming tenant, who would by the custom be the person primarily bound to pay him. Indeed, there might be no incoming tenant, and as, in that case, the custom would in the absence of agreement fix the landlord with the liability to compensate according to the custom, it is clearly to the landlord's interest to have his liability carefully defined by the lease.

<small>CHAP. I.
Sect. 3.
The Subject-Matter of the Lease.</small>

The question of purchased food will be found alluded to as one of "unexhausted improvement;" the several acts of husbandry to be compensated for will be discussed in the chapter on valuation.

<small>Compensation for acts of husbandry.</small>

There is a further observation to be made under this heading, namely, that if (see Example A., clauses 34 and 36) the letting is a Michaelmas one, provision must be made for outgoing occupation by the outgoing tenant of barns, stabling, &c., and for part or whole of the house until the month of May following, to enable him to thrash his corn. This is not necessary in a Lady-day entry, which is one of the advantages of that season. The point will, however, be noticed hereafter.

<small>Temporary occupation of buildings by outgoing tenant after expiration of term.</small>

In the event of non-payment of rent within a specified period, generally three weeks from the date of collection, whether notice or not has been given, it is necessary to give the landlord power to re-enter and occupy as in his former state. The power is also generally made to come into operation in the event of any breach of covenant; and this takes in a point to which the steward's attention should be particularly directed, as such a wording of the clause adds greatly to the landlord's protection, and is not invariably adopted. The power may also be made operative in case the tenant becomes a bankrupt, or liquidating, or compounding debtor; but this is not essential if the landlord is enabled to re-enter so soon as any term or agreement in the lease is broken.

<small>Lessor's power of re-entry.</small>

SECTION IV.

COMPENSATION FOR UNEXHAUSTED IMPROVEMENTS.

AGRICULTURAL HOLDINGS ACT, 1875—ERECTION OF BUILDINGS—LAYING DOWN OF PERMANENT PASTURE—MAKING AND PLANTING OF OSIER BEDS—PLANTING HOPS—RECLAIMING WASTE LAND—CHALKING LAND—CLAYING LAND—CLAY-BURNING—BONING LAND—LIMING LAND—CONSUMPTION OF CAKE AND OTHER PURCHASED FOOD—APPLICATION OF ARTIFICIAL MANURES—ADVICE TO LAND STEWARDS.

CHAP. I.
Sect. 4.
Compensation for Unexhausted Improvements.

Agricultural Holdings Act, 1875.

THE ordinary acts of husbandry, compensation for which is always sufficiently provided for either by custom or contract, are to be distinguished from what are called "unexhausted improvements." Concerning the latter the Legislature, thinking tenants insufficiently provided with means of compensation, pretended to come to their assistance by the Agricultural Holdings Act, 1875. But, as this Act leaves the parties at liberty to exclude its operation by agreement, it has practically scarcely any operation at all.

The student should here refer to the terms of the Act as set out in the Supplement (*post*). Although it is usual, as we have said, to exclude its operation, and to make compensation a matter of bargain between landlord and tenant, the Act contains a useful summary of the matters concerning which the question of compensation may be raised, and it will be observed that it includes in its list of "improvements" the consumption of purchased manure and of purchased foods—acts to which we have already alluded as taken in the nature of ordinary farming operations than of "improvements." Proceeding now to consider the question with reference to the three classes of acts or processes mentioned in the statute as "improvements," we may say that, assuming the operation of the Act to be excluded, the subject presents itself to the steward under two aspects. He has, firstly, to consider, on letting the land, for what acts the tenant shall be compensated as a matter of right under the terms of the lease; and we have above stated the points (the consumption of purchased manure and foods) which the provisions of the lease should in any case cover, although the nature of the holding may not unfrequently be such as to make it desirable to extend the provisions to other points also. But, secondly, after the lease has been executed, the tenant will often apply for leave to perform acts of improvement on the terms of having compensation allowed him for so much of the operation as he cannot himself profit by; and then the landlord or his agent has to decide whether or not the proposed operation is a desirable one, and he must approach the subject in a reasonable and liberal spirit, and not in a spirit of determination to insist upon the lease and nothing but the lease. _{Chap. I. Sect. 4. *Compensation for Unexhausted Improvements.* *Application by tenant to perform special acts.*}

For it is often impossible, in taking a farm, for a tenant to know what special acts will be required of him for the full development of the resources of his holding, and often as impossible for the steward to provide clauses in the lease to meet every case, no matter how ready the latter may be to meet the tenant in a reasonable and liberal way. It is therefore highly necessary that special contracts during the existence of the lease should be granted freely and fully, when applied for by a good tenant, for such acts as will materially benefit the land. *Advisability of granting special contracts.*

But with reference to acts not provided for by the lease, the question may often arise whether they are best performed by the application of the landlord's capital or the tenant's. In our opinion, those acts referred to under Class I. in the Agricultural Holdings Act are such as should be, with four exceptions, undertaken by the landlord; such exceptions are: *Whether landlord's or tenant's capital should be employed.*

   Laying down of permanent pasture.
   Making and planting of osier-beds.

CHAP. I.
Sect. 4.
Compensation for Unexhausted Improvements.

Erection and enlargement of buildings.

Planting of hops.
Reclaiming of waste land.

With regard, for instance, to the erection and enlargement of buildings, one of the subjects comprised in Class I., the expenditure of tenant's capital for this purpose is not to be encouraged. When buildings are really required, most landlords, upon a fair payment of interest, will carry out the work. When the landlord cannot find the sum necessary, he is able to borrow and to secure the repayment of the loan by creating a rent-charge upon the property sufficient to pay capital and interest; so that, if the rent-charge is borne by the tenant, there is really no excuse for the non-carrying out of necessary improvements. It is to the landlord's interest to leave the tenant's capital unshackled for the direct benefit of the land. Good and sufficient farm-buildings are of course necessary, and money judiciously laid out in this respect will yield a fair and reasonable return; for the farm will let at a figure proportionately higher, to the extent of, at least, 5 per cent. upon the outlay. For example: supposing a farm of 500 acres is let with old and insufficient buildings for 450*l.* a year, or 18*s.* per acre. Let 1500*l.* be laid out in the building of cottages, warm sheds, covered yards, and other conveniences, and we have an extra sum of 75*l.* a year as interest, to meet in the shape of extra rental, or 3*s.* per acre only—an increase of rental which most tenants would consider to be made up to them by the increased accommodation.

Acts in Class II.

Those acts, however, which are comprised in Classes II. and III. are what most concern us here. These acts are:

CLASS II.
Boning of land.
Chalking of land.
Claying of land.
Burning of clay.
Liming of land.
Marling of land.

Class III.

Application to land of purchased artificial or other manures.

Consumption on the holding by cattle, sheep, or pigs, of cake or other feeding stuff not produced on the holding.

Such acts as these are clearly operations to be undertaken by the tenant with his own capital.

The improvement caused by most of the acts contained in Class II. should, in our opinion, be considered as exhausted in a much shorter period than that suggested by the Act, which defines the period in each case as seven years. Three or four years is generally sufficient; compensation after that is buying what may exist, but what nevertheless is very difficult to appreciate. The benefit derived from the operation has become so merged in the soil as to make it almost impossible, practically, to set a money value upon it.

Under Class III. one year's compensation is ample, and often more than is necessary, as will be hereafter shown.

We will now proceed to discuss in order the various operations and applications which appear suitable for performance by the tenant, and explain the circumstances under which they may be deemed necessary and beneficial, and the mode of performing them, and the amount of compensation to be given.

A tenant, without special agreement, will not, of course, desire to lay down permanent pasture unless he has several years still to run, so that he may expect to reap the advantage of his outlay. If his tenancy is of short duration, and he feels that such an act would be beneficial to his holding, he will, if he is wise, consult his landlord and obtain his sanction. As the laying down of land to permanent pasture is generally looked upon in these times as wise and judicious, he is not very likely to meet with a refusal. The sanction, however, if given, should be conditional on the work being done thoroughly, and with care and judgment, and on the seeds being bought from an approved firm, for

Chap. I. Sect. 4. Compensation for Unexhausted Improvements.

Acts in Class III.

Laying down of permanent pasture.

**Chap. I.
Sect. 4.
Compensation for Unexhausted Improvements.**

there should be no haphazard about a work of such an important nature. In some cases the landlord may possibly be willing to find the seed, and the tenant the labour. In that case the agreement (which should be in writing) to give compensation may be made on the following scale : If the term expire the first year after the operation, the tenant to receive 20s. per acre; if the second year, 15s. per acre; if the third year, 10s. per acre. But beyond that period no compensation should be allowed.

If, on the other hand, the tenant finds the seed as well as the labour, the figures may be raised in each case 20s., 15s., and 10s. respectively. There may, of course, be reasons why the laying down of certain fields in pasture may be of doubtful benefit; in fact, a future tenant may consider the value of the farm decreased by the alteration.

The land chosen should be near homesteads, low-lying bottoms well watered, oddly shaped fields difficult to cultivate, or otherwise specially adapted.

Making and planting osier-beds.

The method of planting of osier-beds is fully explained under the head of "Willow" (*post*), and it is, therefore, unnecessary to state it here. The operation is one that will only occasionally present itself to the land steward as the act of a tenant. When, however, a tenant desires to perform it, his offer to do so should be in most cases accepted as a decided improvement, and worthy of encouragement. If the tenant has a considerable time still unexpired, he may be content to perform the operation without compensation, as the osier crop soon reaches a profitable growth, and quickly repays any outlay that may have been incurred. But in case he holds by the year, or has only two or three years of his lease still to run, he is not likely to undertake the operation without first arranging a fair basis of compensation. Such a basis appears to us to be :

If the term expire the first year after the planting—the full cost.

If the second year—two-thirds.
If the third year—one-third.

CHAP. I.
Sect. 4.
Compensation for Unexhausted Improvements.

This is an expensive operation, and is generally looked upon as a marked improvement to an estate, so that the tenant can scarcely need the sanction of the landlord. When, however, the term is short, and the tenant seeks compensation, he must apply for permission, as he cannot expect his landlord to submit to a demand for compensation, if the application is first made when he leaves the farm. One matter that must weigh with the steward is, whether the proposed planting will entail the necessity for extra kiln room. If this is the case, it at once opens up a fresh outlay, and consequent increase of rent in shape of interest. This is mentioned simply to impress upon the reader the necessity for foresight and care.

Planting hops.

Compensation for three years, by which time the new garden will be in full bearing and consequent profit, will fairly meet the case; *e.g.*, a fair basis for compensation seems to be:—

If the time expire the first year after planting—full cost.
If the second year—two-thirds.
If the third year—one-third.

The reclaiming of waste land is an operation of great importance upon many estates; but it is seldom undertaken by tenants. When, however, tenants perform it, the best compensation that can be given them is a lease of considerable length, at a nominal rent. If this is resorted to, it is of course necessary to secure a man of capital and character. To arrange a basis for cash compensation before the reclamation is a very difficult matter; for it is impossible often to estimate either the extent to which the tenant may within a short period of years recoup himself for his outlay, or the additional value which that outlay may, at the end of such a short period, have given to the land. To go generally, however, into the subject of reclamation is not within the purpose of this work.

Reclaiming waste land.

There are other acts, such as drainage of land, and

CHAP. I.
Sect. 4.
Compensation
for Unexhausted Improvements.

making of ponds, wells, &c., which may possibly be done by the tenant by arrangement; but, as a rule, they are best done by the landlord as already expressed.

We come next to the operations under Class II., all of which, to entitle the tenant to compensation, must, like those above considered, be done by arrangement with the landlord or his steward, either by conditions in lease, or by special written contract. They are all expensive and heavy operations, though often in the highest degree desirable. We shall dismiss, with a few passing remarks, those operations which are to a certain extent local, and speak with more detail of the more general operations of boning and liming.

Chalking land. Chalking of land must of course be confined to those farms where chalk is procurable close by, as the heavy cartage makes it impracticable in any other. In any case the tenant should not expect large outlay for this purpose to be made good to him by compensation.

It acts to a certain extent as lime, but is more slow in its effect. It should be applied in winter, or better still in autumn, so that the frost may pulverise it. Frost is a most perfect pulveriser. Chalk contains such a large amount of water, that the expansion caused by the act of freezing quickly bursts large lumps on which a hammer has but little effect. The action of chalk will be explained more fully under the head of "Liming."

Claying land. Claying is a heavy operation, but one nevertheless of great importance upon light sandy soils, provided the supply of clay is close by. Under such conditions, it is a proper subject for compensation, for, say, three years.

Clay burning. The burning of clay is an important operation when the soil is very plastic and tenacious. Burnt clay never returns to its original state when exposed to the action of the weather, so that when mixed with a heavy clay it serves to make the soil more kind and workable. To conduct this operation thoroughly, however, is very expensive, and it is seldom resorted to. Where it is done with the landlord's concurrence, he may properly regard it as being during four years a fit subject for compensation.

Marling was once greatly resorted to, as the pits in many parts of England fully testify. Marl is carbonate of lime in a soft state, and mixed with clay and sand. Marls vary in value in accordance with the carbonate of lime they contain. Some contain but little, say 10 to 20 per cent., others as much as 80 per cent. Beds of marl are found in the greensand formation containing a considerable quantity of phosphate of lime. When this is the case, it becomes a very valuable dressing. This substance is found in nearly all marl, but often to such a limited extent as to be almost untraceable. When found, however, in the greensand, it sometimes amounts to 10 per cent.

This operation, therefore, when the lime contained in the marl is of fair proportion, may be classed as highly effective, and one that should be fully encouraged. It is important, however, that the steward should be alive to the quality of the dressing; he may otherwise pay heavily for a dressing of simple clay, of little or no value, possibly even injurious. He can test the substance fairly well by pouring on a heap of the substance a weak solution of muriatic acid. Effervesence will be produced if carbonate of lime is present, for the carbonate of lime consists of carbonic acid and lime in combination; but the lime has a greater affinity for the muriatic acid than for the carbonic; and therefore immediately unites with the former, and releases the carbonic acid, which escapes in gaseous form, causing the effervescence. This operation, when the marl is really good, may rank for compensation for five years.

Boning requires fuller consideration, as it is more resorted to at the present time than many of the operations already described. Bone ranks high as an improver, and, generally speaking, the operation is one which merits full compensation. The dressing is principally applied to pastures, especially in those districts where cheese is made and where young stock are reared, the object of it being to return to

Chap. I. Sect. 4. Compensation for Unexhausted Improvements.

Marling.

The method of testing marl.

Boning land.

Chap. I. Sect. 4. Compensation for Unexhausted Improvements.

Visible effect of bone-dressing.

the soil the phosphate of lime extracted by the constant production of milk and bone.

But little effect is visible to the eye, and many have very little faith in the dressing on this account. We have in one case found by careful experiment that the weight of hay obtained from a plot dressed with half-inch bone has been less for the first two years than upon the plot unmanured, although the third year has shown a slight increase (see the list of "Experiments upon Top-dressing of Pastures," chap. vii.).

Object of bone-dressing.

But, although visible effect must not be looked for, it is nevertheless a valuable dressing. Its tendency is to promote the growth of the firm grasses. The fact that every ten gallons of milk contains about half a pound of bone-earth, and every 100lb. of cheese contains $2\frac{1}{2}$lb. of the same substance, is of itself suggestive of the necessity for restoring to the feeding ground the substance so extracted from it. If a pasture is grazed for years by cows, and no attention is paid to this important fact, it would seem that the natural result must be the exhaustion of the soil, so far as regards this particular element.

Again, when we consider the amount of the ingredients constituting bone-earth which are requisite to supply young stock with bone, and how year after year pastures are grazed and no attention whatever paid to this, the probability would seem that our stock must degenerate for want of necessary material, unless we replenish the exhausted stores. In Cheshire and other cheese-producing counties we believe the application of bone is made compulsory, and it ought to be so to some extent on all farms where pastures form an important feature of the holding.

Compensation.

The plan which commends itself to us is to dress to the extent of 7cwt. per acre once in seven years, giving compensation for the whole of the period, *i.e.*, one seventh of the dressing being treated as exhausted each year.

We recommend the use of half or quarter-inch bone, *i.e.*, crushed bones that have passed through meshes of such sizes; and we give the preference to raw bones on account of the gelatine they contain, this being an extra nitrogenous manure, although the presence of gelatine retards to some extent the necessary decay. Bone dust is, of course, more rapid in its action, but it is so liable to adulteration, and the adulteration so difficult to detect, that its use is attended with considerable anxiety. Applying once to one of the first manure manufacturers' in England for bone dust, their reply was that they could supply bone dust, but only at considerable expense, as it must come direct from their own works, for they could warrant none bought elsewhere. *Chap. I. Sect. 4. Compensation for Unexhausted Improvements.* *Adulteration of bone-dust.*

Compensation over so extended a period should, however, be allowed only when the dressing is of raw or undissolved bones. When dissolved their action is more rapid, and therefore the effect is less permanent, and the operation merits compensation for a shorter period, only such compensation, in fact, as would be applicable to a dressing of manure under Class III. *Compensation to apply to undissolved bones only.*

The cost of boning is heavy. The market price varies, but 9*l.* 10*s.* per ton may be taken as an average price, to which must be added cost of application. It is evident, therefore, that though absolutely necessary, the application must be made with judgment. Soils vary much with regard to the phosphate of lime they contain; for instance, the soils of the *upper greensand* are rich in such ingredients, consequently the application of bone to such land is less imperative than upon other soils where they are almost absent. This proves the necessity for some knowledge of geology in the proper management of estates (see *post,* chapter viii.). *Price of bone.*

Undissolved bones are sometimes applied to arable land, and the practice is to be much recommended. Where, however, it is resorted to, compensation must extend only to three years, as the conditions render the action more rapid. *Application undissolved bone to arable land.*

Liming is a most important operation upon most farms, and one too often neglected. There are few soils that would not repay a dressing of lime. All plants need lime *Liming land.*

E 2

CHAP. I.
Sect. 4.
Compensation for Unexhausted Improvements.

directly; it also acts upon the vegetable matter or "humus" contained in the soil, and renders it soluble, and fit for plant food; it combines with the acids in the soil, and removes sourness, and also upon mineral matters, fitting them for entering into the roots of growing plants.

Reasons for applying lime.

The reasons for applying lime, and not chalk or other limestone, are twofold. In the first place, this course is a great saving of labour. When chalk or other limestone is burnt in a kiln, the carbonic acid which it contains is driven off, leaving behind the lime only. This substance is quick or hot lime. If water is poured upon this, or if it is left exposed to atmospheric action, it falls into a fine powder, and is said to be "slacked." If applied to land in its quick or caustic state, its action is more rapid, but this application is only recommended in the reclamation of peaty or heavy clay soils. It is best to leave it in a heap for a year, when by the action of the atmosphere it crumbles gradually, and having a great affinity for carbonic acid, attracts it from the air, and again becomes a carbonate, but reduced to a fine state of powder, and much lighter than in its original form. A ton of chalk when burnt will produce only $11\frac{1}{4}$ cwt. of lime, therefore, if we cart chalk, we cart $8\frac{3}{4}$ cwt. in every ton of matter not required. Such a great saving in cartage is effected only in the event of the lime being carted in a caustic state; if allowed to slack (or slake as it is often called) it gains weight, one ton of pure lime becoming $26\frac{1}{2}$ cwt. of slacked lime. But in either case, it is clear that a great saving is effected in labour. The other and more important reason for the use of lime is, that in the state of powder, it acts at once and vigorously.

Lime to be applied superficially.

The application should be superficial, its tendency being to work down. It should not, therefore, be ploughed in, but be used as a top-dressing.

Quantity required.

The quantity used will depend upon the length of time between the application. Some prefer, little and often, others a heavy dressing once in eight or ten years. A full dressing is 1 bushel to the rod, or 160 bushels per acre.

This is expensive, and only necessary under extraordinary conditions. No rule as to compensation can be laid down, but it is a safe subject for full and free acknowledgment. The cost of the lime (perhaps sixpence per bushel), and of the cartage and application, can be easily obtained from the outgoing tenant, and the necessary amount of compensation can be reckoned in accordance with the time that has expired since the application. A full dressing, in our opinion, may be considered as not exhausted till the expiration of seven years.

With regard to the compensation for the acts comprised under Class III., it may, as we have stated, be foreseen and provided for in the lease.

It is as necessary for the land steward to provide compensation for consumption of cake and other purchased food, as for the tenant to exact it, as it is this full feeding of cake and other purchased foods to the last day of the term, that determines in a great degree the future letting value of the land. And it is not likely, as already expressed, that a tenant, shortly bound to quit a farm, will purchase food which he knows will only partially benefit himself, without feeling sure of repayment for that portion that lies buried in the soil. This portion is so exactly defined by analysis, that the basis of compensation becomes a simple matter of arithmetic. The only difficult matters are to be sure of the pureness of the article consumed, and of the actual finding of it in the land. So much rubbish is now forced into the market, with the brand of "pure," that we have to use all our diligence to prevent the payment of compensation for an expenditure for which we have not a sufficient equivalent. These difficulties can only be overcome by generating a feeling of trust, or by unobtrusive but keen supervision.

Those who have fed cake upon the land know well its marvellous effects upon the succeeding crop; the outline of the folds can be distinctly traced in the luxuriant growth and dark colour of the herbage. Upon those farms where sheep can be folded throughout the year, there is no better

CHAP. I.
Sect. 4.
Compensation for Unexhausted Improvements.

plan of distributing manure than by the feeding of sheep; the heavy operation of the dung cart is much reduced, and the application is more effective. Also in pastures, where beasts are fed with cake, the benefit is very marked. As a matter for compensation it has this advantage—that what we pay for we see, and feel before the year is out.

Compensation for cake consumed.

The amount of compensation is generally one-third the amount of cake consumed upon the farm during the last year of the term, provided such expenditure does not exceed that of the two or three previous years, but so that compensation shall not extend to that consumed upon land from which a corn crop has since been taken, or to that purchased from money obtained from the sale of hay or straw: (see the clause in the lease, p. 11.) The amount of one-third is fixed because the analysis proves that one-third of every ton of oil cake is left upon the farm in the form of manure. In case of cotton cake, two-thirds are left, and this peculiarity is sometimes noticed and allowed for in compensation.

We have not alluded to other articles of food; compensation can only be given for expenditure on such as may have been purchased, not for such as have been grown upon the farm, and the manure left from consumption of corn is, in our opinion, too small to merit compensation.

The one-third should not certainly apply to the whole bill of purchased foods.

Artificial manures.

The application of artificial manure merits but slight compensation as applied to arable land. The benefit derived from them is so very transient that we are of opinion that the outgoing tenant reaps what he sows. This does not apply, of course, to such as may have been applied to crops growing at the time he quits. For this he will, of course, be paid as an ordinary act of husbandry of which he does not reap the benefit. Neither does the same principle altogether apply to pastures. If the reader turns to the list of " Top-dressing " experiments, he will find what a marked effect guano had for three years, and will see that for such a result substantial compensation can hardly be withheld.

Let your leases be drawn up in accordance with each individual letting, and do not too strictly enforce a *set form*. Give liberty of action to a good man, but secure to yourselves a means of checking bad farming. Let your enforcement of due attention to the conditions of the lease involve the smallest possible interference with the tenant. Be ready with advice when applied for, be backward in giving it unasked. Be liberal in compensation agreements and otherwise, when the value of the holding will be thereby advanced; but grant no terms without first instituting full inquiry. As you are the medium between the landlord and the tenant, remember that the interests of the two are identical, and that the tenant cannot be alienated in feeling from the landlord without injury to the latter.

Chap. I. Sect. 4. Compensation for Unexhausted Improvements.

Advice to land stewards.

CHAPTER II.
FARM VALUATIONS.

SECTION I.
Valuation Generally.

VALUATION FROM OUTGOING TO INCOMING TENANT—VALUERS: THEIR APPOINTMENT AND PROCEDURE—VALUATION OF TILLAGES—ALLOWANCE OF RENT, RATES, AND TAXES—MICHAELMAS VALUATIONS: GROWING CORN, ROOT CROPS, PREPARATION FOR WHEAT FALLOWS, CLOVER LEYS—CLOVER AND GRASS SEEDS—STRAW AND HAY—FARMYARD DUNG—LADY-DAY VALUATIONS: HALF TILLAGES, WHEAT CROP, SEEDS, SAINFOIN ROOTS—SURVEY OF DILAPIDATIONS—FIXTURES.

Chap. II. Sect. 1. Valuation Generally.

FARM valuation is an important branch of estate management, and every land steward should have a full knowledge of the subject, whether he is called upon to act on behalf of his employer or not. He may, for instance, when farms usually let change hands, have to act in the capacity of valuer for his employer as outgoing or incoming tenant, as the case may be. Even if he be authorised to employ a practical valuer on behalf of his principal, he should nevertheless be possessed of the necessary knowledge, or he cannot fully protect the interests which he represents. Again, annual valuation will always be necessary upon the home farm for the purpose of the annual balance sheet.

Valuation from outgoing to incoming tenant.

When, however, the farm passes directly from one tenant to another, the question of valuation is primarily one between the outgoing and the incoming tenant, and in that case the land steward may have no special concern with it, but will only have to see that the outgoer has so far performed his covenants that there will be no difficulty at the outset in enforcing the performance of the like covenants from the new tenant: (see the remarks on dilapidations at the end of this section.)

CHAP. II.
Sect. 1.
Valuation Generally.

With regard to the ordinary valuation of those acts of husbandry or those substances which it is customary for the incoming tenant, or, if there is no incoming tenant, for the landlord to pay for, as representing the outlay incurred by the outgoer from which he cannot reap the benefit, it is to be observed that there are certain fixed principles of valuation generally understood and admitted, but that the exact limit to which the principle of compensation is to be carried in any particular case, is a matter on which it is difficult to lay down decided and absolute rules. In the first place, the outgoer has to look to his lease or agreement, which does in many cases, and should in every case, lay down the limit. But in the next place, if the outgoer's right to compensation has not been thus settled by agreement between himself and his landlord, he has still the custom of the country to rely upon. The custom of compensation varies greatly in different districts, but when the outgoer has ascertained it definitely, and is able to prove its existence, he is legally as safe as though he had an agreement on the subject. Local valuers are the only reliable authorities where nice points of valuation are to be decided according to the mode sanctioned by the custom. But every valuer must of course be acquainted with those general principles, without which no valuation can be made at all.

Custom of country.

In order to act as a valuer or appraiser, a man must be licensed to act as such. This licence can be obtained for the sum of two pounds on application to the collector of Inland Revenue residing in the district. These licences expire on the 5th day of July of each year. Anyone signing an award without such licence is liable to a penalty.

Valuers, their appointment and procedure.

CHAP. II.
Sect. 1.
Valuation Generally.

The appraisement, *i.e.*, the inventory of goods with the value attached, must be written upon stamped paper and signed by the valuer or valuers as the case may be. The only exemption, bearing upon estate management, is when the appraisement is for the purpose of probate.

Stamp duties.

The following are the stamp duties:—

	£	£	s.	d.
Not exceeding	50	0	2	6
Exceeding 50 and not exceeding 100	100	0	5	0
Exceeding 100 and not exceeding 200	200	0	10	6
Exceeding 200 and not exceeding 500	500	0	15	0
Exceeding 500 and not exceeding 1000	1000	1	0	0

The award.

The form of valuation, or the award, is simply the bill or account from the one party to the other. When signed by the respective valuers, it is presented by the person acting for the outgoer for payment, either to the other party direct or to his valuer. When paid, a receipt is given for the money on the award, no further stamp being required. It is then held by the incoming tenant as proof of payment, a copy (which requires no stamp) being furnished to the outgoing tenant.

The valuer acting for the outgoing tenant takes the initiative in settling the values, his task therefore is somewhat more onerous than that of his fellow.

It is clear that no satisfactory result could be arrived at if the detailed figures adopted by valuers were made known to the respective parties. No gentleman could undertake the task of valuation if he knew that every figure he decided upon would be subjected to the cross-examination of the parties most interested. Therefore it is the practice to render to the incoming tenant a full inventory of the items under question, but as to the value the sum total only is added. To explain this more fully an example is given of both the fully-priced inventory, and the same as it is forwarded to the respective parties: (see p. 76—80.)

Appointment of valuers.

The outgoing and incoming tenants each select and appoint a valuer; these valuers, when they meet, select on their part a third, or "umpire." This they do in writing, *i.e.*, they make an entry in their books somewhat to this effect, viz.: {*Chap. II. Sect. 1. Valuation Generally.*}

> We hereby agree, in the event of any dispute arising in the valuations upon _____ Farm, to submit the same to A. B., and we agree to accept his decision upon all points as final.
>
> (Signed)   C. D.
>   E. F.

In the event of a dispute arising a joint letter is written to A. B., informing him of the fact of his appointment as umpire, and requesting him to meet the parties in consultation at such and such a place, and at a specified time; or, when possible, the subject is submitted to him by post for his decision. {*Reference to umpire.*}

He will reply to each party; and, his decision having been given, he will forward a moiety of his charges to each. This charge will vary in accordance with circumstances, but is seldom less than three guineas, and from that to six. {*Umpire's fee.*}

We may here mention that valuers' charges are based, as a rule, upon the amount of the award. In some counties they are paid by the day, probably about three or five guineas, and expenses. When by percentage it will range from $2\frac{1}{2}$ to 5 per cent. The expense of the stamp is shared, *i.e.*, a moiety is paid by each party. {*Valuers' charges.*}

We shall confine our observations in this section to the valuation of those acts and substances which are left generally upon the farm, assuming that all live stock and implements have been sold by private treaty or auction. Nevertheless, arrangements are often made, whereby the whole of the farmer's stock passes to the incomer by valuation; this, however, is not to be encouraged.

The term tillage represents those acts of husbandry which are essential to the cultivation of the holding, and which consist in the working of the soil, viz., ploughing, harrowing, drilling, labour on manure, and such like. {*Valuation of tillages.*}

All these operations cost money, cause wear and tear of

ESTATE MANAGEMENT.

Chap. II.
Sect. 1.
Valuation Generally.

machinery, cause risk to horses, and require the farmer's skill. The value, then, of these respective acts is the cost of them reckoned upon the above bases.

Example of cost of tillage.

Take ploughing as an example:—

Suppose it requires two horses to plough a certain soil the calculation is made as follows:—

	s.	d.
Keep and risk of a horse per day..................	3	6
Ditto. Ditto.	3	6
Ploughman's Wages	2	6
Wear and tear of plough and harness.................	1	0
	10	6
Farmer's skill, and interest on capital, and loss of time in bad weather	1	6
The cost of ploughing one acre	12	0

Tillage must be properly performed.

An important matter to bear in mind, however, is, that all operations, to merit their full value, must be well performed; it would be obviously unfair to the incoming tenant and also to the painstaking outgoing tenant to charge the same for an acre of land, whether well or ill-ploughed. So much more than is generally supposed depends upon good cultivation that this is all important.

Cost of various tillages.

All the acts of husbandry are reckoned in this way, and we give the following list with the prices which we have found suitable in Hampshire. They will, of course, vary more or less in other places.

	s.	d.		s.	d.	
Ploughing, from	12	0	to	16	0	per acre.
Harrowing „				8		per tine.
Dragging „				1	0	„
Drilling „	3	0	to	3	6	per acre.
Pressing „	5	0	to	7	6	„
Cultivating „	3	6	to	5	0	„
Sowing broadcast, from	0	4	to	0	8	„
Horse hoeing, from	0	8	to	1	0	„
Rolling (light or heavy), from	1	0	to	2	0	„
Filling, carting, and spreading dung, from	10	0	to	12	0	„
Hand hoeing, from	4	0	to	7	0	„

When valuing tillages, therefore, the fields are visited in

rotation by the valuers, and the acts of husbandry, given by the farmer or bailiff, are entered in their respective note-books. The full value of those operations only must be allowed from which the outgoing tenant has reaped no benefit, and which are as beneficial as they should be to the incomer. For if the object of the cultivation has not been arrived at, owing to imperfect execution, it is unfair to charge it all to the incoming tenant. For example :—A fallow, thoroughly performed, has been money well expended, and no incoming tenant will grudge the amount; but if the fallow, after an apparently full tillage has failed in its object, if the land is still foul, it is hard and unfair to charge the full amount to the incoming tenant. Some portion must be borne by the outgoing tenant, who must suffer from the incompleteness of his work.

CHAP. II.
Sect. 1.
Valuation Generally.

Method of procedure.

On the other hand, when the farmer has done his best to secure a crop, and the crop, through no fault of his, fails, it would be hard upon him to suffer the loss. The result of this would be to leave a large acreage uncultivated at the end of the term ; as, if a farmer felt that repayment of his labour was subject to the success of the crop, he would prefer not risking it.

Failure of crops.

All the incoming tenant under the same circumstances could do would be to sow, and leave the result to Him who gives the increase. Therefore, where a root or other crop fails from no fault or neglect, the full amount expended upon it should be paid by the incoming tenant without question.

The matters submitted to valuation will, of course, vary with the period. If the change of tenants takes places at Michaelmas the items to be considered will vary considerably from those presenting themselves at a Lady-day valuation.

Allowance of rent, rates, and taxes.

In a Michaelmas valuation in some counties we have to deal with rent, rates, and taxes, in others they are not allowed at all. Fallows and root crops receive at Michaelmas in some districts the full amount of these

CHAP. II.
Sect. 1.
Valuation Generally.

paid by the outgoer, in others the charge is not made at all.

At Lady-day, however, some allowance must be made as will hereafter be explained.

Michaelmas valuation.

In a Michaelmas valuation we may have to deal with growing corn, and we shall also have to consider such tillages as bear upon the root crop, the preparation of clover ley for wheat, summer fallows, and clover seeds.

Growing corn.

In some instances a Michaelmas valuation will include the growing corn. When this is the case, the decision upon quantity must be arrived at in July, as it is impossible to value quantity when in stack. When, therefore, an arrangement of this kind has been entered into by the respective parties, they will communicate with their valuers, who will before harvest, together or separately, as they may deem best, walk through and inspect each field. In their notebooks they will enter the name of the field, acreage, kind of corn, and their opinion as to quantity. These figures they will compare, and when they have arrived at their decision, the values will be left until Michaelmas and decided in accordance with the market price at the time. Such values, will be less the cost of threshing and dressing and conveyance to market. In the case of wheat 20s. per load or 4s. per quarter may be reckoned as a fair deduction. In barley and oats 2s. 6d. or 3s. per quarter. Much care must be taken in valuing standing corn, and perhaps nothing tests the ability of a valuer more. He must take into consideration the straw, the quality of the grain, the ear, whether well filled or deficient, the blights to which the crop is subject, and whether the attack is likely to decrease the yield, or injure the quality. To be able thoroughly to comprehend this, he must have, if not a scientific, at least a practical knowledge of blights, for the wheat crop is subject to at least four or five enemies in the form of blight, to a greater or less extent every year. This subject will, however, be spoken of hereafter.

Method of valuing growing corn.

Sometimes root crops are valued by the value of the crop per acre; but it is more often reckoned at the cost of the cultivation. When the former method is resorted to the outgoing tenant, if the crop is a heavy one, will reap a decided advantage; when, however, the crop is light or a partial or full failure, the result to him would be disastrous. If this plan is resorted to, the valuer proceeds to arrive at the quantity per acre, and to reckon the same at its feeding value. A proportionate part of an acre is measured off in a portion of the field where the crop represents a fair average (a square rod, *i.e.*, 5½ yards square, is a useful size), the roots from this are carefully weighed, and this result multiplied by the acreage of the field gives a fair idea of the total quantity. The feeding value of roots may be roughly stated to be at the present time as follows:

Mangold .... 12s. per ton.
Swedes, from .... 12s. to 13s. per ton.
Turnips ,, ... 8s. to 10s. ,,

The fairest way, however, of valuing a root crop is to take the sum it has cost to produce. This sum includes, perhaps, three or four ploughings (unnecessary on clean land), repeated draggings and harrowings, drilling, seed, and manure, application (occasionally) of dung, hoeing, &c.; in some districts even rent and taxes are included. The cost, therefore, under any circumstances is heavy, ranging often from 5*l.* to 7*l.* per acre.

Preparation for wheat may be by summer fallow, and on heavy clay lands, such is often the case. The cost is very heavy, especially when a year's rent and taxes are allowed, as is the case in some parts of Sussex and Surrey. It is not an unusual thing for a fallow to cost under the latter circumstances 7*l.* or 8*l.* per acre. Four, or even five ploughings with their accompanying dressings may be allowed, but valuers should not allow more than this; the land ought not to require it.

It is unnecessary to describe a fallow, it has been so

CHAP. II.
Sect. 1.
Valuation Generally.

often done, and the reader can refer to many good authors upon the subject. It is necessary, however, to state that, except upon heavy clay lands (where the practice is absolutely necessary to secure a heavy crop of wheat), it is not only a proof of the foul state of the farm, but is absolutely ruinous; and as it ought not to be necessary, great care must be taken by the valuer for the incoming tenant to protect his client against any such claim. The incomer should only pay for as much of the operation as would have been necessary were the farm clean and in good condition.

To obtain the full value of a "fallow" no crop of any description must have been taken off the land since the previous harvest, *i.e.*, the land must have rested for one year.

Clover leys.

In the preparation of clover leys for wheat, we shall have, at this early period, little but the labour on the dung, ploughing, and pressing.

The valuer here will have to exercise great judgment as to the quality of the ploughing; a good furrow alone will secure the necessary firm bed, and the "tread" so much desired for wheat depends almost entirely upon this operation.

Clover and grass seeds.

Clover and grass seeds are the seeds sown with the late grain crop, and intended for the following year's hay crop.

The value is the cost of sowing and of the seeds. If the seed bills can be obtained, they are generally entered in the valuation as they are, in full; if not, a sum supposed to represent the value may be taken—about 12*s.* per acre is a fair amount for an ordinary mixture of grass and clover seeds.

Failure of clover.

This crop, like the root crop, will sometimes fail. When this is the case, the amount must be paid by the incomer, unless the failure can be proved to be due to carelessness or neglect.

Sainfoin.

Sainfoin roots will be mentioned when we treat of a Lady-day valuation. Special acts of husbandry we need scarcely mention, they are all based upon the same principles, viz., giving to the outgoing tenant a return of his money judiciously expended.

Straw and hay are reckoned at either market or feeding value, as may have been agreed upon. The usual method of valuing straw is by the acre, not by the ton or load, as is the case with hay. *The feeding value* is generally 7s. or 9s. per acre of wheat straw, and about 2s. more for that of barley and oats.

The *market value* is about 30s. or 40s. per acre, according to the market and the nature of the soil on which the straw has been grown, some lands being capable of growing very heavy crops of straw, whilst others will carry but little.

When straw, however, is in stack, and the acreage unknown, it must either be measured or trussed out; about eighteen to twenty yards may be taken to represent a ton.

Straw is often left upon the farm free of charge, the incoming tenant taking it away from the machine at his own expense; but this custom varies much, and this matter should, as already stated, be provided for by the lease. If no charge is made, the outgoing tenant has no interest in it; he is consequently careless about it, and much loss is the result.

Hay is also valued at either market or feeding price. The difference between the two is generally about 20s. per ton, or a sum sufficient to *cut* and carry it to market. The method of measurement and computation of weight is given on page 71.

With regard to straw and hay, and also with regard to dung, the right of the outgoing tenant to compensation, or the manner of computing it seems, when it is left to custom to vary so much in different counties that it is preferable in this (as in all other matters) not to rely upon the custom, but to have the understanding of the parties expressed in the lease.

Farm-yard dung is often left free of charge upon the

CHAP. II.
Sect. 1.
Valuation Generally.

farm, the outgoing tenant receiving only the amount of labour he has expended upon it.

Value of farm-yard dung.

In some counties, however, the dung itself is paid for. Where a proportion of the cake consumed has been allowed for, it will be unfair to add a value to the dung on this account; where, however, no allowance of this description has been made, and much cake has been consumed, the increased value may be looked upon as considerable.

Weight of farmyard dung.

It is necessary when dung has to be valued, to get it into heaps, so that the quantity may be arrived at by measurement.

A cubic yard of dung will weigh about 15 cwt., equal to a small cart load, a large cart will hold nearly one and a half a yards. The value will range from 3s. to 5s. per load, when the value of the cake has been taken into consideration elsewhere. If it has not been the value may range from 7s. to 10s. per load.

Cost of labour on farmyard dung.

When labour alone is considered, the amount for filling, carting, and spreading is reckoned at 1s. per load, or 10s. to 12s. per acre.

When in mixens or heaps, at 9d. per yard, or a little more when the distance of cartage is considerable.

The heap or mixen should be well made to prevent loss by exposure to rain. When carelessly conducted, but a small allowance should be made. Reference is made to the chapter upon "The Home Farm" for further remarks upon this important subject.

The above form the principal features of a Michaelmas valuation. We will now proceed to discuss the like points as they present themselves to us in a valuation at Lady-day.

Lady-day valuations.

The acts of husbandry and other matters which we must note on a valuation at Lady-day, differ considerably from those to be dealt with at Michaelmas. For we enter the farm in the middle of the farmer's year, whilst Michaelmas, of course, represents the close of his year in a financial point of view. We find, therefore, his wheat and oat crop sown, his root crops nearly fed off, and much of his land either sown or prepared for sowing with barley. Therefore, whilst the principle of the valuation remains the same, the result will be widely different.

Chap. II.
Sect. 2.
Valuation Generally.

The customs concerning entry at this period, as well as all others, differ greatly in nearly every district; we do not profess to enumerate them. The desirable object to attain is to do away with the necessity for joint occupation. The practice of entering months before to prepare for the wheat crop, or in February to prepare for sowing Lent corn, or the practice of sharing the crop, *i.e.*, the incomer reaping and harvesting the whole, and having the right to a portion as repayment, are all objectionable. We have known compensation so successfully managed as for a tenant to enter at Lady-day, and not even to come in contact with the outgoing tenant at all.

The matter which will principally require our consideration is that of half-tillage. When the roots were fed off the land, the sheep carried to market only a portion, the rest they returned to the soil in the shape of dung. The outgoing tenant naturally claims this dressing. He says, "If you do not allow me something for this, I ought to reap my own crops and take from them what you refuse to give me." His demand is a just one.

Half tillages.

Joint occupation, however, for so long a period, would be undesirable, therefore either custom or the agreement of the parties usually provides some arrangement to obviate this. Half the cost of the cultivation of the root crop is given to the outgoer, hence the term "half-tillage" is given to it. This is, however, not very fair. The sheep have not left one half of the crop behind them. In our practice in this matter we have not followed the usual course, but have endeavoured, whilst giving a fair compensation to the outgoing tenant, to secure to the incomer a fair dressing for a fair price. In agreements, therefore, for Lady-day, we allow "*compensation for roots fed off*," but limit the amount to 30s. or 40s. per acre. If the root crop has been a heavy one, the full amount may be given, if it has been a light one 15s. or 20s. may be quite sufficient.

F 2

CHAP. II.
Sect. 1.
Valuation Generally.

The plan has, however, this disadvantage, that when land has been ploughed and sown, it is difficult to know whether a heavy or a light crop has been consumed off it, and we have only the tenant's word to guide us; but even with this disadvantage it is fairer, in our opinion, than subjecting an incoming tenant to a payment for a heavy dressing which he has not obtained; or, if "one-third tillage" instead of "half tillage" was resorted to, the case would be still more fairly met.

Wheat crop.

The tillages of the wheat crop will, of course, be paid in full, and will consist of ploughing and pressing, after the spreading of manure, dragging and harrowing, drilling, and seed, and other acts of tillage, that may have been deemed necessary—as already mentioned in a Michaelmas entry. An important item, however, in this case is the repayment of half a year's rent, taxes, rates, and tithe rental. It is clear that this is fair and reasonable. The outgoing tenant has paid half a year's rent upon land from which his successor will reap all the benefit, and the crop would be reaped but for this, for only half a year's rent. The half year's tithe rent-charge, too, being upon the crop under question, as already explained in the last chapter, must also be paid by the incoming tenant.

In the event of the wheat crop being sown upon a fallow, the valuation would extend to the whole of the operation.

Seeds.

Many farmers are tempted to feed young seeds early in spring, especially when they are quitting the farm. Shepherds are particularly inclined to this when they can get the opportunity. It ought, however, to be strictly discouraged, and we have in our Lady-day leases provided for this, by disallowing compensation in every case when it is resorted to.

If the seeds are a full plant and have not been fed off, the valuation will consist of seed and labour, and half a year's rent, rates, taxes, and tithe rent-charge.

If the plant has failed or partly failed, the compensation should be withheld or only a portion paid, for this reason, that a clover crop ought not to fail when the farm is properly managed. If by a repetition of broad clover at too short intervals "clover sickness" results, the incoming tenant should not be called upon to bear the loss.

Sainfoin roots.

Sainfoin roots may be met with at Michaelmas or Lady-day. If the crop has been sown the previous season, and has not been fed off since harvest, the outgoing tenant may claim at Lady-day half a year's rent, rates, and taxes, as in seeds. In addition to this he may receive from 30s. to 40s. per acre for the first year, 20s. to 30s. for the second, and 15s. to 20s. for the third. It is only on the Lady-day after sowing, that all rents and taxes are allowed.

Compensation for sainfoin roots.

Laying down land to sainfoin is an expensive operation when well performed, but upon limestone soils it is such a valuable crop that full compensation shall not be withheld. It should not, however, extend beyond three years.

Half a year's rent, rates and taxes, and tithe rent-charge, are sometimes claimed for the whole farm at a Lady-day term, but we are of opinion that it should only extend to those cases named.

A farmer entering on a farm and paying the outgoing tenant compensation according to the custom of the country, has the satisfaction of knowing that at the end of his term he will, by the custom, have a similar right to compensation from his successor. Where the custom is departed from, and the outgoer is compensated according to some special terms contained in his lease, the incomer may be content to deal with him on the footing of those terms, provided the same terms are inserted in the new lease so as to give him the like rights against his successor.

We have already stated that custom and opinion differ to such an extent that it is difficult to lay down absolute rules upon the subject of valuation to meet all cases. Sufficient has perhaps been said to enable a young land-steward or pupil to understand the general principles upon which the operation of valuing depends. He must, to a great extent, work out in his own mind the actual bearings of all cases

CHAP. II.
Sect. 1.
Valuation Generally.

as they present themselves to him. Common sense will guide him, when set rules would often confound. He must bear in mind, that compensation must be given cheerfully for all acts that visibly affect the value of the land, and for which the operator has received no benefit; and must be withheld for all acts injudiciously and extravagantly carried out; but that compensation (unless in such special matters as we have noticed) should always be within the value of the benefit.

Extinguishment of objectionable rights.

We would here remark what an excellent investment of landlords' capital presents itself in some districts in the purchasing of objectionable "tenants' rights" and merging them in the soil. An extra rent might safely be charged, if by the extinguishment of old fashioned rights, the tenant's capital instead of being applied on entry in purchasing them, could be retained for immediate use upon the farm.

Survey of dilapidations

It may be useful here to notice a point which should always, on the determination of a tenancy, engage the attention of a steward. It should never leave the state of repair of the property, or, in other words, the dilapidation which it may have suffered, as a matter to be settled between the outgoing and the incoming tenant. Unless the steward is absolutely satisfied on the point, the best course is for the landlord and tenant to join at the end of the term in appointing a competent surveyor to draw up a schedule of the repairs which, according to the term of the tenant's covenant, he may be bound to execute, and to affix to the schedule an estimate of cost, the document being stamped with an appraisement stamp. If the tenant refuses to agree to having his liability in respect of repairs ascertained in this way, it will nevertheless be the right and prudent course for the landlord to have the report of a qualified person in order to preserve evidence of the actual state of the premises, and such a report the steward should take care to procure. But any difference of this kind would be so injurious to both parties, in the influence which it might have upon the finding of a new tenant, that it is very much to be deprecated. If the matter is amicably settled, the new tenant, aware of the precise requirements of the landlord in the matter of repairs, may be willing to enter at once and even to execute them himself, a sufficient allowance being made him by the outgoer for that purpose.

<small>Chap. II.
Sect. 1.
Valuation Generally.</small>

It will also be the steward's duty in every case to see that the outgoing tenant does not attempt to remove any fixtures which by being affixed to the soil have become the property of the landlord. But on this point we may refer to the Supplement.

<small>Fixtures.</small>

SECTION II.

RULES FOR ASCERTAINING WEIGHTS OF HAY AND CATTLE AND CONTENTS OF ASH HEAPS.

TO ASCERTAIN THE WEIGHT OF HAY BY MEASUREMENT.

The weight of hay will, of course, much depend upon the nature of the herbage from which it was taken; also upon the state of it when carried.

<small>Weight of hay by measurement.</small>

Well heated hay sets closely, but late cut hay, when exposed to rain and carried dry, heats but little and consequently settles lightly.

The difference between the two leaves room for, and requires judgment.

The rule is, to measure the length and breadth and height, multiplying the same together and dividing the product in yards by the number of yards which under the circumstances may be considered to be equal to a ton of hay. This number may vary from ten to thirteen—ten cubic yards of well made and old hay being equal to a ton, whilst it may take thirteen yards of inferior hay to weigh that amount.

<small>Rule.</small>

CHAP. II.
Sect. 2.
Rules for ascertaining Weights and Measurements.

Method of arriving at contents.

In practice it is usual to measure the height only a little above the eaves; if the full measurement of the roof is taken, the sum arrived at will be greatly in excess of the real quantity.

The density of the stack may be arrived at by thrusting in the hand, or by forcing in a sharp stick or rod, or by cutting out a piece with the hay-knife. The latter practice is often resorted to when the quantity is large, and in the event of any dispute between valuers. A cut is made from the top, about the middle of the stack, to the bottom, and about two trusses in depth; this gives a thorough insight into the quality of the rick, and if the same be weighed and the cavity measured, a very exact computation may be arrived at as to weight.

If the contents be taken in feet, we may reckon a foot to weigh from 8lb. to 9lb.

Examples.

Example:

Suppose a stack of well-heated and old meadow hay, measures 33ft. in length, 17ft. in width, and $9\frac{1}{2}$ft. in height, what is the tonnage?

$33 \times 17 \times 9\frac{1}{2} = 5329\frac{1}{2}$ cubic feet.
$5329\frac{1}{2} \times 8$ (weight per foot) $= 42636$lb.
$42636 \div 2240$ (lb. in 1 ton) $= 19$ tons.

Or,

$5329\frac{1}{2}$ cubic feet $\div 27$ (cubic feet in 1 yard) $= 198$ yards (nearly).
198 yards $\div 10 = 19.8$ tons.

Again—

A hay stack measures 33ft. in length, 17ft. in width, and $9\frac{1}{2}$ft. in height. Quality, dry and light. Required, the tonnage?

$33 \times 17 \times 9\frac{1}{2} = 5329\frac{1}{2}$ cubic feet.
$5329\frac{1}{2} \div 27 = 198$ cubic yards.
$198 \div 12 = 16\frac{1}{2}$ tons.

Second cut clover hay will require a still larger divisor, say, 13 to 14.

Hay should not be measured, when great accuracy is required, before Michaelmas.

To ASCERTAIN THE WEIGHT OF CATTLE BY MEASUREMENT.

To arrive at this there are various rules. It is, however, necessary for accuracy that the measurer should have a considerable knowledge of the points of a fat beast, and also be cognisant of the facts connected with the feeding, the length of time in stall, and the nature of the food. When these points are thoroughly understood and considered, it is astonishing how very accurate the calculation becomes.

Chap. II. Sect. 2. Rules for ascertaining Weights and Measurements.

We have measured cattle of shorthorn, Devon, and Highland breeds, and, comparing the result of the calculations with the actual weight afterwards arrived at by the butcher, have found it often within 4lb. of the actual weight. The rule we have found most reliable is the following, but one, nevertheless, needing more than any other, the above qualifications.

Take the girth immediately behind the shoulder, drawing the tape fairly tight, then take the length from the shoulder to the *tail-head*, each place being determined by an imaginary perpendicular line, let fall and clearing the fore and hind-quarters respectively. Thus—

Method of measurement.

MEASURING CATTLE.

Next proceed with your calculations as follows:—Square the girth in feet, and multiply the result by the length, and the product again by a decimal selected from the following table, striking off to the right as many points as are contained in the decimal, and the result will represent the weight of the beast in imperial stones:—

Rule.

ESTATE MANAGEMENT.

CHAP. II.
Sect. 2.
Rules for ascertaining Weights and Measurements.

TABLE OF DECIMALS APPLICABLE TO BEASTS OF VARIOUS CLASSES.

A moderately fat beast .... ·23
A fat beast .... ·24-·25
A prime fat beast .... ·26
A very fat beast .... ·27

To reduce Imperial stones to Smithfield stones of 8lb., multiply by 7 and divide by 4. To reduce imperial stones to the score of 20lb., multiply by 7, and divide by 10. To reduce Imperial stones to a cwt. of 112lb., divide by 8. The process may be reversed by multiplying by the second figure, and dividing by the first.

Another rule is to multiply the square of the girth in inches by the length in inches, and divide the product by 7238, and the quotient will be the weight in imperial stones.

Another rule is to multiply the square of the girth in feet by five times the length in feet, and divide by 21, and we have the same result.

Examples:

A fat ox measures 7ft. 4in. in girth, and 4ft. 6in. in length. Required, the weight.

RULE I.
$7\frac{1}{3}^2 \times 4\frac{1}{2} = 53.77 \times 4.5 = 241.965$
$241.965 \times .24 = 58$ imperial stones.

RULE II.
(Girth in inches) $88^2 \times 54$ (length in inches) $= 418176$
$418176 \div 7238 = 57.7$, or 58 imperial stones (nearly).

RULE III.
Girth, in feet $^2 \times 5$ lengths, in feet $\div 21$
$53.77 \times 22.5 = 1209.825$
$1209.825 \div 21 = 57.6$ imperial stones.

One-tenth to one-twentieth of the weight may be added in rules 2 and 3, when the beasts are prime or very fat, to correspond with the decimals by rule 1.

To ASCERTAIN CONTENTS OF ASH AND SAND HEAPS.

Ash and sand heaps for measurements should be in the form of cones. It is often necessary to calculate the contents of such. The contents are generally considered in cubic yards or bushels. In the case of ashes, the labour of burning is mostly performed by the bushel; in the case of sand, it is generally sold or bought by the yard.

The rule to find the contents of a cone is, to multiply the area of the base by the height, and divide by 3, or by formula:—

$$\frac{\text{Area of base} \times \text{height}}{3} = \text{solid contents.}$$

Therefore to find the contents of a heap of ashes, proceed as follows:—

Take the diameter of the base and the height, and proceed according to the foregoing rule.

Example:

A heap of ashes or sand measures 12ft. in diameter and 8ft. in height. Required, the contents in cubic yards.

(By rule of circles, *post*).

12 × 3·1416 = 37·699 (circumference).

Then half the diameter × half the circumference.

6 × 18·85 = 113 (area of base).

Area of base × height.

113 × 8 = 904

904 ÷ 3 = 301⅓ cubic feet.

301⅓ ÷ 27 = 11 cubic yards.

1 cubic yard contains about 20 bushels.

SECTION III.

Forms of Valuation.

Form of a Michaelmas Valuation in "Detail."

TILLAGES.

Chap.	A. R. P.		s. d.	£ s. d.	£ s. d.
Chap. II Sect. 3. *Forms of Valuation.*	4 0 0	*Mangold.*	*Faithful's Green.*		
		3 ploughs	12 6	1 17 6	
		6 drags.........................	1 0	0 6 0	
		2 rolls	1 0	0 2 0	
		Drilled..........................	3 6	0 3 6	
		4 harrows	0 8	0 2 8	
		4 lb. of seed	1 0	0 4 0	
		4 cwt. mangold manure......	8 0	1 12 0	
		4 cwt. salt	1 3	0 5 0	
		Filling, carting, and spreading (F. C. S.) 12 loads ...	1 0	0 12 0	
		3 hand hoeings	4 6	0 13 6	
		2 horse hoeings	0 8	0 1 4	
				5 19 6	23 18 0
	2 0 0	Same as above failed. Half dressing allowed.*			5 19 6
	2 0 0	*Cabbages.*	*Faithful's Green.*		
		2 ploughs......................	12 6	1 5 0	
		F. C. S. 12 loads	12 0	0 12 0	
		2 drags...........................	1 0	0 2 0	
		2 harrows	0 8	0 1 4	
		1 roll	1 0	0 1 0	
		Planting	12 0	0 12 0	
		3 hand hoeings	4 0	0 12 0	
				3 5 4	6 10 8
		15,000 cabbages	3 0		2 5 0
	4 0 0	*Wheat.*	*Eighteen Acres.*		
		1 plough		0 12 6	
		Pressed		0 6 6	
		F. C. S. 12 loads		0 12 0	
				1 11 0	6 4 0
	5 0 0	F. C. S. 12 loads			3 0 0
			Carried forward		47 17 2

* Notice of this is taken upon p. 61.

FARM VALUATIONS.

Chap. II. Sect. 3. *Forms of Valuation.*

A. R. P.		s. d.	£ s. d.	£ s. d.
		Brought forward		47 17 2
5 0 0	*Mangold.*		*Oaklands.*	
	1 plough	12 6	0 12 6	
	6 drags	1 0	0 6 0	
	4 harrows	0 8	0 2 8	
	2 rolls	1 0	0 2 0	
	Drilled	3 6	0 3 6	
	4 cwt. turnip manure	6 6	1 6 0	
	5 cwt. salt	1 3	0 6 3	
	F. C. S. 12 loads	12 0	0 12 0	
	4 lb. seed	1 0	0 4 0	
	2 horse hoes	0 8	0 1 4	
	3 hand hoes	5 0	0 15 0	
	Labour on ashes	0 3	0 0 3	
			4 11 6	22 17 6
6 0 0	*Turnips.*		*Oaklands.*	
	1 plough	12 6	0 12 6	
	1 duck foot harrow	2 6	0 2 6	
	4 drags	1 0	0 4 0	
	4 harrows	0 8	0 2 8	
	2 rolls	1 0	0 2 0	
	Drilled	3 6	0 3 6	
	3 cwt. superphosphate	6 0	0 18 0	
	3 lb. seed	0 8	0 2 0	
			2 7 2	14 3 0
0 2 0	*Cabbages.*		*Oaklands.*	
	3500 plants		} 0 15 0	
	Planting			
9 0 0			*Forrester's Pond.*	
	F. C. S. manure, 12 loads		0 12 0	5 8 0
3 3 0	*Faithful's Green.*		*Swedes.*	
	5 ploughs	12 6	3 2 6	
	8 drags	1 0	0 8 0	
	6 harrows	0 8	0 4 0	
	3 rolls	1 0	0 3 0	
	Drilled	3 6	0 3 6	
	4 cwt. turnip manure	6 6	1 6 0	
	Broad cast, half manure	0 4	0 0 4	
	3 lb. seed	0 5	0 1 3	
	Harrowed across drills		0 0 6	
	3 hand hoes		0 14 6	
	2 horse hoes		0 1 4	
	Labour with ashes		0 0 3	
			6 5 2	23 9 3
		Carried forward		114 9 11

ESTATE MANAGEMENT.

CHAP. II.
Sect. 3.
Forms of
Valuation.

A.	R.	P.		s.	d.	£	s.	d.	£	s.	d.
						Brought forward	114	9	11		
7	0	0	*Swedes.*			*Faithful's Green.*					
			3 ploughs...............	12	6	 1	17	6			
			4 harrows	0	8	 0	2	8			
			3 drags.................	1	0	 0	3	0			
			2 rolls	1	0	 0	2	0			
			Drilled..................	3	6	 0	3	6			
			3 lb. seed.............	0	5	 0	1	3			
			4 cwt. turnip manure........	6	6	 1	6	0			
			Half sown broadcast	0	4	 0	0	4			
			1 horse hoeing	0	8	 0	0	8			
			3 hand hoes........................			 0	14	6			
						4	11	5	31	19	11
2	2	0	*Mustard.*			*Faithful's Green.*					
			1 plough	12	6	 0	12	6			
			2 drags.................	1	0	 0	2	0			
			2 harrows	0	8	 0	1	4			
			1 roll	1	0	 0	1	0			
			Broad cast	0	6	 0	0	6			
						0	17	4	2	3	4
2	0	0	*Rape.*			*Clay Piece.*					
			2 ploughs...............	12	6	 1	5	0			
			4 drags.................	1	0	 0	4	0			
			3 harrows..............	0	8	 0	2	0			
			Clod crushed	2	0	 0	2	0			
			2 rolls	1	0	 0	2	0			
			3 cwt. manure..............	6	0	 0	18	0			
			4 lb. seed.............	0	5	 0	1	8			
			Broad cast	1	0	 0	1	0			
						2	15	8	5	11	4
7	0	0	*Fallow.*			*Clay Piece.*					
			2 ploughs...............	12	6	 1	5	0			
			4 drags.................	1	0	 0	4	0			
			2 harrows	0	8	 0	1	4			
			Clod crushed	2	0	 0	2	0			
			Spreading lime	1	6	 0	1	6			
						1	13	10	11	6	10
			150 bushels of lime, at 5d. per bushel						3	2	6
3	0	0	*Fallow.*								
			1 plough			 0	12	6	1	17	6
			Clearing and stacking hop poles and ploughing alleys..						7	0	0
									£177	11	4

FARM VALUATIONS.

			£	s.	d.	£	s.	d.
Hay.	1 stack of meadow hay	3 tons	4	0	0	12	0	0
	Stump of old clover hay	6 ,,	2	10	0	15	0	0
	1 stack of new clover hay	15 ,,						
	,, second clover hay	7 ,,				115	0	0
						142	0	0
Fixed machinery	} Turnip pulper, horse gear, chaff cutter					12	10	0
Sundries	22¼ acres of hop poles					150	0	0
	77 acres of straw at fodder price, 7s.					26	19	0
	Mixens by roadside					10	0	0
	Proportion of fur waste and hoofs, as per agreement					15	0	0
	Proportion of oil and cotton cake					70	0	0
	Seeds, 23½ acres, as per seed bill, or 12s. 6d. per acre					14	13	9
	Tank, 1½ ton of coal, 4 bundles of brooms, 2 new coops, 8 old coops, 80 head of poultry, 50 bavins, 3 augurs, handsaw, hammer, 4 tin milk-pans, strainer, skimmer, milk-can, 2 buckets, 1 lanthorn, 2 beer stands, 10 hop bags, machine for bagging, 3 baskets, numbers, 47 frames, bedstead, 3 tons of culm, ½ tub of brimstone, 9 bags, 44 hop garden bags, 46 surplices					48	0	9

CHAP. II.
Sect. 3.
Forms of Valuation.

TOTAL.

	£	s.	d.
Tillages	177	11	4
Hay	142	0	0
Fixed machinery	12	10	0
Hop poles	150	0	0
Straw	26	19	0
Mixens	10	0	0
Proportion of manures	15	0	0
,, ,, cake	70	0	0
Seeds	14	13	9
Sundries	48	0	9
	£666	14	10

CHAP. II.
Sect. 3.
Forms of Valuation.

THE SAME VALUATION AS PRESENTED TO THE PARTIES AFTER HAVING BEEN SETTLED BY THEIR RESPECTIVE VALUERS.

Valuation of tillages, hay, and straw, and other effects, from Mr. ———— to Mr. ————.

September 29, 187 .

A.	R.	P.		TILLAGES.
4	0	0	Faithful's Green.	Mangold.
				The tillage, labour, and seed.
2	0	0	,,	Failed, proportion only allowed.
2	0	0	Faithful's Green.	Cabbages.
				The tillage, labour, and plants.
4	0	0	Eighteen acres.	Wheat.
				The tillage, labour, and seed.
5	0	0	Eighteen acres.	Clover-ley.
				Manured.
5	0	0	Oaklands.	Mangold.
				The tillage, labour, and seed.
6	0	0	Oaklands.	Turnips.
				The tillage, labour, and seed.
2	0	0	Oaklands.	Cabbages.
				The tillage, labour, and plants.
9	0	0	Forrester's Pond.	Clover-ley.
				Manured.
3	3	0	Faithful's Green.	Swedes.
				The tillage, labour, and seed.
7	0	0	Faithful's Green.	Swedes and turnips.
				The tillage, labour, and seed.
2	2	0	Faithful's Green.	Mustard.
				The tillage, labour, and seed.
2	0	0	Clay Piece.	Rape.
				The tillage, labour, and seed.
7	0	0	Clay Piece.	Fallow.
				The tillage, labour, and lime.
3	0	0	Hop kiln field.	1 plough.

Collecting and stacking hop poles, ploughing alleys.

1 stack of meadow hay.
,, new clover hay.
,, second cut clover hay.
1 stump of old clover.

FARM VALUATIONS.

CHAP. II.
Sect. 3.
Forms of Valuation.

FIXED MACHINERY.

A.	R.	P.	
22	2	0	Turnip pulper, horse gear, and chaff cutter.
77	0	0	Hop poles.
			Straw at fodder price.
			Mixens by road side.
23	2	0	Seeds, as per bills (or per acre.)
			Proportion of fur waste and hoofs.
			Proportion of oil and cotton cake.

SUNDRIES.

Tank, 1½ ton of coal, 4 bundles of brooms, 2 new coops, 8 old coops, 80 head of poultry, 50 bavins, 3 augurs, 1 hand saw, hammer, milk can, 4 tin milk pans, strainer, skimmer, 2 buckets, 1 lanthorn, 2 beer stands, 10 hop bags, 3 baskets, machine for bagging, set of numbers, 47 frames, bedstead. 3 tons of culm, ½ tub of brimstone, 9 bags, 44 hop garden bags, 46 surplices.

The items before mentioned are valued by us in the sum of six hundred and sixty-five pounds fourteen shillings and tenpence.

£665 14*s.* 10*d.*

A. B.
C. D.

Memo :—The sum of half the stamp is generally added to the valuation.

FORM OF A LADY-DAY VALUATION AS PRESENTED TO THE PARTIES.

Inventory and valuation of tillages, hay, and straw, and compensation in lieu of "half-tillages," &c., upon   Farm, from Mr.   to   Mr.

March 25, 187 .

A.	R.	P.	TILLAGES.	
14	0	0	Upper Berry Down.	Wheat.
			Tillages, half rent, taxes, and tithe rent-charge.	
6	0	0	Upper Berry Down.	Swedes.
			Compensation for roots fed off.	
9	0	0	Lower Berry Down.	Fallow.
			The tillage.	
9	0	0	Lower Berry Down.	Turnips.
			Compensation for roots fed off.	
16	0	0	Windmill Field.	Turnips.
			Compensation for roots fed off.	

G

CHAP. II.
Sect. 3.
Forms of Valuation.

A.	R.	P.		
7	0	0	Windmill Field. The tillage.	Fallow.
12	0	0	,, ,, ,,	Seeds.

Seeds, tillage, half rent, taxes, and tithe rent-charge.

10	0	0	Windmill Field. The tillage.	Fallow.

Hay, straw, &c.

1 stump of hay.

13	0	0	Wheat and oat straw at fodder price.

One-third value of oil cake fed off.

The above-mentioned items are valued by us in the sum of one hundred and fifteen pounds five shillings and twopence.

£115 5s. 2d.

A. B.
C. D.

CHAPTER III.
TIMBER TREES.

SECTION I.

TIMBER AND TIMBER-LIKE TREES; THEIR HISTORY, PROPAGATION, TREATMENT, AND USES.

THE OAK (*Quercus robur*) has ranked, and probably always will rank, as the most valuable of our timber trees. It requires a rich, strong soil in which it can strike down its roots to attain to its full magnitude. On light, open soils it comes to a premature maturity, and often shows signs of early decay; this shows itself in the growth of moss and lichens, dead branches, and late development of leaf; and, when cut, an unsoundness is generally found about the heart, near the base. It delights in tolerably high situations, and thrives best in woods and plantations.

The oak is propagated entirely from seed, and great care should be taken to select acorns from well-developed trees, as otherwise all care and attention may end in disappointment. The acorns may be planted any time between October and March in properly prepared nursery beds, and when one year old may be transplanted into rows. Here they must be well hoed, and kept free from weeds. At the end of the second year they should be again transplanted, and the following year, or year after, they will be fit to move to their final destination. The effect of this repeated transplanting is to encourage root fibre.

The oak seldom bears fruit until twenty years old; though this depends much upon soil and climate. When felled the stump shows great vitality, throwing out abundant shoots, which makes it a valuable underwood plant.

<small>Chap. III. Sect. 1. *Timber.*</small>

<small>Treatment of young plants.</small>

Young plants, when taken from the nursery, should be lifted carefully, and, if they possess a tap-root, it should be cut off; they should be planted in holes dug some weeks before, that the soil may be well pulverised, and sufficiently large to take the plant without the use of force. When the earth is thrown in the woodman should lift the plant up and down to allow the earth to find its way amongst the fibres, and finally tread the earth well all round. They should be planted 20 feet apart, and in rows at a like distance, the rows being interlined with fir or other trees for the object about to be mentioned.

<small>Period of planting.</small>

The oak is best planted early, that it may become established before the heat of summer sets in; and care should be taken to plant it in such situations and in such soils as it is likely to thrive in. It should also be planted with faster growing trees than itself, especially when planted in exposed places, as it is, when young, peculiarly liable to injury by frost. The trees, however, which are planted as nurses should not be allowed to smother the oak, but should be removed when they have accomplished their task; as otherwise the oaks become drawn and delicate.

<small>Trees to be planted as nurses.</small>

<small>Surface drainage.</small>

<small>Pruning.</small>

Young plantations of oak should be carefully attended to. Where the soil is retentive, and apt to hold water upon the surface, open drains or watercourses should be cut to carry it away, as standing water is fatal to the oak. Pruning must be judiciously done, as a too vigorous use of the knife and saw is worse than no use at all. Branches low upon the stem, or unshapely, may be removed, care being taken to cut in such a way as to allow water to run off from the surface of the cut. It is best to cut the branch about two inches from the stem. The young tree should not be robbed of its leaf more than is necessary, as lung-power is absolutely necessary for its full development. Here and there may be found a "hide-bound" tree; a gash up and down with a knife will sometimes rectify this. A healthy, growing

<small>Hide-bound trees.</small>

oak may be known by the condition of its bark, which should be cracked up and down, all over, as if the rapid growth was too much for its skin. Chap. III.
Sect. 1.
Timber.

The uses to which Oak is applied are too numerous to admit of enumeration. The texture is so firm and close as to fit it for all purposes where strength and durability are required. It bears immense strain, thus fitting it for machinery of all descriptions. In fact, it is adapted to nearly all uses, from the building of our largest vessels to the most delicate piece of household furniture. Being very straight in the grain, it readily splits, and this quality fits it for laths, spokes, and palings. Uses.

In addition to its qualities as a timber tree, it produces the most useful bark for tanning purposes; in fact, almost the only bark used commercially in this country. Other barks are used, viz. that of Birch and Larch, but only to a small extent, and in a few districts; the latter is very light, and consequently very bulky and hardly worth the cost of carriage. Owing to this value of oak bark it is necessary to fell the tree in the spring, contrary to the treatment usual in the case of other trees. The sap must commence to circulate before the bark will separate from the stem; and it is only from the commencement of the circulation to the bursting of the leaf-buds that the separation is practicable, as directly the leaf expands and performs its function, the bark again adheres closely to the trunk and branches; The barking season is therefore limited. Bark.

It takes place in April and May according to the soil and climate. In localities where the soil is rich, the work is often completed before more exposed districts have commenced; thus enabling the workers to pass from one district to another. The work is performed by gangs of men, known as "Strippers," and is contracted for by the ton of bark. The contract includes, felling, stripping, and harvesting, *i.e.*, rendering it fit for stacking. The lop and top is left until the stripping is done, when it is made into bavins and stackwood. The usual sum paid for filling, stripping, Season of barking.

Strippers.

Cost of barking.

ESTATE MANAGEMENT.

Chap. III.
Sect. 1.
Timber.

and harvesting is 30*s*. to 35*s*. per ton. Tying bavins and stacking stack-wood, about 2*s*. 6*d*. per hundred for bavins, and 3*s*. to 4*s*. per stack of stackwood.

Method of barking.

Bark is taken first from the stem, in 2 feet lengths; it is cut through with an axe at equal distances, and is then forced off with an iron made for the purpose. Where it will not readily separate from the tree it is beaten with a wooden mallet until it starts. This trunk-bark is then set aside and barking the branches is proceeded with, down to the lesser branches an inch in thickness. When all the bark is stripped, the men cut forked props from the branches about eighteen inches long and drive them into the ground, and upon these lay straight hazel or ash rods; against these props the bark is set up, the small branch-bark first, the best of the trunk-bark being used for covering over the top. Bark should always be set up with the inner side well protected. In some districts they erect stages, by cutting forked props three feet long, laying across these pieces of small wood, and again upon these transversely other pieces or small poles, to serve as a kind of table to hold the bark.

Treatment of bark.

When dry, it should break when bent, and not bend like a green stick. If in good order the inside will be of a pale creamy colour; if dark, it is a sign of the presence of but little tannin—the quicker it is dried the better. If rain sets in, it is best to leave it alone, only looking to it regularly to set up what may have fallen; by no means turn it. When fit, it is either tied in bundles with withies, or carted away loose or cut up into small pieces and placed in sacks. It is sold by the ton, and generally delivered by the seller to the nearest town at his own expense. The price of bark varies, but may be stated at 4*l*. 10*s*. to 5*l*. per ton.

Price of bark.

Proportion of bark to timber.

About one ton of bark may fairly be expected from every three or four tons of timber.

In plantations of underwood, the oak is the only class of timber that should be admitted; and this only to a limited extent where the underwood is considered of value.

There are many varieties of oak, but it is unnecessary to mention more than two or three, as the common oak *Quercus robur* is the only one we meet with in practice. We have the *Q. r. pedunculata* and *Q. r. sessiliflora*, both varieties of the robur, but classed by some as distinct species; *Q. cerris* (Turkey Oak) and *Q. ilex* (Evergreen Oak.

Chap. III. Sect. 2. Timber.

Weight of Oak, 36·20 cubic feet = 1 ton.

The common English ELM (*Ulmus campestris*) is not a native of this country, but there is no trace of its introduction. From the fact of its not seeding here, there can be no doubt of its foreign origin. It is found in the central parts of Europe and in Western Asia, and in the latter country seeds freely. It is propagated in this country from suckers, in the following way:—an established tree is felled, and from the stool of this suckers will shortly appear; when these have attained a season's growth they are laid over, and the base covered with four or five inches of earth, whereupon they take root and may be separated the following season, and planted in nursery lines; the stool will again throw out, and may be treated in the same way the following and successive years. The Elm throws out very fibrous roots, and may consequently be transplanted when of considerable size. It will also throw up suckers at a great distance from the bole, especially on light loams; these are, however, of little value, as if transplanted they seldom attain size, and decay early.

Elm.

Propagation.

It grows very rapidly and comes to early maturity, and with, perhaps, the exception of the oak, is one of the most common of our timber trees.

The largest specimens are found near old dwellings, churches, and monastic buildings, but the most useful are generally found in hedgerows. The trees attain considerable height, and possess large, well developed boles, free from lateral branches, furnishing thereby excellent planks.

The branches are very brittle, and large ones should not be allowed to overhang public paths or buildings, as

CHAP. III.
Sect. 1.
Timber.

Uses.

Price.

Wych Elm.

Propagation.

these often fall without any apparent reason and sad accidents have thus arisen.

The timber is durable and not liable to crack, making it useful for purposes where lateral strength is required. It is much used by wheelwrights for wheel-boxes, sides of carts, waggons and wheel-barrows. It is also used by undertakers, being one of the most valuable timbers for coffins; and by shipwrights for blocks and portions of rigging furniture. It is also used for pumps.

The price may be stated at 1s. to 2s. per cubic foot, according to size and quality. It is covered with a thick bark, the thickest in fact of any tree in this country. In measuring, therefore, an allowance must be made, which however will be hereafter explained. The allowance will be from 1in. to 1½in. for every foot of quarter girth.

As an ornamental tree it ranks high, being thick and massive in foliage and of tall upright growth. It attains size only in rich soil; it is therefore an excellent guide when valuing land for fixing rent.

There is only one other variety in this country of any value as a timber tree, viz. :

The WYCH ELM (*Ulmus montana*) is a native of Scotland, and unlike the common Elm, yields no suckers, but seeds freely. It is propagated entirely from seed. It blossoms very freely in April, before the full expansion of leaf; and the seed ripens in June. They should be collected and sown immediately in a rich seed bed; a light loam being the best soil for the purpose. The beds should be four feet wide, and one bushel of seed will sow nearly twelve square yards. They should be covered with half an inch of mould. The young plants appear very soon after sowing, and if the weather is hot and dry it will be necessary to shade and water the beds. If not too close the young plants may be allowed to remain two years in the seed beds, when they should be transplanted into nursery lines, about one foot apart and two feet between the lines, and allowed to remain there for two years, when they will be ready for planting out. The wych elm thrives best on open subsoils. It never attains the size of a well developed common elm, but becomes at an early age a very useful tree. It is used much by agriculturists for farm purposes, being very elastic; and sells for 2s. to 2s. 3d. per foot. When well veined, as it often is, it is much prized for veneering, and sells at a high figure.

It should not be pruned until it reaches ten or twelve years of age, the leaders may then be shortened and some of the strongest laterals cut back. The wych elm differs in appearance considerably from the common variety. The branches are more drooping and the foliage larger, and the leaves are placed upon the twigs with great regularity, alternately on each side. It is also of a pure character, showing very little tendency to degenerate; whilst the common elm degenerates to a very marked extent.

Weight of Common Elm, 46·66 cubic feet = 1 ton.

The ASH (*Fraxinus excelsior*) as a timber tree stands second to none for usefulness and beauty, and for agricultural purposes it rivals all. It is a native of this country, and is propagated from seed; these are ripe in November, when they may be collected; care, however, should be taken to select them from well grown and healthy trees. When gathered, they must be placed in pits and mixed with double their amount of sand, and be turned repeatedly for the first few months. Here they may remain for twelve or fifteen months. The latter time is best, as if sown in the autumn the young plants are apt to become injured by frosts. The seed beds should be four feet wide, and the soil a light sandy loam. They should be sown tolerably thickly and covered with half an inch of mould. They may remain, if not too thick, for two years in the seed bed, and then be transplanted in lines 6in. apart and 18in. between the lines. Whilst in lines they must be kept from weeds and grass. After the expiration of four years dating

*Chap. III.
Sect. 1.
Timber.*

Soil.

from the time of sowing, they will be ready for planting out permanently.

To secure decided success, it is advisable when practicable to trench the soil, as this tree rejoices in a free growth. The soil best adapted to it is a rich loam. When the growth is slow, the timber is of little value, being brittle and loose in texture. Where, however, the growth is rapid, it is tough and elastic. Great care is required in selecting sites for ash plantations; if chosen upon high and exposed situations, whether for timber or coppice, the end is failure and disappointment; if chosen in rich and sheltered situations, perhaps no tree gives greater satisfaction. The soil may be moist, but if it contains stagnant water the tree soon fails. Draining, therefore, is highly necessary.

Drainage necessary.

It is better in every way to plant ash by itself, or at least with nurses only, with the ultimate view of removing the latter. It is peculiar in its light and airy foliage, and becomes smothered when in company with heavy-headed timber. The best nurse, perhaps, for this purpose is the Scotch fir, as it shelters without shading. As an underwood or coppice plant it will be hereafter noticed; but when planted for timber the distances may be twenty feet. A timber plantation may be formed from an ash plantation of underwood by leaving standards at correct distances. It should be borne in mind that air and light alone give leaf, and the plant without leaf is like an animal without lungs; therefore, do not shade, but protect from colds winds and frosts.

Nurses.

Felling.

The sap of the ash is highly fermentable; it is therefore necessary to fell the tree when the sap is dormant. It has been proved that in July and August the state of dormancy is more absolute than at any other period; the operation, therefore, can take place during these months if convenient. If this is not attended to, decay soon sets in. For all high class work that which has grown rapidly should be employed, and only when it has attained maturity. When young the sap wood is very thick, which may be seen by cutting a stick across. It is out of all proportion to the heart wood, but as age advances the latter increases.

The uses to which it is applied as timber are too numerous to detail fully. It is used by agricultural implement makers more than any other tree, as it is better able to stand constant strain, being very elastic and pliable. Wheelwrights use it for spokes of wheels, shafts, sides of carts and waggons, ploughs, barrows, and drags; handles of forks, spades, shovels, and picks.

The carriage-builder uses it for his finer class of work; the shipwright for oars and paddles; the cooper for hoops; the cabinet-maker for furniture. In fact, as already stated, it is unsurpassed. The price is much higher now than formerly. For good boles as much as 3s. per foot may be obtained; but perhaps, if of an average size and quality, 1s. 8d. to 2s. per foot represents the fair market value. In measuring the ash an allowance must be made for bark, as in oak and elm; but it will vary of course in accordance with the situation upon which it has grown.

Weight of Ash, 47·15 cubic feet = 1 ton.

The trees already discussed, namely, the oak, the elm, and the ash, appear to be the only trees which at all times and everywhere in this county have been considered as timber trees. But amongst those which we are about to enumerate will be found other

TREES OF SCARCELY LESS IMPORTANCE AT THE PRESENT TIME FOR THE PURPOSES OF TIMBER.

The BEECH (*Fagus sylvatica*) is by some considered the most stately of our timber trees, and certainly, when seen in its full and perfect growth, it forms a most pleasing feature of the landscape. It is a native of this country. By nature it is very umbrageous, but by thick planting it may be made to produce long sticks of timber free from branches for a height of 50 feet or more from the ground.

CHAP. III.
Sect. 1.
Timber.

Soil.

It grows freely on the chalk, and often on apparently barren soil reaches both size and grandeur. In Hampshire many magnificent specimens may be seen, perhaps more than in any other county. A tree of great age and size, which is unsurpassed for beauty by any we have ever seen, grows upon a poor soil, suitable only for purposes of plantations. Its girth, 4ft. from the ground, is 26½ft.; and the diameter of the ground it covers is 68ft. The branches are not only wide-spreading, but most eccentric in form and entanglement. In the immediate vicinity there are many others partaking of the same characteristics, but unequal in size and beauty.

As a park tree the beech is perhaps unsurpassed for beauty and shelter. As a timber tree it is valuable only when grown closely in woods; when grown in the open it yields little but firewood. In the former case it not only reaches to a great size, but the grain is very fine, resembling satin wood in many of its features; and then it commands a high figure.

Uses.

The uses to which it is applied are very numerous, one of the principal being chair-making. It is also used for cheap furniture, being often stained to represent mahogany, and passing as such. It is used by wheelwrights for felloes, by builders for weather-boards, and for many other purposes where great durability is not required. It may also be split very thin, and is consequently used for bandboxes, sword-scabbards, toy boxes, measures, shovels, and dairy utensils. It will not bear a great strain, being somewhat brittle.

Propagation.

It is propagated from seeds; these are found as nuts in prickly husks called "mast." They are ripe in October and may be collected by beating the tree and allowing the nuts to fall into a sheet. A great many so collected will be of little or no value; they may be separated after gathering by throwing all the mast into a vessel of water, when the empty, or partially-developed ones, will float, and may be skimmed off. The good ones when dry should be placed in sacks or barrels with about double the amount of sand, and kept so until April. If planted in the autumn the young plants, being peculiarly susceptible, are often carried off by late spring frosts. In April these seeds may be planted in well-prepared beds, and covered with an inch of soil; before covering them, however, it will be well to fix the seeds by blows from a spade, as this prevents their being dragged to the surface when raked over.

<small>CHAP. III.
Sect. 1.
Timber.</small>

The young plants must be kept free from weeds. If too thick they should be removed into lines. They should at the end of the first year be removed into nursery lines, and the following year they may be transplanted, if they have made good use of their time; if not, they should be allowed to remain one more year. This period, however, should not be exceeded, as, if allowed to remain too long in the lines, they often become "bark-bound" when finally planted out.

<small>Planting.</small>

If required for timber, they should be planted together somewhat closely, and to prevent lateral growth they should be kept thick for some years. If side branches are cut off, or if pruning is injudiciously performed, they are very apt to become bark-bound as well as in the case already mentioned.

<small>For timber purposes.</small>

As a hedge-plant the beech is invaluable, but as such it will be fully considered under the head of "fences."

<small>Beech as a hedge plant.</small>

A peculiarity in the beech is its wonderful natural propensity to spring up from the earth where old beech trees have been removed. Remove one or two, and no young seedlings appear; remove all, or all from a considerable space, and they almost immediately appear, and if allowed to remain form valuable plantations.

The "mast" is an excellent food for pigs, and on commons where the beech grows, large herds are often fed. The ancient common-right of "masting" pigs was often a valuable thing, particularly in the case of common-rights in the Royal forests.

<small>Masting.</small>

The price of beech timber varies in accordance with the

<small>Price.</small>

CHAP. III.
Sect. 1.
Timber.

quality. Some years ago it was considered one of the cheapest timbers, and good beech was often sold for 4*d*. a foot; it may now be quoted at 10*d*. to 1*s*. 4*d*. The latter sum we have obtained.

Weight of Beech, 51·49 cubic feet = 1 ton.

Horse chestnut.

The HORSE CHESTNUT (*Æsculus hippocastanum*) is not a native of Great Britain. Its original *habitat* is doubtful, but it is supposed to have been introduced about the sixteenth century from the East. It is one of our most beautiful flowering trees, and as such is grown; its timber bearing no special value.

It attains great size in good situations, throwing out long and drooping branches, often sweeping the ground; forming splendid shelter for deer and cattle.

But a short time elapses between the first forming of the bud and the full expansion of the leaf and flower; the full umbrageous head of the tree forming a great contrast to the surrounding trees, whose leaves take more time to burst through their covering.

When in full flower it forms a lovely addition to the landscape, and the seed, which ripens early, is also very beautiful, as it forces its way through its thorny cover; forming not only a favourite toy for children, but a rich meal for deer.

Propagation.

It is readily propagated from seed. They may be sown any time in winter; if the beds are 4ft. wide, one bushel of nuts will sow a bed 20yds. long. The young plants are left in the seed bed one year, when they are transplanted into nursery lines 1ft. apart, and 2ft. between the lines. When they have been two years in the lines they are ready for planting out permanently. Owing, however, to the fibrous nature of the roots, the chestnut may be planted out when it has attained considerable size, thus fitting it for parks and avenues. Owing to the plant maturing its young wood early, it is capable of standing frosts better than many other kinds.

It should be protected when young from bite of cattle and deer, as the foliage is much relished by them.

On rich loams this tree should never be forgotten, when laying out parks and woods, especially when in prominent situations; it should, however, in all cases form an outside tree.

Weight of Horse Chestnut, 64 cubic feet = 1 ton.

The SPANISH CHESNUT (*Castanea vesca*) derives its name from Kastanea, a city in Pontus, in Asia, of which locality it is a native. It is supposed to have been introduced into Europe by the Greeks 500 years B.C., and brought into England by the Romans.

It is a highly ornamental tree both in foliage and fruit. It flowers in May and June, and ripens its fruit in October. The flowers (that is the male flowers) are long catkins, growing in bunches, the fruit or nut is inclosed in prickly husks, each husk inclosing three nuts. The nuts are farinaceous and sweet, hence its name "sweet chestnut." In this country the fruit seldom ripens, or even attains full development, but in the south of Europe, particularly in Spain, it is a produce of importance, and is exported largely into England.

The young wood, unlike the common chestnut, ripens late, and is, consequently, unable to withstand early frosts. When established, and for the first twelve years, it grows very rapidly, often three feet or more each year. The growth is often of a twisted or spiral form, which shows itself in the bark; in some cases this is most marked.

The tree attains to very great size, and almost fabulous measurements are given by various writers. The timber is very valuable, being very hard and durable; it ranks with the oak, and may be used in its place when procurable. Unlike the oak, however, the timber is most valuable when young; when old it becomes brittle. It is most valuable as an underwood plant, being a free grower from stools when "lopped over." It will, however be noticed as such in the chapter devoted to underwood.

CHAP. III.
Sect. 1.
Timber.

Propagation.

English seeds should be use for propagation, as those obtained from abroad, though much finer, are often kiln dried before being exported. They are sown in drills sixteen inches apart, and covered with one inch of soil. They should be sown in April, as if sown in Autumn the late frosts in Spring often destroy the young plants. They are allowed to remain one or two years in the seedbeds, they are then transplanted, and when this is done they should be separated into sizes. Before being planted also, the tap-roots should be cut off; this is highly important in all fruit-bearing trees. They should be left two years in the lines, when they will probably be about three feet high, and may then be finally planted out. If large trees are required for special purposes, they should be transplanted every two years, that their roots may become fibrous, being each time allowed more room. The price of young and well-grown boles may be stated at 2*s.* per cubic foot.

Price.

Walnut.

The WALNUT (*Juglans regia*) is grown for its fruit, but is at the same time ornamental, and useful as a timber tree. It is a native of Persia, and was introduced into this country about 300 years ago. Being a *bonâ fide* fruit tree, it should be grown as such, and consequently should be transplanted two or three times before its final planting, taking care, as already stated, to cut off the taproot. When this is neglected, or when they are allowed to grow without attention, or from self-sown seed, the fruit neither fills nor ripens, and the tree will be tardy and late in growth.

Treatment.

Fruit.

It flowers in May, and ripens its fruit about October. The seed is enveloped in a husk, but bursts from this when fully ripe.

Propagation.

It is propagated from seed (fully developed nuts should be selected), the treatment being very similar to that of the chestnuts. Sow in autumn, and cover with two inches of earth. When the young plants appear, cover them with larch trimmings, or rough litter, as they are easily injured by frosts. They should be left in the seed bed until the following year, when the strongest plants may be transplanted into lines. The weaker ones being left another year in the seed bed. At the end of the second year transplant again as already explained.. {CHAP. III. Sect. 1. Timber.}

The timber is very useful, and a high price can be obtained when old and well matured. It is then dark in colour, but when young almost white. It often yields a beautiful grain, especially near the bottom, and is much prized for purposes of high class veneering. It is susceptible of a high polish. The roots also yield a beautiful grain. It is used for drawing-room furniture, pianos, and gun-stocks. A dye is extracted from the roots, and an oil from the nuts. {Uses of the timber.}

It is impossible to quote a price, as when it possesses the above qualification it is almost invaluable. {Price.}

The POPLAR (*Populus*) is a deciduous tree. It is unisexual and diœcious, *i.e.*, having but one sex upon each flower, and these upon different trees. It is a genus of many species, and each species possesses many varieties. Some of these are natives of Great Britain, but they are found more or less throughout the world. It is not necessary, however, to dwell upon any except those that are met with in this country, and that at the same time bear ornamental or commercial value. {Poplars.}

They grow rapidly, and are therefore selected where shelter is needed in open and exposed situations and around new houses. When well grown they are very ornamental, being very light and airy in appearance, the leaves, too, being suspended upon delicate stalks, tremble with every breath of wind.

The upper surface of the leaf (which is entire, round at the base, and lanceolate at the apex) is dark green and very glossy; in some of the varieties the under side is white and silvery, and this gives to the tree a very beautiful appearance. This is especially the case in the white poplar (*P. Alba*).

H

CHAP. III.
Sect. 1.
Timber.

As a nurse.

As a nurse to more slow growing trees, such as the oak, silver fir, and others, the poplar is invaluable, as it rapidly grows to a size which admits of its being utilized when it is necessary to cut it out. Neither is it by nature a tree that smothers, like some nurses do.

It grows from stools, and may therefore be used as an underwood plant. It soon arrives at maturity, and when this is attained it should be at once converted, as decay then rapidly sets in. This shows itself but little outwardly, decay taking place in the centre, and for this reason this tree should not be planted near buildings, paths, or roadways, as it sometimes falls bodily, and often with but little notice.

Liability to decay.

Uses.

The timber bears but little value. It is white and soft, and possesses the merit of not warping and is consequently used for doors, packing-cases, and wheelwright's work. It is also used near fireplaces and in the erection of kilns, as it is less liable to take fire than any other kind of timber.

Price.

Its value may be stated at 6*d.* to 8*d.* per cubic foot.

Propagation.

It is propagated by layers. These may be separated and transplanted into lines (as has already been explained with regard to elms) the first year and the second year may be planted where required.

Species of poplar.

The most common species are the following :—

Populus canescens, or grey poplar, a native of Great Britain. Flowering in April, with a profusion of catkins.

Populus alba, or white poplar, a native of Flanders. White on the under side of the leaf.

Populus tremula, the trembling-leaved poplar or aspen, a native of Great Britain. A beautiful and stately tree, thriving in high and exposed situations. Its leaves are round and entire, and hang on a long and slender stalk, and tremble with every breath of wind; hence its name. This peculiarity, however, as already noticed, belongs to the whole of this tribe, but is more noticeable in this than in any other species. The foliage passes through many shades of colour, from the most beautiful green to bright yellow, and adds greatly to the beauty of the landscape in autumn.

Populus fastigiata, or Lombardy poplar, is known by its straight upright growth, and is beautiful only from its contrast to surrounding trees. Its growth is very rapid, but like the rest of its class it decays early.*

The BIRCH (*Betula alba*, Lin.) is a native of Great Britain and the high lands of Europe. It is exceedingly hardy, being found at great heights, often several thousand feet above the level of the sea. It also thrives in northern latitudes, almost to the extreme limit of vegetation.

There are two kinds, the *B. alba*, and the *B. pendula*, the latter being the most valuable, though not so common as the former.

In Scotland, it grows in coppices, glens, and ravines. It is able to resist drought, but will, nevertheless, grow on swampy soils; it will also grow where fir plantations have been removed, and soon makes good cover under those circumstances. The birch is peculiar in this respect, as but few ligneous plants will grow where firs have been, owing to the peculiar exuviæ from their roots.

It ripens its seeds in September, and they are collected and placed in thin layers until dry, when they may be packed in casks or boxes until March, when they may be sown in seed beds. The best soil for this purpose is a friable peat. A bushel of seed will sow a bed four feet wide and thirty yards long. If the soil is light they may be trodden in, and may then be left. At a year old the plants will be six or eight inches high. If too thick they should be thinned, those taken out being planted into nursery lines. The others may be left for another year, being kept free from weeds. When two or three years old they may be planted out.

---

* A feature peculiar to this, and a few other classes of trees, is the large size of the leaf upon young wood. Some species of poplar also when young show a tendency of the leaf to a lobate form, which disappears with age.

CHAP. III
Sect. 1.
Timber.

Uses.

Twigs of the birch are used for broom making, the larger stuff for hoops. The timber is white with pink centre, and of loose texture. As a fuel it bears but little value, but the smoke it evolves is considered the best for drying herrings. Its bark is valuable, but cannot rank with oak; for tanning fishing nets, however, it ranks high. As a charcoal it is much esteemed by gunpowder makers.

In parks and ornamental planting it should be allowed a prominent place, as its delicate foliage and silvery bark give a very pretty and pleasing effect.

Alder.

The ALDER (*Alnus glutinosa*) is an aquatic tree. In moist situations it will attain considerable size, sometimes a height of fifty or sixty feet with a corresponding girth. It matures early, and if not cut when maturity is reached, it soon decays. As an ornamental tree it is not to be recommended. On low-lying and wet meadows it is useful, both as a profitable crop and a reclaimer, serving not only to dry the soil, but to add to its fertility by the fall of leaves. As a hedge plant it is valuable in swampy districts. As a nurse it is often useful, owing to its rapid growth.

Price.
Uses.

As a timber it may be sold for 1s. to 1s. 3d. per foot. It is used by last-makers, turners, cabinet-makers, clog-makers, and by agriculturalists for cart bottoms, handles to farm tools, &c. In districts near the sea-shore it is used for fish barrels, being fit for this purpose when twenty years old.

Immersion in water before use.

As the timber is very subject to the attack of insects, it is necessary to immerse it in water for two months after felling, first stripping off the bark, and if one bushel of lime is thrown in to the water it will greatly assist the process. When thus treated it can be used for purposes for which it is otherwise unfitted, as this process hardens the grain.

Propagation.

It is propagated from seed, which may be collected at the end of October. The seeds are contained in a kind of small cone. The cones should be placed in a dry room, about six inches thick and constantly turned over until April, when they may be thrashed, sifted, and cleaned.

They must then be moistened with warm water, only just off the chill, and dried; they are then ready for sowing.

Beds four feet wide may be prepared for the seeds in moist meadow land, being dug with a spade. The seed must be sown thickly and trodden in, it being quite unnecessary to cover them very carefully.

By the autumn they will be nine or twelve inches high, when they may be planted into nursery lines. Here they may remain for two years, being kept free from weeds. At the end of this period they will be ready for planting permanently where required.

By river sides, swamps, water-meadows, and in odd wet corners they may be advantageously grown. Plant 4ft. apart in rows, and give them fair attention, as pruning and thinning must go together. But always keep a good head of leaf and do not sacrifice a limb except when absolutely necessary. The thinnings can be sold for hoops, barrel-staves, and faggots, and, as they advance in size, for other purposes.

Plantations of alder are often sold by auction, when they are generally purchased by charcoal burners; the charcoal being highly valued for the manufacture of gunpowder and for use in chemical works. *As a charcoal.*

When cut young, dyes can be extracted from the catkins and twigs. *As a dye.*

From the foregoing remarks it is clear that this tree possesses merits, which by no means permit its being overlooked in the improvement of estates, situated in fens or low lying districts.

The LIME TREE (*Tilia Europæa*), sometimes called the Linden or Teil tree, is supposed by some to be a native, but it was probably introduced into this country about the sixteenth century from Germany, Russia, and other parts of Europe. Most of the foreign trees now looked upon by many as natives were introduced about this period, by enterprising planters. *Lime.*

CHAP. III.
Sect. 1.
Timber.

The foliage of the tree is exceedingly beautiful and graceful. The leaves are entire and very umbrageous. It flowers very freely in July, yielding a strong scent and a great quantity of honey, and ripens its seeds in October. The seed-pods are in the form of small balls, hanging in clusters on delicate thread-like stalks, each pod containing several seeds in a cotton-like substance. They may be sown in April, and their treatment is similar to that

Propagation. already discussed. When, however, purity is required it is necessary to propagate by layers or suckers; as this tree has a peculiar tendency to degenerate by hybridism. Layers or suckers always turn out the exact reproduction of the parent tree.

It is used principally for avenues, but is also a beautiful park tree.

Uses. The timber is soft and white, sometimes yellowish. It is used for carving and fret-work, moulds for foundries, and model-making. The inner bark also forms an important item in the value of the tree, being used by gardeners for tying plants, making mats, &c. When the utilisation of this bark is intended, it is necessary to fell the tree in spring, when the sap is rising, in order that the bark may separate freely from the stem. But the collection of this is confined to Sweden and Russia and is not practised in this country. The wood forms when burnt a charcoal useful for the manufacture of gunpowder.

It stands any amount of cutting, and is therefore suitable for gardens and drives. As a pollard it is unsurpassed.

Treatment of stools. The treatment of the suckers is so similar to that of the elm already described, that it is unnecessary to repeat it here. It grows freely from stools, and if the stools are occasionally manured, they throw out strong plants each year, which, if moved into lines, will be ready the following year for final planting.

By repeated transplanting, however, to encourage root fibre, this tree may be planted when of considerable size.

The Sycamore (*Acer pseudo-platanus*) was introduced at an early period from the central parts of Europe.

<small>Chap. III. Sect. 1. *Timber.*

Sycamore.</small>

As a timber tree its value consists in its close texture, which fits it for furniture making. Often, however, when its growth has been retarded, the wood which should be white has a pinkish hue, which seriously affects its value.

In form it is an exceedingly ornamental tree; its leaves are deeply lobed and palmate, but they are apt to exude a sticky substance called honey-dew, which retains the dust, and gives to the tree a dark and dull appearance. What honey-dew is, is still a matter of dispute. By some it is supposed to be a sweet exudation from the leaf, by others to be the deposit of aphides. It is, however, clear that upon the leaves of the hop plant it does not show itself until after the presence of the fly. Whether, therefore, the fly actually deposits the substance upon the leaf, or whether it punctures the leaf so as to allow of the exit of a natural juice, must still remain undecided. <small>Honey-dew.</small>

It is propagated from seed, which is ripe in October. It may be collected when ripe, and mixed with double the amount of sand, and kept until April, when it may be sown in seed beds as already described. It grows rapidly, and is therefore wisely selected where shelter and blinds are required. , It is very umbrageous, and throws an impenetrable shade. <small>Propagation.</small>

It is exceedingly hardy, and stands almost any amount of exposure. When white the timber is worth 1s. to 1s. 3d. per cubic foot; if pink in tint, 6d. to 8d. <small>Price.</small>

The Plane (*Platanus Orientalis*) is somewhat similar in foliage to the sycamore, hence the name of the latter *pseudo-platanus*; and in many parts of Scotland the two trees are confounded. The leaves are five-lobed and palmate—*i.e.*, hand shaped; on the young wood they often attain great size. The seed is ball-shaped, hanging grace- <small>Plane.</small>

fully to a delicate thread-like stalk, giving a very beautiful appearance to the tree.

It is a native of South Eastern Europe and Western Asia, and from its origin is very susceptible to frost. It is not, therefore, suitable for exposed and cold situations. It blossoms in May, and ripens its seed in October. It is generally propagated from seed, the seed pod being first broken to extract the seed from its downy bed. It is sown in March in seed beds, the following year the young plants are placed in nursery lines, when they are left two years, and then finally planted out.

It may also be propagated by layers, like the elm and lime.

It is grown for ornament; its timber though used like the sycamore for domestic purposes, bears but little value. The plant attains in South Eastern Europe to a great size and grandeur. On the Bosphorus there are some grand specimens, under which it is stated a regiment of soldiers may take shelter.

The WILLOW (*Salix*).—This genus posesses a great many species, and is a native of all parts of the world. The species vary so much in height that whilst one is measureable in feet, the height of another must be expressed in inches. Probably the large subdivision of the genus into species, and of these again into varieties, may be due to hybridism, for this, from the nature of the flowers, can be easily imagined as likely to take place. Each species consists of a male and female plant, but the pollen from the male flower of one plant falling indiscriminately may alight upon the pistil of a flower not identical, and if fertilisation takes place, a new variety may be the result.

The foliage also varies very much in the same species in accordance with age and situation, so that a considerable amount of confusion attaches to this group.

The most common in this country are the *Salix caprea* and *Salix alba*.

The *S. caprea*, or goat willow, is useful as a coppice plant, being used for hoops, hop-poles, rods for crates, and other purposes. The kind known as the red-hearted willow (similar to the white in other respects) is very durable and well fitted for hop-poles, the *white* does not last so long. It may be cut every three or four years hence its value as compared with other descriptions of coppice. It may be remarked that sheep hurdles made from this plant are very durable, and being exceedingly light are easily carried about by the shepherd.

As a pollard, by banks of rivers, it is exceedingly profitable, a healthy stock often producing in one year a full sheaf of straight shoots eight to twelve feet long, which are sold to basket-makers.

It is propagated by cuttings, the cuttings being taken from shoots of one year's growth; they should be one foot long, and if the soil is moist and good they may be put in direct, about three to four feet apart; if the soil is poor it will be best to plant them in a nursery for one year first.

The leaves and bark of the willow are astringent, and the bark is used for tanning.

On good soil and if left to attain maturity they sometimes grow to considerable timber, in which case a fair price per foot can be obtained. Where Larch and Scotch fir have been the willow will grow and form good cover; and as there are but few plants which grow under these circumstances, it is well to bear the fact in mind.

For embankments near water, it is invaluable; stakes taken from full-grown coppice plants driven into the ground and interlaced with branches of the same will take root and grow, and so form a barrier of great strength and durability.

The timber is white, soft and light, and is used for the same purposes as the alder.

The dwarf willow, or Osier (*Salix rubra*) bears a high value, as it yields an unusually large income to the owner.

Plantations of these are found near rivers, for example, at Staines, Windsor, and other places near the Thames; and

CHAP. III.
Sect. 1.
Timber.

Drainage.

Propagation.

Uses.

Weeping willows.

Elder.

Medicinal and other uses.

many acres of marsh land now valueless might be made to yield a considerable annual income, at a very moderate outlay.

All that is required is to cut surface drains in such wet parts of a meadow as it may be considered advisable to plant, such drains should be 1½ft. wide and deep enough to carry off the surface water, and 10ft. or 12ft. apart. Then take cuttings from one year old shoots about, 14in. long, and thrust them into the soil about two-thirds of their length.

They should be 18in. from each other in lines, the lines being 3ft. apart. In three years they will attain full growth, when they may be cut, after this they come to cut annually. The shoots should not be allowed to stand more than one year.

They are tied in bundles and sold to basket makers.

Weeping willows being of feeble growth, are best exhibited by being grafted upon stems of the common willow, and are much prized for garden and ornamental trees, especially near ponds and rivers. There are several kinds of weeping willows, but few of striking appearance, except where propagated as above.

The ELDER (*Sambucus nigra*).—There are several species of this tree, but it will be only necessary to consider the common elder (*S. nigra*).

It is a native of Europe, Asia, and Africa. By nature it is more of a bush than a tree; but as the stems when fully grown possess a special value we have considered it best to include it in the list of timber and timber-like trees.

It produces in June large clusters of creamy white flowers, produced in terminal cymes, and these in their turn, in the autumn, yield large masses of black berries. It is by no means a desirable plant to have near a dwelling, having little beauty, and emitting a sickening odour when in flower. As a medicinal plant it has various uses; the flowers are used for the manufacture of lotions and ointments, and are also convertible into a kind of wine. When dry they can be used as a tea, which is very debilitating in its effects, producing great perspiration. The inner bark is an active cathartic, and from the berry is made the well-known elder wine, so much prized with chestnuts round the village Christmas firesides.

In bleak situations, and near the sea, it forms a very useful shelter; the points of the branches become injured by the wind and salt air, but they throw out fresh lateral shoots, and so become thicker and more dense, thus turning what might be a disadvantage into an actual benefit.

The growth of the young plants is very rapid on suitable soil; the young shoots will sometimes attain a growth of 5ft. in one summer.

As a hedge plant it is useless, and in fact, when present in any old hedge, it will be best to exterminate it by grubbing. As a shelter, however, round young plantations, it is valuable. *Useful for shelter.*

It is propagated readily by cuttings. Take the new growth, and cut into lengths of 1ft. or 14in., leaving a bud at the bottom and at the top; and plant them any time from November to March in lines 2ft. apart, and at a distance of 1ft. from each other in the lines; when a year old they may be planted out. *Propagation.*

When young the stem contains a large pith, which, however, as the plant advances in age, disappears. When old the wood is yellow and glossy, and will take a fine polish. It is used for the manufacture of mathematical instruments and shoe-makers' pegs. *Uses.*

With all these merits, however, it is a plant but little grown, and may be deemed a weed amongst trees and shrubs.

In addition to the foregoing list of timber and timber-like trees we may mention in conclusion the following; but as they are principally grown for ornament, it is unnecessary to do more than tabulate them:

CHAP. III.
Sect. 1.
Timber.

Wild cherry.
Mountain ash.

Maple.

Norway maple.

English maple.

Large-leaved maple.

Red maple.
Oregon maple.

The WILD CHERRY (*Cerasus sylvestris*) a native of this country.

The MOUNTAIN ASH (*Pyrus aucuparia*), a native of this country, thrives well in exposed and high situations, hence its name.

The MAPLE (genus *Acer*) is found in Europe, Asia, and America. It is looked upon principally as an ornamental tree, but some of the species have nevertheless uses of a marked character. The sugar maple (*Acer saccharinum*) of North America yields an abundance of sap, rich in sugar, and though not used much in commerce, is very useful to the settler.

The NORWAY MAPLE (*Acer platanorides*) is a hardy species, and yields a useful timber. Amongst the varieties of this species, we have the cut-leaved or eagle's claw maple, very beautiful, and readily propagated by grafts upon the stem of the common sycamore; a species belonging to this genus which we have already discussed.

The COMMON ENGLISH MAPLE (*Acer campestris*) bears an uncertain value. The timber is sometimes beautifully grained, and capable of taking a fine polish, and when knotted forms the well-known bird's-eye maple; other species also have this peculiarity.

The most ornamental of this genus for garden purposes, which may all be propagated by grafts upon the sycamore stock, are:

The LARGE-LEAFED MAPLE (*Acer macrophyllum*), a native of North America.

The RED or SCARLET MAPLE (*Acer rubrum*).

The OREGON MAPLE (*Acer circinatum*) which is pendulous in character, and yields leaves which turn to a brilliant scarlet in autumn.

Perhaps of all the deciduous trees the maple is the most varied and beautiful. Recently marked variegated forms of it have been much introduced into gardens; and as it is easily propagated by grafts, is likely to continue a favourite. Some of the varieties form a pleasing feature in the fine nursery gardens, in the neighbourhood of Bagshot and Sunningdale.

Chap. III. Sect. 1. Timber.

The LABURNUM (*Cytisus Laburnum*).—This tree is a native of Europe. It is grown only for the fine effect of the flowers. The timber, however, is very beautiful, and used by the turner when procurable.

Laburnum.

The SLOE or BLACK THORN (*Prunus spinosa*).—This plant is a native of this country. It ranks more as a hedge or underwood plant than a timber tree. It is much in request for whips and walking-sticks.

Sloe.

SECTION II.

THE CONIFERÆ, OR CONE-BEARING TREES; THEIR PROPAGATION, TREATMENT, AND USES.

LARCH—SCOTCH FIR—COMMON OR NORWEGIAN SPRUCE—COMMON SILVER FIR.

IN addition to the deciduous timber trees which we have just considered, we have to speak of another and important class of trees—most important indeed in this particular, that it is the class which will, perhaps, more than any other, force itself upon the attention of the land steward. We allude to the "Coniferæ" or cone-bearing trees, a natural order containing many genera. The most important are the *Larix* or Larch, the *Pinus* or Fir, the *Abies* or Spruce, and the *Picea* or Silver Fir, and in this order we will consider them.

The LARCH (*Larix Europœa*).—This tree belongs to the natural order Coniferæ, and is the only one of the tribe that is deciduous.

Larch.

It is a native of the French and Swiss Alps, Appennines and Tyrol, and was introduced into England early in the seventeenth century.

CHAP. III.
Sect. 2.
Cone-bearing Trees.

It rejoices in open, but flourishes in all situations, whether high or low, provided it can have air and light and a dry subsoil; the roots ramify near the surface, but it cannot live with stagnant water beneath. On hillsides, or near running streams, it reaches perhaps to its greatest dimensions. It is a monœcious plant, bearing its pistils and stamens in different flowers on the same tree, as already explained.

In Scotland it attains maturity earlier than in England, and is more hardy, owing to the situation being more in conformity with its natural tastes.

It blossoms early, and in spring forms, with its light green leaves or spines, and its brilliant vermilion flowers, a beautiful object; forming a striking contrast to the surrounding trees, still enshrouded in their winter garb, and the contrast, though different in kind, is scarcely lessened as the season advances, and the tree attains full development of foliage.

Treatment of cones.

The cones, for purposes of propagation, should be carefully selected from well-grown and healthy trees. They are collected at the latter end of winter, and the seed is extracted from the cones by various processes.

The most approved method is to lay the cones on a timber kiln about six inches deep, and expose them to a heat of 100° Fahr., turning them twice or three times with a shovel. Ten hours ought to be sufficient to attain the object, if the temperature has been carefully kept up; if not a longer period will be required.

The heat will not separate the seed from the cone; when dry they must be taken from the kiln and threshed, and then dressed with ordinary fanners.

Price of seed.

The cost of this process may be reckoned at 3*d.* per lb., and the usual price of seed is 1*s.* to 1*s.* 6*d.* per lb.

Propagation.

The seed should be sown in April in a light sandy soil, and covered to the depth of a quarter of an inch. One pound of seed will suffice for a bed of four square yards. The soil in which they are sown should not be dressed with any manure, but a soil from which a crop has been taken, and which has been manured for that purpose, will probably be beneficial.

CHAP. III.
Sect. 2.
Cone-bearing Trees.

The young plants will appear in about three weeks; weed them carefully, and protect with branches from late frosts. They will be six or eight inches high in September; if too thick they must be thinned, and those taken out should be planted in rows about fifteen inches apart. They should not be allowed to remain in the seed bed more than two years. If strong plants are required, they should be transplanted into rows and allowed to remain one or two years, as may be necessary, according to the purpose required. For moorland they may be taken direct from a two-year-old seed bed, but for more open and exposed situations they should be taken from lines of two years standing.

They are sold from the seed-bed for transplanting into rows at from 3s. to 5s. per thousand, and from the lines at from 8s. to 10s. per thousand.

Price of young plants.

Whilst in nursery lines they must be kept carefully hoed and free from weeds, and they will in two years reach from two to three feet in height. On moorland, when taken from the seed-bed they are generally planted in the "slit." A man goes forward with a spade and makes two cuts, lifting slightly with the second, a woman or child following with the young plant and inserting it in the slit, the man then treads it down and passes on to the next. This is a cheap and speedy process. In more exposed situations and for large plants, holeing must be resorted to, and if this is done a few weeks before planting, to ameliorate the soil, it will be found beneficial.

Methods of planting.

This process is conducted by a gang of men. The foreman goes forward marking with his fork, or what is still better a "beck" or mattock, the spot where the holes are required, the next set following and forking, and the next with spades to complete the holes. Before planting, the trees are laid out by the foreman, placing here and there a

Chap. III.
Sect. 2.
Cone-bearing Trees.

Fill up gaps.

Diseases of larch.

Thinning.

hardwood tree or ornamental pine, and the men following, plant and tread them in. It is necessary sometimes to cut and clear the grass and undergrowth, and great growth sometimes results from this course, but in very exposed situations the undergrowth often acts as a shelter, and may be safely left. The following year it will be wise to look over the plantations and fill up all gaps, selecting strong plants for the purpose.

The larch flourishes in almost all soils, except when the subsoil is wet, as already stated. When in low and damp situations it is subject to the attack of insects, the chief being the *Coccus Laràcio*. Healthy plantations, open and exposed, seldom if ever suffer from this pest. For those plantations attacked there is no remedy except by such acts as will serve to promote the more rapid growth of the trees. They suffer most after early frosts when the leaves or spines die, leaving little for the insect to feed upon, when it attacks vigorously the buds, and thus causes decay and death. It is also subject to another disease called "rot." This often shows itself in plantations which have been planted on ground from which trees have been removed, the decaying roots and fungi caused thereby, and the spawn or white fibrous matter yielded by the decaying timber, acting upon the tap roots and causing early decay. This form of disease produces a hollow stem, and is consequently called by some "pumping," owing to the pipe-like form of the diseased tree. It is also sometimes caused by the application of dung, and also by a wet subsoil, which often produces a ferruginous crust fatal to tree growth. All surface-rooted trees are more or less liable to this disease, but none so much so as the larch.

The plantations should be judiciously thinned, but this will hardly be required for ten years, except in soils where an unusual growth is obtained, and this only when close planting is resorted to. When four feet apart, a longer period may elapse before the woodman's axe is heard within the limits of the plantations.

We have found in exposed situations, 2ft. 6in. apart a useful distance, the plants growing more rapidly and straighter; but under these circumstances they must be thinned early, as otherwise they are apt to become covered with lichen.

Chap. III. Sect. 2. *Cone-bearing Trees.*

When thinning, the decayed, injured, or ill-grown trees should be removed, leaving those of good growth for timber. The lower branches of those left should be broken off with the back of the axe or billhook, or a stick; by no means cut them if it can be avoided. When felled they must be dragged out to the nearest ride or roadway, and there trimmed, the trimming being tied into faggots for brick-burning or other purposes, the poles being laid into lengths for hop-poles, or for whatever purpose they may be required. Larch hop-poles are very valuable; we have obtained in the wood about 20s. per hundred for mixed poles from 12 to 16 feet long. The expense of such thinning may be covered by the faggots, provided they can be sold for four shillings or five shillings per hundred.

Thinning of plantations.

After this first thinning they may be left for another term of 10 years or so; they may then be sold at prices ranging from 4l. to 7l. per hundred trees, and in twenty to thirty years they may attain in good soil to timber size, and sell for 1s. per cubic foot. In this condition they become valuable timber, none perhaps more universally valuable is grown in Great Britain. For estate purposes it is almost necessary, and for the economical working of an estate it is unsurpassed. It is used for all kinds of roofing timber, except perhaps beams and king-posts, for rafters, plates, battens, puncheons, boards, joists, posts and rails, gates, and other purposes too numerous to mention. It is also easily convertible, and may be used seasoned or unseasoned. Its bark is also used in some districts for tanning, but it is bulky, contains but little tannic acid, and is sold for about half the price of oak. Venice turpentine is extracted from it, and becomes, on the Continent, an export of some importance. For this purpose a

Uses.

Venice turpentine, and method of collecting.

I

CHAP. III.
Sect. 2.
Cone-bearing Trees.

Yield of turpentine.

full-grown tree is selected, and pierced to the centre with an auger, a tube is placed in the hole, and the turpentine collected in troughs, the only preparation needed being straining through a hair-cloth. Seven or eight pounds yearly is considered a fair yield, and this will continue sometimes for fifty years. The run takes place from May to September. After this, of course, the timber bears no value.

Larch as a reclaimer.

The larch also bears a value as a reclaimer of waste lands; the deposit formed by the fall of leaves is exceedingly rich, and, when exposed to atmospheric influence, becomes a most fruitful soil. Land comparatively useless when planted, will, after the lapse of years, when the trees have been removed, bear a high agricultural value. It has been estimated that some of the poor land on the Rotherfield Estate, in Hampshire, planted many years ago with larch, has yielded an average annual return from date of planting three times the amount of its original rental value, and this after making fair allowance for labour of planting, compound interest on capital, and cost of final realisation.

Planting of larch has, in fact, become a matter of national importance; and those landlords who plant large areas of poor land with larch and other fir confer not only an immediate benefit upon themselves, but upon their successors, and upon their country generally.

Weight of Larch, 67·86 cubic feet = 1 ton.

Scotch Fir.

SCOTCH FIR (*Pinus sylvestris*).—This genus is perhaps the most valuable of all ligneous plants, and includes many varieties. Like the larch it belongs to the coniferæ, but it is unlike it in the fact of its being evergreen. It is a native of Europe, Asia, and America, and is valuable for its timber and resin-producing qualities. But the only one of the genus which it is necessary to consider is the well-known Scotch fir (*Pinus sylvestris*), that being the only species grown largely in Great Britain.

Its habitat.

We find this species throughout the kingdom, mostly in high situations and on soils of a poor character. It delights in poor sandy soil, and will not thrive in rich land, except when high and dry. As a shelter, under these circumstances, there is no more useful tree; its growth being rapid and formal. As it advances in age the larger branches die away, leaving a bare but picturesque stem, of a rich sienna colour, contrasting very beautifully with its dark green foliage. Where the birch grows, naturally, the Scotch fir seems to thrive, and this may be borne in mind when arranging plantations on waste lands.

CHAP. III.
Sect. 2.
Cone-bearing Trees.

The treatment is similar in almost all respects to the larch, and it is planted under very much the same circumstances. Acres, however, are often planted from ignorance of the surpassing value of the latter. The larch is valuable from its first thinning until attaining maturity. The Scotch fir is valuable only when maturity is arrived at. It is monœcious, and flowers in May and June, but does not ripen its cones the same year. To separate the seed, the same process is resorted to as described already with reference to larch, with the exception that greater heat is required for the first four hours. When the seed has been collected immediately on becoming ripe, a heat of 130° Fahr. may be applied; when however the seed has been exposed to the heat of the sun, a temperature of 100° Fahr. will be sufficient. It is well to lay some boards on the floor of the kiln about one inch apart, so that the seed escaping when the cones are turned may be collected. They should be allowed to cool before being turned, the heat being again applied for a few hours, when they may be finally turned and sifted. The seed should then be soaked for a while in water to separate the husk. It should be sown in April. The seed-bed, which must be light and sandy, should be covered about a quarter or half an inch with fine mould and protected from birds. Weeding and thinning must of course be attended to, and those that are thinned out may be placed in nursery lines. They will be fit for use according to the situations for which they are required, either as one year's seedlings or two years old

Treatment.

Preparation of the seed.

Sowing the seed, and treatment of plants.

CHAP. III.
Sect. 2.
Cone-bearing
Trees.

Selection of seed.

seedlings which have been twice transplanted, and they will range in price from 2s. to 8s. per 1000.

It is highly necessary to secure seed from districts where the tree is known to attain a healthy growth. That obtained from Highland forests is the best. Individual trees also vary much in quality, even where growing close together; some being red and hard, and others white and soft; if, therefore, cones from the former can be collected, the opportunity should not be neglected. The careful selection of seeds is the more necessary from the natural inclination of this class of trees to degenerate.

Uses.

It grows in a wild state in Norway, Sweden, and Poland; and often in large masses, to the exclusion of other growth. It flourishes in high situations, and grows naturally near the extreme limit of plant life. The use to which the timber is applied varies of course in accordance with its age. When young it bears but little value, being liable to early decay. It is used, however, for pit-props, paling, staves, and laths. As timber it is used as deals for boarding, and

Price.

ordinary carpenter's work, and its price may be estimated at from 1s. to 1s. 3d. per cubic foot. These remarks do not of course apply to certain districts where the tree reaches great dimensions, as under these circumstances a much higher value will be obtained. Such exceptional size is only attained, however, in a few high situations in the Highlands of Scotland, and on northern slopes.

It may be remarked that this is the only species of the pine tribe indigenous to Great Britain.

Weight, 66 feet = 1 ton.

There are many other species of the pine grown in this country, but chiefly for ornamental purposes. Amongst them may be mentioned the following:

Pinus Pineaster.—Chester or Star Pine: a native of India, China, and Japan.
,, *Austriaca.*—Austrian Pine.
,, *Strobus.*—Weymouth Pine.
,, *Insignis.*—Remarkable Pine: a native of California.

And many others; some well known, others of more recent introduction. All ornamental, and, as a rule, hardy and easily treated and propagated.

<small>CHAP. III.
Sect. 2.
Cone-bearing Trees.</small>

The COMMON or NORWAY SPRUCE (*Abies excelsa*).—There are several species of the genus to which the common or Norway spruce belongs, but it is the only one which we need specially consider. <small>Common Spruce.</small>

It is a native of northern Europe, also of Asia and America. It is not indigenous to Great Britain, but was introduced, it is supposed, about the fifteenth century, the exact period is however unknown. Although it grows in high and exposed situations, it reaches great size only in low moist bottoms. It is the most lofty tree in Europe, sometimes reaching a height of 150 or 170 feet. It blossoms in May and June and ripens its cones in the following winter. The cones are pendent and form a beautiful feature in the tree. <small>Its habitat.</small>

The treatment of the cones is similar to that of the Scotch fir cones, already described, and need not, therefore, be repeated. <small>Preparation of seed.</small>

The roots of this tree are very fibrous and ramify near the surface; it is therefore treated somewhat differently to other conifers. The young plants should be left two years in the seed-bed, and if not too thick may be even left three years before being transplanted into lines. But this treatment is scarcely suited to any other of the tribe. <small>Treatment o plants.</small>

For planting in moorland, two years' seedlings once transplanted are the best. By being transplanted they become hardier, but do not increase much in size.

When transplanted for use as above, they may be planted in rows nine or ten inches apart and three inches between the plants.

If they are to remain two years in the lines, they should be one foot apart and four inches between the plants.

Nurserymen sometimes plant closer and remove every other line as time progresses.

CHAP. III.
Sect. 2.
Cone-bearing Trees.

For plantation purposes, two or three years' transplanted plants are best; *i.e.*, plants which have been taken up and replanted twice or three times. They are very fibrous and bear removal well.

Useful as nurses.

Owing to their lower branches retaining foliage, they form an excellent shelter, and are therefore useful as nurses.

If required for timber purposes they should be planted very close together, so that the lower branches may decay and fall off, as the spruce should never be pruned under any circumstances. By this method the timber is obtained free from knots. The thinnings may be used for pit-props, and when further advanced for scaffold poles and sleepers; some of the best may be used for the masts of small vessels, and, when full growth is reached, for planks. The timber is soft and white and of fine grain. It does not, however, reach a high figure; when fully grown 1*s*. to 1*s*. 3*d*. per foot is the full value.

Pruning.

Uses.

Price.

Some magnificent specimens of this tree, and also of larch, Scotch, and silver fir are to be seen in Windsor Park, near Virginia Water.

They grow slowly until they become fully established, when their growth is rapid, and on good moist soils they attain a great height in a few years.

Burgundy pitch, and method of collecting.

From this tree is obtained the Burgundy pitch. This substance is the congealed sap, melted and clarified by boiling in water.

The tree should, where circumstances are favourable, take its place to some extent in all plantations; where, however, ornament is required, it should form the outside lines. It is seldom that it can be recommended as a timber tree, as the larch will grow under similar circumstances, and come earlier to a profitable maturity.

It is best adapted to belts, park circles, and shrubberies.

Silver Fir.

The COMMON SILVER FIR (*Picea pectinata*.)—This is one of the most ornamental and useful of the coniferæ. It is a native of Europe, Asia, and America, and the northern parts of Africa. In the Black Forest and in the glens of Germany it attains great size.

CHAP. III. Sect. 2. Cone-bearing Trees.

It was introduced into England about the year 1600, and has now become a tree of some importance.

It is very similar, in many respects, to the spruce, but the foliage is darker and more lustrous or metallic; the cones, also, are erect, not pendent like the spruce. As the cones ripen the scales fall off and liberate the seed, therefore no such artificial process for liberating the seeds as has been described in the case of the larch and Scotch fir is required.

Treatment of seed.

When young it is the most tender of its class, and needs shelter in the seed-bed; but when it becomes established it is not only hardy, but grows with great rapidity.

Treatment of plants.

It grows best on rich, deep loams; and perhaps for such soils a better tree cannot be selected. For timber purposes it should be planted thickly, under which circumstances it grows straight and soon attains considerable girth, a greater girth than the branches would indicate.

It is also useful in filling up gaps in plantations, as it grows freely in shade.

The seedlings are best transplanted into lines when they have been two years in the seed-bed. They should be left one year in the lines and then transplanted again, giving them more room. This practice makes them hardy and more fibrous-rooted, which latter adapts them for final planting.

From this tree is obtained the well-known Strasburg turpentine, used for fine varnishes and artists' colours, the only turpentine, in fact, fitted for this purpose. It is obtained from the resinous exudations found under the outer skin or bark.

Strasburg turpentine.

The timber is white and soft, and when free from knots makes good planks, which may be used in the place of foreign deals. It fetches in the market from 1s. to 1s. 3d. per cubic foot.

Price.

SECTION III.

TIMBER MEASUREMENT.

MEASUREMENT OF STANDING TIMBER—MEASUREMENT OF SAWN TIMBER—SUMMARY OF RULES WITH EXAMPLES—INSTRUMENTS USED IN TIMBER MEASUREMENT—SLIDING RULE—ITS DESCRIPTION AND USE.

TIMBER MEASUREMENT, WITH A VIEW TO VALUATION AND ULTIMATE REALIZATION.

Chap. III. Sect. 3. Timber Measurement.

HAVING now described the various kinds of timber and timber-like trees and their treatment, we must ask the student's attention to the very important subject of measurement, as, of course, correct knowledge of contents is absolutely necessary before setting a value upon timber with the view to its final realization. To arrive at a quick perception of contents and value, the student will need care and patience. He must cling closely to the set rules, doing nothing by guess work, but proceed methodically with tape and rule, until by degrees his eye acquires such a training as to enable him, by its aid alone, to compute with accuracy; even then, however, he cannot altogether set formal methods of measurement aside.

MEASUREMENT OF STANDING TIMBER.

Rule.—To ascertain the contents of round timber, take the girth in inches in the middle, divide it by four, and square the result (which gives the mean sectional area of the trunk). Multiply the product by length of tree in feet, and divide by 144, and the quotient is the contents in cubic feet. (See rule, page 123).

The result can also be quickly and accurately obtained by use of the carpenter's rule, a description of which will be found hereafter.

Allowance for bark. Where there is bark an allowance must be made, or a false quantity will be obtained. In oak and elm the usual allowance is half to one-and-a-half inches to every foot of quarter girth; thus, the total quarter girth being 24 inches, and the bark being thick, a deduction of two or three inches would be necessary, the quarter girth being taken at 21 or 22 inches.

<small>Chap. III.
Sect. 3.
Timber Measurement.</small>

When trees are measured standing the girth must be taken as high as can be reached, and an allowance made for *fall*, i.e., the natural slope of the tree, which must, of course, be regulated by the regularity or irregularity of such slope. Where the tree tapers gradually, and where the height is considerable, six inches may be deducted from the total girth.

<small>Measurement of standing timber.</small>

The height of standing trees may be judged by using a 20-foot rod, or by the rod made expressly for the purpose in sliding joints, or, when too high even for this, the simple instrument hereafter described may be used: (see pages 125, 126.) The student, however, after a little practice, will generally succeed in forming a correct estimate without the use of this instrument. To arrive at accurate results each tree must be carefully measured, and nothing decided at random. Each tree should be marked when measured, or it may easily be measured by mistake a second time. This remark applies also to felled timber. Therefore a cross should be cut with a razing knife upon each tree as soon as measured. As the measurements are taken, entry must be carefully made in a book ruled for the purpose, and the contents of each quickly reckoned on the sliding rule, or worked out after in the office. A book ruled as follows will be found well adapted to the purpose:—

<small>Method of ascertaining height of trees.</small>

No.	Description.	Length.	Quarter Girth.	Contents in feet.	Price per foot.		Value of tree.		
					s.	d.	£	s.	d.
1	Oak ...	25	17	50	2	0	5	0	0
2	Elm ...	40	25	170	2	0	17	0	0
3	Ash ...	15	14	20	2	6	2	10	0

CHAP. III.
Sect. 3.
Timber Measurement.

Allowance and value of bark.

Dressing bark.

A more elaborate book may be used, but in practice these entries are sufficient. It may be said that this takes no account of the limbs and small wood, or "lop and top." It is however found that as a rule the sale of this about covers the cost of felling, and the timber being valued at the price when felled, the required result is arrived at by leaving its value out of the calculation. When oaks, however, are measured standing, it is necessary, as before stated, to take account of the bark, and for the value of that a sum must be added. This sum must be calculated according to circumstances: where oaks grow together in copses the bark is thin, but at the same time more valuable from the fact of its possessing more tannin, or in a woodman's phrase, "more virtue" than oaks of the same size growing in the open. The bark in the latter case is thick and woody, and requires dressing before a full price can be obtained for it; by dressing is meant the paring off the outside of the bark which is valueless for tanning purposes. Experience only can enable a valuer easily to estimate the value of the bark on the trees which he is valuing. But the student may perhaps be assisted if we repeat the observations made when speaking of the oak tree, namely, that about one ton of bark may fairly be expected from every three or four tons of oak timber, and that 36·2 cubic feet of oak weighs one ton.

Where timber is felled for use on the estate, or for sale after felling, and when oak is stripped by the owner and the bark and timber sold, accurate results are of course obtained, but selling timber standing is a very general custom, and here it is that skill and care are required to ascertain the correct quantities and values. This subject, however, will be further treated of under "Auctions and Sales."

MEASUREMENT OF SAWN TIMBER.

Sawn timber.

It is highly necessary that the student should know how to measure sawn timber. A great deal of practice is required to measure correctly after a sawyer, and as all sawing is done by the "piece," it is important that the account of work given should be duly checked. In sawn timber the superficial foot, not cubic foot, is to be considered, for sale the superficial foot is reckoned at one inch thick. Suppose an oak plank to be three inches thick, the area of the plank would be multiplied by three to arrive at the correct contents. Half-inch plank or any measurement below an inch counts with reference to cost of sawing as one inch, as the labour is of course as great.

CHAP. III.
Sect. 3.
Timber Measurement.

For pit sawing—plank and boards, joists, quartering, &c. —the sum generally given is from 5s. to 7s. per hundred feet, if sawn by steam, 1s. for the same quantity, the estate finding engine-driver. For slabs the sum given is 3s. including hewing-cut.

Cost of pit sawing.
Cost of steam sawing.

Planks are generally cut into fixed lengths, which of course necessitates only the measurement of the width in the middle, or each end if tapering, and then by a rapid calculation on the rule the superficial content is arrived at, and chalked on the plank, and the plank set up for seasoning.

Measurement of slabs and planks.

Where the planks are less on one side than the other, *i.e.*, where the bark or rind adheres it is to be measured on the lesser side.

Rule.—Multiply the mean breadth in inches by the length in feet, divide the product by 12, and the result will be the superficial contents.

Rule.

By the Sliding Rule.—As 12 upon B. is to the breadth in inches upon A., so is the length in feet upon B. to the contents upon A. in feet and fractional parts.

SUMMARY OF RULES WITH EXAMPLES.

1. To ascertain cubical contents of trees; *i.e.*, *saleable* contents.

Rule.—The quarter girth in inches squared multiplied by the length in feet, and divided by 144 = saleable contents.

This rule gives the contents less the sap-wood, which is hewn before sawing.

2. To ascertain the *exact* cubical contents.

124 ESTATE MANAGEMENT.

CHAP. III.
Sect. 3.
Timber Measurement.

Saleable contents.

Exact contents.

By sliding rule.

Superficial measurement.

Rule.—Multiply the area of the circle of which the girth is the circumference in inches by the length in feet, and divide by 144 = exact contents.

Examples :

Rule 1.—Find the contents of a tree 25ft. long whose quarter girth is 16in.: $16^2 = 256$, $256 \times 25 = 6400$, $6400 \div 144 = 44 \cdot 4$ cubic feet. Saleable contents of tree.

Rule 2.—Find the contents of a tree 25ft. long whose total girth is 64in.: area (see Circles), $2 \cdot 368$; $2 \cdot 368 \times 25 = 59$ft. A correct but not practical result.

3. To ascertain the cubical contents of a tree by sliding rule.

Rule.—As the length upon C. is to 12 upon D., so is the quarter girth in inches on D. to contents upon C.

This latter is a quick and easy method, and generally resorted to by timber measurers.

4. To ascertain the superficial contents of a plank.

Rule.—The length in feet multiplied by the mean breath in inches and divided by 12 = superficial area.

Decimals and duodecimals are rules useful for the above; and are more fully described hereafter.

Examples :

Required the superficial contents of a plank whose length is 20ft. 6in. and breath 1ft. 4in.

By fractions $20\frac{1}{2} \times 1\frac{1}{3} = \frac{41}{2} \times \frac{4}{3} = 1\frac{64}{6} = 27\frac{1}{3}$.

By *Decimals.*	*Duodecimals.*
20·5	20 6
1·33	1 4
·615	20 6
6·15	610 0
20·5	
	27 4 0
27·265	

5. To ascertain the superficial contents of a plank by sliding rule.

By sliding rule.

Rule.—As 12 upon B. is to the breadth in inches upon A., so is the length in feet upon B. to the contents upon A. in feet and fractional parts.

TIMBER TREES. 125

INSTRUMENTS USED IN TIMBER MEASUREMENT. CHAP. III.
Sect. 3.
Fig. 1. The razing-knife. This knife can be purchased Timber
for 2s. 6d. or 3s. at any ironmonger's. It is used for marking Measurement.
trees. Razing-knife.

Fig. 2 is the "needle" for assisting the measurer in Needle.
girting the tree with string. When felled, timber lies close
upon the ground, it is often difficult to force the string under
it. This simple instrument overcomes this entirely. It may
be made by any blacksmith for 1s. 6d. (Note.) The two
figures represent the same instrument from different views.

Fig. 3 is the "girt-strap" for girting standing timber. Girt-strap.
It is a strap about six feet long and ¾ or 1 inch wide, having
at one end a loop for the hand, and at the other a weight.
Standing close to the tree, the operator throws the weight
round, which he catches, and thus girts the tree. It is
necessary, however, to be careful, as the weight comes
round with considerable force, and is apt to strike the
operator's face rather unpleasantly.

The strap is divided into inches, which are marked
¼, ½, ¾, 1, &c., each inch being reckoned a quarter, thus
showing at a glance the quarter girth of the tree.

Fig. 4. To find the height of a tree, a simple instrument To find the
may be made by any village carpenter, as follows:— height of a tree.

Take a square-sided staff of some light, but tough wood,
6 feet in length, and divide it into feet for the sake of
taking distances.

Upon this staff, fix at convenient height an oblong piece
of board (mahogany is best), 8in. long and 4in.
broad, and ¾in. thick (or any other size, provided the
length is exactly double the breadth). At the corners A
and B (see fig. 4, page 126), fix two nails or brass pins,
allowing them to project from the board; at C and D fix
two more, making A B equal to A C and C D. At X, fix
an eyelet to admit of the suspension of a plummet. Let
the staff be pointed and shod with iron, that it may be fixed
readily into the ground.

The instrument is then complete, and is used as follows:—

126   ESTATE MANAGEMENT.

CHAP. III.
Sect. 3
*Timber
Measurement.*

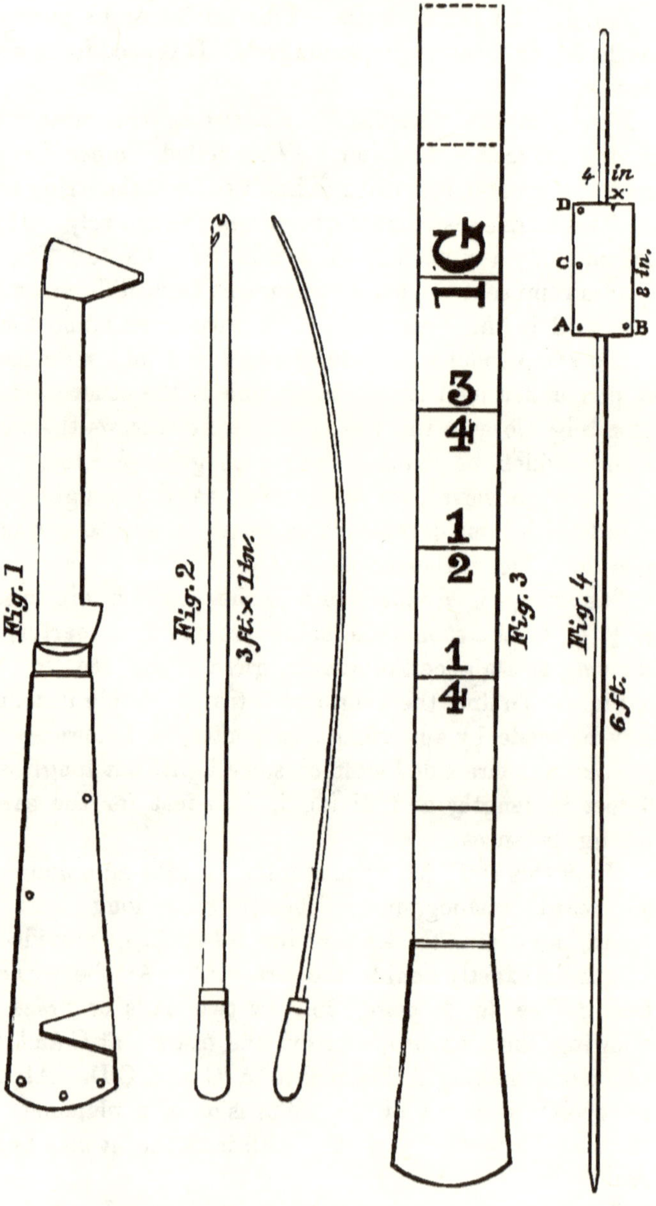

Fig. 1

Fig. 2
3 ft. × 1 in.

Fig. 3
1G
3/4
1/2
1/4

Fig. 4
4 in.
8 in.
6 ft.

Keep the dial face edge-ways, so that the points A, C, D, are towards the tree, and the point B towards the observer. Then fix the staff in the ground perpendicularly by aid of the plummet, at such a place that by looking across B C you can see the top of the tree. The height of the tree will then be equal to the distance of the staff from the base of the tree, plus the height from the ground to the measurer's eye.

If it is more convenient, owing to underwood or other obstruction, to place the staff nearer the tree, fix the staff at such a place that, acting as before described, by looking across the sights B D, you see the top of the tree. The height of the tree will then be equal to double the distance, plus the height from the ground to the eye.

With the addition of a carpenter's rule, book and pencil, and a piece of string 6ft. long, the measurer is equipped.

Sliding Rule—Its Description and Use.

Although it is not easy to make this instrument intelligible by mere written description, the following quotation from Nesbit's Mensuration will probably enable the student to understand and apply it so soon as he has it actually in his hands.

"This instrument is commonly called 'Cogeshall's Sliding Rule,' and is much used in measuring timber and artificers' work; not only in taking the dimensions, but also in casting up the contents.

"It consists of two pieces of box, each 1ft. in length, connected together by a folding joint. One side or face of the rule is divided into inches and half-quarters or eights; and on the same face there are also several plane scales, divided into twelfth parts, which are designed for planning such dimensions as are taken in feet and inches. On one part of the other face are four lines marked A, B, C, D; the two middle ones B and C being upon a slider.

Three of these lines, viz., A, B, C, are exactly alike, and are called double lines because they proceed from 1 to

10 twice over. The fourth line, D, is a single one, proceeding from 4 to 40, and is called the "girt line." The use of the double lines A and B, is for working proportions and finding the areas of plane figures, and the use of the girt line, D, and the other double line, C, for finding the contents of solids.

When 1 at the beginning of any line is accounted 1, then the 1 in the middle will be 10, and the 10 at the end 100, and when 1 at the end is accounted 10, then the 1 in the middle is 100, and the 10 at the end 1000, &c., and all the smaller divisions are altered in value accordingly. Upon the girt-line are also marked W G at 17·15 and A G at 18·95, the wine and ale gauge-points, to make the instrument serve the purpose of a gauging rule. On the other part of this face there is commonly either a table of the value of a load or fifty cubic feet of timber, at all prices 6d. to 24d. per foot, or else several plane scales divided into twelfth parts, and marked 1, ¾, ½, and ¼, signifying that the 1-inch, ¾-inch, &c., are each divided into twelve equal parts.

The edge of the rule is generally divided decimally, or into tenths, namely, each foot into ten equal parts, and each of those into ten other equal parts. By this scale dimensions may be taken in feet, tenths and hundredths of a foot, which is a very commodious method of taking dimensions, when the contents are to be cast up decimally.

SECTION IV.

Sale of Timber.

SALE BY PUBLIC AUCTION — BILL OF EXCHANGE — SALE BY TENDER — PRIVATE SALE.

Realization of Timber.

These methods of sale present themselves to the land steward, from which he must select in accordance with the custom of the district, his own views, or the requirements of the estate. The first and, perhaps, that most resorted to is

> CHAP. III.
> Sect. 4.
> *Sale of Timber.*

SALE BY PUBLIC AUCTION.

After having decided what timber is for sale, he will choose an auctioneer known for his business qualities and uprightness, and arrange with him place of sale, date, and hour, and also give him the quantity and description of timber for sale, in order that he may insert proper advertisements in the local and other suitable newspapers. *Sale by auction.*

Having done this, he will either authorise the auctioneer or employ his own woodman to mark and number in paint the various lots of timber. This is done by scraping off the moss, and, with a paint brush, making a bold number in white or red paint, each tree being marked on the same side, so that, by walking through the wood in one direction, the marks readily catch the eye. It is, however, a good plan when thinning, in addition to the number to paint a ring round the entire stem, so that it can be seen from all directions. *Method of lotting timber for sale.*

The next process will be to go with the woodman and measure and value each lot (in accordance with the foregoing rules), entering the same carefully in a memorandum book. At the time of sale these values will be given to the auctioneer as the "upset" or reserved price. *Valuations of lots.*

At the time of sale the auctioneer then will be in possession of the number of trees of each kind, the woods in which they stand or lie, and the proximity of roads; he will also have prepared conditions of sale, drawn up in accordance with the views of the steward, such rules embodying strict conditions as to payments, and the fufilment of certain obligations. The sale will then proceed. If the timber is good and useful, if the advertisements and postbills have been widely and wisely circulated, and if the auctioneer is known, there is every prospect of success.

It is very necessary that the sale should be extensively known, as, when local merchants only are present, it is a very common practice to combine and keep down the prices; *Publicity of auctions.*

K

CHAP. III.
Sect. 4.
Sale of Timber.

when, however, buyers come from a distance this is almost impossible.

An auctioneer's form of conditions and the usual memorandum of agreement are annexed, which will serve as a guide, and help to make clear the foregoing remarks.

Auctioneer's duties.

The auctioneer after the sale will collect the money in accordance with the conditions (the conditions having been read aloud previous to the sale). Within a week or so he will forward to the steward a statement of accounts, showing the expenses connected with the sale—printing bills and catalogues, posting bills, marking and lotting, "expenses out of pocket," and commission; the latter depending upon circumstances, but it will vary from $2\frac{1}{2}$ to 5 per cent. upon the gross sum obtained. The balance, after these deductions are made, he will cover by a cheque, and at the same time he will inclose a list of the purchasers, their names and addresses, with the respective balances due from them. The steward will then proceed to draw upon each in the usual way, which will be hereafter more fully described.

When auction is not advisable.

The plan of auction is generally strongly to be recommended. It brings what is highly necessary, viz., keen competition, and as a rule gives general satisfaction. The practice, however, is not desirable in the case of small sales. When the sum expected is less than 200*l.*, it is scarcely advisable.

Lotting.

When trees are standing or lying altogether, lots of twenty will be found a useful number; when scattered, the lots may consist of fewer, and sometimes even of single trees. When felled, they may of course be collected and drawn into lots and into suitable situations, and when this can be done it will be wise to select with judgment, so that each lot may be valuable for special purposes.

Settlement after purchase.

In settlement it is sometimes wise to allow a discount for cash payments, *i.e.* for the balances due after payment of the stipulated deposit. Five per cent. discount will almost invariably induce cash payments when the purchaser is sound, but 2½ per cent. will seldom do so. The allowance, however, of 5 per cent. is a matter of importance in a pecuniary point of view, and it is doubtful policy to take it from a thoroughly trustworthy man (and on this account provided for in condition 4).

Bills, though often absolutely necessary, should be, where possible, discountenanced.

Where necessary to resort to the practice, the form is as follows :—

[Handwritten bill form]

£ . s . d   London (or other abode), date.
Three months after date (or other period) pay to my order the sum of   pounds,   shillings, and pence, for value received.
To M. A.   Y. Z.

This form, filled up with the amount due, must be forwarded to A.B., the party upon whom it is drawn, with a request that he will accept it and return it at once. In the event of his sole acceptance being considered satisfactory, no further step is required; if, however, there are doubts existing as to his ability to meet his engagement, he must be requested to furnish another signature to the bill, the party attaching such signature being responsible in the event of the failure of the drawee.

The acceptance must be written across the bill (as above) and should be made payable at a banker's. This bill is then either kept by Y. Z. the drawer (in this case the steward) until it becomes due, or deposited with his bankers for collection at maturity; or he may, if he desires it, discount it at the current rate of interest. The act, however, of discounting does not remove from the drawer any responsibility in the event of the bankers becoming losers by the failure of the drawee.

The bill being made to "order" will require the signature of the drawer on the back, previously to payment.

It must be written on paper stamped, according to the

CHAP. III.
Sect. 4.
Sale of Timber.

Bill stamps.

amount for which it is drawn, the stamp duties being as follows:

BILLS OF EXCHANGE, ON DEMAND, 1*d.*

Bill of any other kind (except a bank note), and promissory note of any kind whatsoever (except a bank note), drawn or expressed to be payable, or actually paid or indorsed, or in any manner negotiated in the United Kingdom, or purporting to be drawn or made out of the United Kingdom, though actually drawn or made within it.

	£	£	s.	d.
Any sum not exceeding	5	0	0	1
Above £5	10	0	0	2
,, 10	25	0	0	3
,, 25	50	0	0	6
,, 50	75	0	0	9
,, 75	100	0	1	0

And for every £100 or fraction thereof, 1*s.*

Rules necessary to secure success.

In conclusion, it may be observed that, in order to insure the success of a sale by auction, the following requirements are necessary :—The selection of a trustworthy auctioneer, wide distribution of notices of sale, comprehensive rules and conditions, and the retainment of power over the timber until payment is made or secured.

CONDITIONS OF SALE.

Conditions of sale.

1. The highest bidder to be the purchaser on being declared such by the auctioneer, whose decision shall be final.

2. No person shall advance less than 1*l.* at each bidding, nor retract his bidding.

3. The sale is subject to a reserved bidding for each lot, which will be made by the owner's agent if necessary.

4. Each purchaser, at the time and place of sale, shall subscribe his name and address (on request) to these particulars, and sign an agreement for the due performance of these conditions. Each purchaser shall, immediately after the sale (or on the fall of the hammer, if requested), pay into the hands of the auctioneer 25*l.* per cent. on the amount of purchase money, and shall, within fourteen days from the day of sale, make and deliver, at his own expense, to the vendor's agent, security to be approved by him for the remainder of the purchase money by an acceptance, payable at a banker's three months after the date of the sale, and shall find also sufficient surety or sureties for payment of the same; or in default of giving such approved acceptance or finding such securities the deposit money shall be forfeited to the vendor, who shall thereupon be entitled to the timber and produce thereof, sold to such

purchaser, for his own use and benefit, as if no such sale had taken place, nor shall the purchaser be allowed to enter on the premises to remove any part of the said timber or trees or produce thereof. Should any purchaser pay the whole of his purchase-money at the time of sale, a discount of 2½ per cent. on the value, after deducting the deposit as above, will be allowed.

CHAP. III.
Sect. 4.
Sale of Timber.

5. If any person shall purchase more than one lot, the lots so purchased by him shall, for the purpose of the fourth condition, be considered as one lot; and the total amount of the purchase money for such lots shall be subject to the same deposit and securities accordingly.

6. If any purchaser shall neglect or fail to pay his purchase money as aforesaid, or shall become bankrupt or insolvent, the vendor or his agent shall be at liberty to secure and prevent the removal of any of the timber, or produce thereof, purchased by such purchaser that shall be remaining on the said manor, and shall be at liberty to sell or dispose of the same, and apply the money arising from the sale thereof towards paying the purchase money of such purchaser, or such part thereof as shall be unpaid, and after deducting all charges of converting and selling the said timber, or produce thereof, shall render the overplus (if any) to such purchaser, or to the person or persons legally claiming under him, but such taking possession or sale shall not discharge such purchaser or his surety or sureties from their respective liability upon any acceptance then unpaid, or any bond or other security, further than to the extent of the net proceeds of such sale.

7. The trees shall be removed and taken off the said premises at the purchaser's expense, on or before the 1st day   187 . And such timber or produce of such timber, which shall be remaining after the said 1st day of   shall be forfeited to the vendor, who may take the same to his own use, without making any satisfaction to the said purchaser.

8. The respective purchasers shall use all possible caution to prevent damage to the adjacent hedges, fences, gates, posts, and rails, and shall, with their horses, teams, carriages, servants, and workmen, keep the accustomed roads to and from the woods, or such other tracks and ways as shall be pointed out by the vendor, or his agents, and shall not, nor will take any dogs or guns into the woods, plantations, or fields of or belonging to the said manor. All injury or negligent damage arising from the breach of this or any other condition, either by the purchasers, or their respective agents, workmen or labourers, horses and cattle, as aforesaid, shall be forthwith made good and paid by the purchaser thereof, and the amount of such injury or damage shall be settled by the vendor's agent, and be thereupon recovered by the vendor as liquidated damages.

9. If any dispute shall arise as to the identity or number of trees or saplings comprised in any lot, such dispute shall be decided by the vendor's

ESTATE MANAGEMENT.

CHAP. III.
Sect. 4.
Sale of Timber.

agent, and no mistake, error, or mis-description whatsoever in the particulars of sale shall vacate or vitiate the sale of several lots or any of them, and no compensation or allowance shall be made, paid or allowed by the vendor or purchasers respectively in respect of such mistake, error, or mis-description, unless the same be declared or pointed out at the time of the sale, or before signing these conditions.

AGREEMENT.

Agreement.

I,   of   , do hereby acknowledge that I have this day purchased by public auction, Lot   of the timber mentioned in the annexed particulars, for the sum of £   and have paid the sum of £   as a deposit, and in part payment of the said purchase money, and I do hereby agree to pay the remaining part of the said purchase money at the time and place within appointed, and in all other respects on my part to fulfil the within-mentioned conditions.

Dated the   day of   187 .
Witness my hand

Purchase money ...	£	Here attach a 6d. Agreement Stamp.
Deposit money ...	£	
Balance due	£	

As Agent for the Vendor, I hereby confirm the same, and acknowledge the said sum of £   to have been paid to me on account of the above purchase money.

SALE BY TENDER.

Sale by tender.

Before resorting to this plan it will be necessary to arrive at the real value of the timber for sale, in order that the tenders received may be fully considered. There will probably be a great divergence in the amount of the various tenders; but this is only to be expected when values are decided by parties wanting the timber for various purposes, and unprompted by the knowledge of competition.

Method of selling by tender.

The method of procedure is as follows :—An advertisement is drawn up somewhat as follows, and inserted in the various local and other papers likely to come under the notice of timber merchants :

Forms of tender.

"*To Timber Merchants and Others.*—Tenders are invited for the purchase of oak (or other) timber growing (or lying) upon the   estate. To view, and for full particulars, apply to Mr.   , woodman of the estate. Tenders to be delivered by the   day of   , 18   , and addressed to Mr.   , steward (address). No pledge is given to accept the highest or any tender," or,

"Tenders are invited for the purchase of timber growing (or lying) upon the   estate, in accordance with the following particulars: Tenders to be sealed and marked 'Tenders for timber,' and delivered by the 6th day of December (or other date). No pledge is given to accept the highest or any tender. To view apply to the woodman,   estate. Tenders to be addressed to A. B. C., steward,   House (address)."

Name of Wood.	Oak.	Ash.	Beech.	Elm.
Great Wood ...	6	12		
High Wood ...	10	3	6	
Church Lane ...				5

This practice is approved of by many. It possesses the advantage of simplicity, and also saves considerable trouble and expense. It fails, however, to produce the necessary competition which can alone secure high figures.

The intending purchasers are also somewhat restricted in their offers by the feeling that they may possibly, to secure the purchase, overreach themselves. They are, to a certain extent, working in the dark, and lose that very necessary element acquired in public auctions of rapid calculation and decision. That buyers are influenced in this way there is no doubt; for we have known the amount of tenders vary to such an extraordinary extent that it has been scarcely possible to believe that they have been based upon the same lots of timber, or that they have emanated at all from practical men.

CHAP. III.
Sect. 4.
Sale of Timber.

In the event of this practice being determined upon, however, the conditions as to payments, and conversion of the timber, will be similar to that already described in the foregoing pages.

PRIVATE SALE.

Private sale.

For small lots, this is perhaps the wisest course, but for large lots the most unwise. But it is to be observed that there are those who are always looking out for bargains, and ready to take advantage of the unwary or inexperienced; and accordingly a private sale is scarcely likely to be satisfactory except where it is made by a man of considerable experience.

It is necessary in this method to measure and value with great accuracy, more so than under the two former plans of sale; this, however, must be evident, as upon the estimate only the steward must make his bargain.

Often on estates there are small lots of timber not required for home use, which may be sold in this way, and which will bring in small sums of money for ordinary outgoings.

In most districts there are men who can better afford to buy small than large lots, and are willing to pay a trifle over the ordinary value rather than lose this advantage. In cases of this sort private sale is useful, and may be safely resorted to; but, for large sales, we are of opinion that the practice is most unwise, and should in every case be discountenanced. It is to be remembered that $1d.$ a foot represents a considerable sum when large quantities of timber are in question.

CHAPTER IV.
UNDERWOOD AND ITS MANAGEMENT.

SECTION I.
UNDERWOOD.

UNDERWOOD AS A SOURCE OF INCOME—SALE OF UNDERWOOD—CUTTING AND SORTING UNDERWOOD—TIME FOR CUTTING—UNDERWOOD IN THE HANDS OF A TENANT—THE PLANTING AND PROTECTION OF UNDERWOOD—TABLES FOR CALCULATING NUMBER OF PLANTS REQUIRED FOR PLANTING DIFFERENT AREAS.

BY underwood is meant coppice, which is growth from stools or stumps. This growth, as a rule, forms an important item in the annual receipts of most estates, and the duty of the Forester is to see that the acreage is so arranged that the same quantity comes to cut each year. For instance, supposing we have upon an estate 100 acres of coppice, and the soil is such as will bring the wood to maturity in eight years, we divide the acreage by eight, which gives $12\frac{1}{2}$ acres as the annual cut. This is highly important in estate management, as the yearly income should be, as nearly as possible, equal, in order that expenses may be regularly met; and also that the owner may know as nearly as possible what income he may expect. Upon rich estates underwood forms one of the most profitable sources of income, and deserves careful attention. The return is regular and the expenses low, as during the growth little labour is required beyond looking to the watercourses and ditches, and keeping down ground game; and, of course, the annual payment of rates. Under these circumstances a return considerably beyond agricultural value may be

CHAP. IV.
Sect. 1.
Underwood.

looked for. On soils, however, of poorer quality, the growth is less rapid, and the quality much inferior; a period of twelve years being often required before coming to "cut." It is highly important, where underwood is looked upon as the chief means of return, that timber should be thoroughly and carefully thinned, as no class of underwood will grow under spreading oaks or beeches. It is also of great importance that ground game should be kept down, as when hazel and ash are barked, or the young shoots nipped off, the value of the next cut is greatly affected. In hard winters, and when game is preserved, the damage done is often beyond calculation.

Sale of underwood.

Underwood, as a rule, is sold by auction, under rules very similar to that of timber: (see p. 132.) It is sold by the acre; the purchaser undertaking to cut and remove, without injury to surrounding growth, within a certain period; also undertaking to cut clean and low, leaving all heirs, saplings, and hollies (these, however, ought first of all to be marked in paint by the Forester) as belonging to the estate. He also makes good all the fences adjoining the portion which falls to him from the growth in proximity, being allowed for the same at a fixed sum per rod on payment of his account. He is also in some cases called upon to leave rods, where the plant is thin, for future layering; and where this is done an allowance is made for every 100 rods so left. The parties purchasing are generally men who make it part of their calling; they consequently know to a nicety what use each separate stick is adapted to. When the work is completed, and the ground clear, the buyer and seller appoint a measurer, who measures off each piece, and it is upon this area that payment is made; the sum per acre being of course fixed when the contract is made. The acreage of each cut is, however, after some years tolerably well known, and consequently a fixed sum may be arranged at the outset. The value of underwood much depends upon the number of ash and other poles which it contains; for these are looked upon as direct profit, whilst the hazel and other small stuff are expected to clear expenses unless the quality is very deficient.

When the sale has been effected, the buyer agrees with a party of men to cut the stuff. This is done also by the acre; the price generally being from 14s. to 15s. They lay it in rows just as it comes. When the whole is felled they return to the place where they began and commence the process of *sorting*. A practised cutter knows in a moment what to do with each piece, and with his sharp bill-hook the work rapidly proceeds; hop poles, hurdle-rods, shores, withes for tying, rods for fencing, hoops, &c., being all sorted and made up by the dozen or quarter of a hundred, and the refuse tied into faggots. This is also done by task work. When this is all completed the men are paid and the buyer commences the act of realisation. One of his first acts in those districts where basket hurdles are made is to send in the hurdle-maker to make up the rods put aside for that purpose. This process is paid for by the dozen hurdles, the price paid being about 3s. to 3s. 3d., a good maker turning out on an average twelve to fifteen hurdles per day. The price of these when sold is about 7s. to 8s. per dozen.

It will consequently be seen that the buyer of underwood must have some amount of capital to enable him to conduct his work. But credit is usually given by the seller. This is of course arranged at the time of sale, and the practice varies in different districts and on different estates.

It is very important that cutting should not commence until the sap ceases to circulate, as otherwise the stumps soon become injured from bleeding. From November to March is the best time. There is also a period at which the growth falls off and rapidly decreases in value. It is therefore necessary to watch the exact period of maturity.

Where underwood is let with the farms, the annual growths are of course the property of the tenant. Upon quitting therefore he is entitled to receive from the incomer a sum representing the value of such growth; this

CHAP. IV.
Sect. 1.
Underwood.

value is determined by valuers chosen in the ordinary way by each party, and, with men of experience, there is little difficulty in arriving at a fair sum. We append for the use of the student a table which we have found of value, and which may act as a guide. Of course, the nearer the growth is to maturity the greater in proportion becomes the value; and as the table is framed on the assumption that the soil will only bring to maturity every twelve years, it will require modification in valuing on a soil where maturity is more rapid.

Table of values.

Value per acre at maturity.	£ s. d. 6 0 0	£ s. d. 5 10 0	£ s. d. 5 0 0	£ s. d. 4 10 0	£ s. d. 4 0 0
Years.					
Value per acre at the end of successive years after last cut. 1	0 7 2	0 6 7	0 6 0	0 5 4	0 4 8
2	0 14 4	0 13 7	0 12 6	0 11 0	0 9 7
3	1 2 8	1 1 0	0 19 0	0 17 0	0 15 6
4	1 11 2	1 8 0	1 6 0	1 3 0	1 0 6
5	2 2 0	1 17 0	1 13 0	1 9 6	1 6 6
6	2 9 10	2 5 0	2 1 0	1 16 6	1 13 0
7	2 19 10	2 15 0	2 10 0	2 4 0	1 19 6
8	3 10 0	3 5 0	2 19 0	2 12 0	2 6 6
9	4 1 0	3 15 0	3 8 0	3 0 0	2 14 0
10	4 13 6	4 6 0	3 18 0	3 9 0	3 2 0
11	5 6 0	4 18 0	4 10 0	3 19 0	3 11 0

The planting and protection of underwood.

In preparing plantations of underwood, it is necessary to drain if the soil be at all wet; and open watercourses should be resorted to. These should be cut with sloping sides, as otherwise in winter the earth falls in and fills up the drain, causing flooding and consequent injury. Covered drains are useless owing to the roots and fibres. Trenching may be advisable, and pay in the long run, but it is too expensive to be generally resorted to. Good fences should

UNDERWOOD AND ITS MANAGEMENT.

also be erected, as the bite of sheep or cattle is injurious to the young plant. Roads should always be so arranged that the cuttings may be carted away with as little injury to the stumps as possible. A cart-wheel will often cause the death of a well-developed stool. The subject of propagation will be treated of under the description of plants suitable for underwood; it should, however, be borne in mind, that in planting, variety is a matter to be kept in view; hazel forms generally the bulk, but it may be interspersed with ash, chestnut, &c. The distance apart should be about four feet, and the planting may take place any time between October and March. Where old plantations require filling up, the writer has found layering better than planting. This process is very simple. Layers, which should be well grown and developed rods, are left standing; then, when the ground is clear, these are cut at the base and bent over and so laid where the bare place occurs; the end, being pointed, is struck into the ground and the layer kept down with pegs and covered at the base where cut, and perhaps in one or two other places, with a sod. Growth soon takes place, and in a few years fresh stumps are formed. They should be laid as close to the ground as possible, as otherwise men and horses often trip over them. A cut on the the under side of the layer will assist the development of roots. It is therefore a good plan to incise the bark with the hook, when layering, in two or three places. From these cuts fibres are thrown out and a separate stool is more rapidly formed. It is important to keep blank spaces always well layered or planted, and injured shoots cut down so as to promote fresh growths. In conclusion, no timber trees but oak should be allowed to be present, and that only to a limited extent. The oak roots strike deeply down, and consequently this tree only affects the growth of coppice by the shade which it produces.

The following Table shows the number of plants on an Imperial Statute, a Scottish, and an Irish Plantation acre, respectively, at various distances of the plants apart each way:

Chap. IV. Sect. 1. Underwood.

Distance of plants.

Layering.

CHAP. IV.
Sect. 1.
Underwood.

Distance of plants apart.	Number of plants on an Imperial Statute acre of 4840 square yards.	Number of plants on a Scottish acre of 6150 square yards.	Number of plants on an Irish Plantation acre of 7840 square yards.
ft. in.			
2 0	10,890	13,837	17,640
2 3	8604	10,933	13,938
2 6	6969	8856	11,289
2 9	5760	7315	9330
3 0	4840	6150	7840
3 3	4124	5240	6680
3 6	3555	4518	5760
3 9	3097	3936	5017
4 0	2722	3459	4410
4 3	2411	3064	3906
4 6	2151	2733	3484
4 9	1930	2453	3127
5 0	1662	2214	2822
5 3	1584	2008	2560
5 6	1440	1830	2332
5 9	1317	1674	2134
6 0	1210	1529	1960
6 3	1115	1417	1806
6 6	1031	1310	1670
6 9	956	1214	1548
7 0	889	1130	1440
7 3	828	1053	1342
7 6	774	984	1254
7 9	725	921	1174
8 0	680	865	1102
8 3	640	813	1036
8 6	603	766	976
8 9	569	721	921
9 0	537	683	871
9 3	509	644	824
9 6	482	613	781
9 9	458	582	742
10 0	435	553	705

SECTION II.

Plants suitable for Underwood.

HAZEL — SWEET CHESNUT — ASH — WILLOW — BEECH — BIRCH — OTHER VARIETIES.

Of the various plants suitable for coppice growth, we may mention, firstly:

The HAZEL (*Corylus avellana*), which is indigenous to the temperate climates of Europe. It is very hardy, and is consequently found in all situations. It is deciduous and monœcious, *i.e.*, it casts its leaves in winter and carries its male and female flowers separate, but on the same plant, the well-known catkin being the male flower, the bright scarlet tuft found on examination, but not easily seen from a distance, being the female flower, or that which contains the pistil.

Its growth in good soils and in sheltered situations is very rapid, often as much as five feet in one season. It forms the most ornamental and useful of all our underwood plants, holding its leaf tenaciously long after frosts have set in, and thus giving the rich colour to the autumn landscape.

The Filbert, the Cob, the Barcelona, and other nuts, are all varieties of the genus to which the hazel belongs. To secure, however, their fruit-bearing qualities it is necessary to propagate them by grafts or layers.

The common hazel, however, for simple underwood purposes, is grown from nuts; these should be selected, which may be done by sifting through a riddle, as weak plants are generally obtained from small nuts. The nut should be planted in a bed in October, and covered with an inch of soil; they will break through in spring, and should be kept clear of weeds. When a year old the strongest plants should be transplanted in rows, the plants at a distance of about one foot apart, and the rows at a distance of from one and a half to two feet. Under ordinary cir-

Chap. IV.
Sect. 2.
Plants suitable for Underwood.

Time for planting.

cumstances they are left in these lines two years, and then removed to their destination. The lines should be kept well hoed and free from weeds throughout their infancy.

Planting hazel may take place from October to spring, provided the weather is open; autumn planting is, however, the best, as the plants are better able to bear the heat of the ensuing summer. Care should be taken in the planting, especially where the plants are large; the holes should be large enough to take them without force. When young and small they may be planted with less care, as they are not so readily checked. After planting, the only attention they will need is to have the vacancies caused by death filled up, and to be kept as much as possible from the bite of ground game. When, however, they are injured by biting, it is best to cut the plant down with a sharp knife, rather than leave the injured shoot to struggle on to a diseased maturity.

As a hedge plant the hazel is comparatively useless; unlike the quick-set it will not bear constant cutting, and consequently the neat and trim appearance so necessary in a hedge cannot be obtained. Where, however, it exists the best plan is to lay it, using as little dead wood as possible.

But to this plant must be given the first place in our underwoods, as at once the most universally useful and profitable.

Sweet chestnut.

SWEET CHESNUT (*Castanea vesca*) may be placed next in order of importance. It has already been noticed under the head of "Timber," but, like many other timber trees, it yields, when cut, a growth of shoots from the stool, which increase in number with each successive cutting. The shoots of the sweet chesnut are very valuable as hop-poles, therefore in hop districts it should never be omitted from plantations. In this use consists its principal value, and for that purpose may be said to rank third; larch and ash being first and second respectively. It will come to maturity as poles in from seven to ten years, according to the nature of the soil upon which it is grown. The propagation for this purpose is similar to that already described, and it is unnecessary to transplant so often as would be the case if the plants were needed for timber, fruit or ornamental trees. It thrives well in the shade, and may therefore be grown amongst fir plantations. It also thrives on light and inferior soils, and this consequently forms another reason why it may be chosen to accompany fir. It is not a favourite plant with rabbits, therefore often escapes injury.

CHAP. IV.
Sect. 2.
Plants suitable for Underwood.

ASH (*Fraxinus excelsior*) is a valuable underwood plant, and, as already stated, its presence or absence greatly affects the value of underwood. It grows from stools, and increases three or four fold with each cutting. It is very liable to the attack of ground-game, perhaps more so than any other, except laburnum. When cut it should be cut clean, and as near the stool as possible.

Ash.

It is propagated as already described in our reference to it as a timber tree, and, like the chesnut, needs but little transplanting for this purpose. It may be planted alone four feet apart, or mixed with other plants in fair proportion. It will be ready to cut, under favourable circumstances, in from eight to twelve years. After the first cutting, gaps may be filled up by layers or by new plants from the nursery. Layering has already been described, but it may be well to bear in mind that no plant is more successfully treated in this way than the ash.

Mode of propagation.

The stools yield large crops of poles, which are used for hop-poles when of proper size, and if too large for this they may be split up for sheep cages, hurdles, whipple-trees, and other purposes.

Hop-poles of this description will always realise a high price. If twelve feet long they will be worth in the wood 12s. to 14s. per hundred; if fourteen feet long, 14s. to 16s.; if sixteen feet, 20s. to 22s. Plantations of ash as under-

Uses and value.

L

<small>CHAP. IV.
Sect. 2.
*Plants
suitable for
Underwood.*</small>

wood will often realise from 30*l*. to 40*l*. an acre. It thrives best on rich soils and in sheltered situations, and cannot be recommended at all for high and exposed situations. For further particulars the reader is referred to the "Ash as a timber-tree."

It will be necessary now to give little more than a list of those plants suitable for underwood, as the plants have already been discussed under the head of "Timber." It must, however, again be stated that what constitutes a coppice plant is its power to grow from stools. Without this quality it is useless. In the following list the plants are enumerated as nearly as possible in the order of their relative merit and importance as growth for underwood.

<small>Plants
suitable for
underwood.</small>

OAK (*Quercus robur*).—Oak, as to which it is to be observed that the younger the stool the better will be the shoots. Stumps of old trees may however be induced to throw out shoots by dressing the surface with an adze to a conical form, and keeping down the surrounding grass for the first year. All lateral or ill-grown shoots should be broken off.

MAPLE (*Acer campestris*).—Maple is useful as a hop-pole plant.

WILLOW (*Salix caprea and others.*)—Willow is also a free grower from stools, and very rapid in growth, and clean in bark. The red-hearted willow forms a valuable hop-pole. Its qualities have, however, been fully discussed.

BEECH (*Fagus sylvatica*).—Beech is grown as an underwood, but is not recommended.

BIRCH (*Betula alba*).—Birch may be profitably grown upon poor soils, but not where plants of more value grow freely. It may be used for hop-poles, but soon rots; 12 ft. poles being worth only 8*s*. to 9*s*. per hundred.

OTHER VARIETIES.—The SLOE or BLACKTHORN (*Prunus spinosa*). The OSIER WILLOW (*Salix viminalis and others*). The HOLLY (*Ilex aquifolium*). BLACK or GREY POPLAR (*Populus canescens*). SYCAMORE (*Acer p. platanus*).

CHAP. IV.
Sect. 2.
Plants suitable for Underwood.

CHAPTER V.
FENCES.

SECTION I.

Their Varieties and General Management.

ECONOMY OF GOOD FENCES—PLANTING OF NEW HEDGES, PREPARATION OF BED—TIME AND MODE OF PLANTING—MANAGEMENT OF OLD QUICK HEDGES—GRUBBING HEDGES—TRIMMING HEDGES—PRACTICAL HINTS AS TO HEDGES GENERALLY—DEAD FENCES OF DIFFERENT KINDS, POST AND RAIL, PALES, PALING, SCOTCH FENCE, OTHER KINDS OF WOODEN FENCES, WIRE FENCING, CONTINUOUS IRON FENCE—WALLS—TABLES FOR CALCULATING THE NUMBER OF PLANTS REQUISITE FOR PLANTING.

Chap. V. Sect. 1. Their Varieties and General Management.

Economy of good fences.

A FENCE may, according to its etymology, be defined as any object, artificial or natural, be it hedge or railing or watercourse, whereby a barrier is constructed between adjoining lands. Good fences, either live or dead, are necessary to good management. Nothing conduces more to give evidence of good management; as, no matter how thoroughly the fertility and general repairs of the estate are kept up, bad fences will give an air of untidiness and slovenliness to the whole. And yet how often do we find estates burdened with badly kept fences and also with unnecessary ones. We say burdened, because with regard to live fences, it may be said that fences in bad repair are not only a constant direct drain upon the pocket, but also a drain upon the woods and plantations for material. Only those acquainted with estate management can form an idea of the amount of material required by tenants and home farm bailiffs for this purpose. This drain can only be overcome by planting good live fences, and by keeping them when planted in repair. When once the work is performed, a small annual outlay only is required; an outlay but little felt, as it may often be done between farm operations, and by old men not otherwise employed. But the time is near at hand, thanks to our enterprising implement makers, when we shall see our fences cut and trimmed by machinery at a fabulously low price per rod. Seeing, then, this future before us, let us, as agents, do our best to fit them for the operation.

CHAP. V.
Sect. 1.
Their Varieties and General Management.

When material is applied for, for new fences, it would be a good plan to insist upon a proviso that a thorn or other live fence be planted at the same time, the landlord finding plants, the tenant labour. So when material is required for stopping gaps, it would be well to insist on filling up at the same time with hollies or some other plant that will grow where others have failed. Where there are hazel and ordinary copse-stuff hedges they should be laid, and only cut when cutting is inevitable. If this is done by men accustomed to the work little dead wood will be required, and, instead of the hedge being filled with dead wood, making the gaps greater, we shall have a live fence pleasing to the eye and easily kept trimmed.

Under the list and description of plants suitable for hedge planting, which will be given hereafter, we shall enumerate those points necessary to remember to insure successful growth; but in any case success is only attained by care and attention when the hedge is young, and by careful treatment in old age. A good hedge may be grown by judicious planting and treatment; but a good hedge may also be obtained from an old and neglected one.

Planting new hedges.

In the first case a good bed must first be prepared according to the situation and nature of the soil. If in a high

Preparation of bed.

CHAP. V.
Sect. 1.
Their
Varieties and
General
Management.

and dry situation it may be prepared on the flat, the ground being dug and trenched to the width of a yard, and some well-rotted farm manure being applied at the same time. If in a wet situation a ditch should be cut on each side, sod banks being formed with the top sods, and the space between them being filled up with the loose earth. For this purpose a width of at least four and a half to five feet will be required. Some manure may also be applied, but the soil should be left exposed to the atmosphere for some time before planting to become pulverised and matured. When on the side of a hill a ditch must be cut on the lower side and a single sod bank formed above, backed by the loose earth; and upon this bank the hedge must be planted. In dry situations and those subject to drought, as in the case of sandy soils, the plants may be put in on the flat, but a drain on each side should be formed to carry off the surface water. In fact, the bed must be prepared entirely to suit the nature of the district and soil.

Time and mode of planting.

The bed being ready, the plants will be laid out either in autumn or early spring, as the case may be, about eight or nine inches apart, and planted alternately in two lines, about five or six inches being left between the lines; when planted they may be cut off with a sharp knife about two or three inches above the ground, as they will root more freely this way than when left their natural height. This being done they must be kept hoed and free from weeds, especially from grass, as they will make no headway if choked with grass and weeds; this will give but little trouble if attended to early.

Protection from bite of sheep.

If in an exposed situation where sheep or cattle graze a fence must be erected at once, as nothing is more fatal than the bite of sheep and cattle to young hedges. Although the first expense is great it is best where practicable to erect a double fence, the hedge being then secured against all injury.

The amount of dung necessary for hedge planting will be about one cubic yard of dung to two hundred yards of hedge one yard wide. It is as well not to apply it directly to the young plants. Therefore, where practicable a crop of some kind, say potatoes or carrots, may be grown in the first instance upon the bed. The result of this course often is to bring down the expense to cost of plants and planting only.

CHAP. V.
Sect. 1.
Their Varieties and General Management.

The treatment of old quick hedges is important, as no matter how old these plants may be, if there are plenty of them, a good fence may soon be made. Quicks or thorns will bear any amount of cutting; in fact, the more they are cut the better they thrive, and this fact may be borne in mind in all treatment of these hedges. Where practicable the hedge may be cut down close to the ground, when the after treatment of the young shoots will be similar to that of a newly-planted hedge. When, however, the hedge forms the fence of pastures where cattle or sheep graze, this cannot be done without the erection of a dead fence, which at once makes the operation an expensive one. The necessity for such an erection can be overcome in the following way: Let the hedge be cut down to fence height, and one side only be cut or "brushed" that season, leaving the side where the cattle range untouched. The old growth which remains uncut forms a blind on that side, and prevents, to a great extent, injury from cattle forcing their way through as they would do were both sides trimmed at once. When this is done let all gaps be substantially filled with stumps and rails. In the summer let the first cut side, which will have made vigorous growth be trimmed, and in the following winter treat the other side in the same way as the first. Thus, in two years you have a well-grown and symmetrical hedge better probably than if newly planted.

Management of old quick hedges.

It must be remembered that new hedges will not grow where old ones have failed, without the earth being taken out and replaced by fresh; therefore, in filling gaps, a trench must be dug out and fresh earth put in before planting the hollies and other plants; which should be of vigorous growth.

152　ESTATE MANAGEMENT.

CHAP. V.
Sect. 1.
Their Varieties and General Management.

Grubbing hedges.

Trimming hedges.

Cost of trimming.

Practical hints as to hedges generally.

When fences have been neglected it often answers to grub them up, especially in situations where shelter is not required. Grubbing is often a less expensive process than the first. The expense will depend of course upon the size of the wood, and the amount of earth upon the bank to be removed, and will vary from $2d.$ to $5d.$ per lineal yard.

A clause should be inserted in all leases and agreements that hedges should be trimmed twice a year, once in winter and once in summer; a neat appearance is thus secured at all seasons. It answers also to do this from a pecuniary point of view, as it is the cutting of old wood that adds so much to both labour and cost. By this plan the undergrowth is also cut and the seeding of thistles, docks and other weeds prevented. The trimmings should always be burnt, as seeds are thus destroyed.

Hedges may be trimmed in summer or winter, for a sum varying under circumstances from $\frac{1}{2}d.$ to $2d.$ per rod.

Upon home-farms the hedges should be cut and attended to by the bailiff whenever possible; but all planting and reclaiming of old fences should be placed in the hands of the forester; the farm, if desired, being debited with the amount of labour. Upon every estate there should be a well stocked nursery, where, amongst other plants, should be a constant supply of thorn and other hedge plants. The propagation however will be dwelt upon under the description of the several plants.

When preparing the trench for reception of the plants, see that the whole length is as nearly as possible of equal quality to insure regularity of growth. A compost of dung and earth is better as a dressing than dung alone; road scrapings also are useful for the purpose. When planting select plants as much as possible of equal size and strength, keep clear of weeds, and hoe regularly for the first two years. Do not trim for two years, but keep overgrown shoots cut back. When trimming for the first time do not cut the bottom too close. Leave three or four inches each year of new growth. Look well to the bottom, the top will take care of itself. Fill gaps the first year with new thorn plants, afterwards with hollies, putting in a few shovelfuls of new earth with each plant. Protect the gaps with stumps and a rail; do not force in bushes. Cut with an upward stroke. Keep water courses clear.

CHAP. V.
Sect. 1.
Their Varieties and General Management.

If these matters are strictly attended to, a good fence will be the satisfactory result.

Before passing on to consider the plants suitable for quick fences, a few words will not be out of place on temporary or "dead" fences. These consist generally of material found in the district. In some localities, for example, in the oolitic formations we have stone, and here stone walls are the characteristic feature of the landscape. Again in heath and moor land, fences are formed of sods; in copse districts of rods; in woodlands of timber; and on marshes and swamps of water-courses; and so on. Railways have however, brought all material so within our reach, that we are now able to erect fences according to fancy.

Dead fences of different kinds.

The kinds of fences we will consider are post and rail, park paling, rod or bush fences, wire, continuous iron, and walls.

Post and rail fences may be of larch or of oak, or of larch and oak, according to what the estate is best able to produce. The fence is stronger and more durable when the posts are large enough to admit of mortising. The posts should be 8ft. 6in. apart, and a stump should be driven in and nailed to the rails in the centre of each panel. The fence may consist of three or four rails, but the latter number is recommended except under exceptional circumstances. The posts should be, if possible, of hard wood. They are generally 6in. by 3in. at the top, and from 5½ft. to 6½ft. long. The rails should be 9ft. 6in. long for a panel 8½ft. in length to admit of lap, and they may be inserted in the mortise either lapping top or bottom by an angular cut of about 45°, or side by side, with a lateral

Post and rail.

CHAP. V.
Sect. 1.
*Their
Varieties and
General
Management.*

cut; the latter plan is perhaps the best. If of larch, they are cut flat and about 5in. wide by 1¼in. to 1½in. thick, according to the length of the panel, and the purpose of fence. Oak rails are generally cut in a triangular form about 5in. wide by 3½in. or 4in. at the sides.

The posts should be dipped in tar at the butts, and the tar burnt off, charring the wood to a certain extent; this should be done where soil and air meet, for it is at this point that decay first sets in. The whole may be tarred, but it is unnecessary for durability; if, however, it is done, let it be a year after the fence has been erected, otherwise decay sets in earlier than if left untarred, as the natural moisture of the wood is unable to escape. This remark also applies to buildings of timber where paint or tar is applied. The tarring should also be done in dry weather.

Cost.

The cost of such a fence will depend to a great extent upon the distance of carriage of material, and whether sawn by steam or hand, but may be stated at 1s. to 1s. 6d. per yard of four rails. So that the expense of such a fence is considerable, but it seldom fails to give satisfaction.

Park palings.

Another and more important kind of fence is what is known as park paling. This consists of oak throughout. The posts are from 7ft. to 8ft. long, large in the butt, being generally cut from small trees. These are sunk fully 2½ft. in the ground and well rammed when possible with chalk. They are mortised for three rails, one at the top, one in the middle, and one at the bottom, about 1½ft. from the ground. The rails are cut triangularly as before stated. At the bottom of all is a foot board from 10in. to 12in. wide, and 2in. thick, dovetailed into the posts. Upon these rails split oak pales about 5in. or 6in. wide, and ¼in. or ½in. thick are nailed, slightly overlapping each other. It is a most complete fence and very durable, but very expensive. The cost may be reckoned at from 8s. to 10s. per lineal yard. The nails used for the pales should be corrugated, the ordinary nails being liable to rust.

Cost.

Scotch fence.

Another kind is the "Scotch fence." This consists

mostly of larch, no other kind of tree being so suitable. The uprights should be not less than 2in., and not more than 3½in. in diameter, being in fact the first thinnings of a larch plantation. They are cut into lengths of 5ft. or 6ft., and pointed top and bottom, and driven into the ground 1½ft., about 6in. or 8in. apart. Upon the top of these is placed a rail, bored with auger holes to match the uprights, a nail being driven here and there to prevent its being lifted off. It has the advantage of being difficult to climb, especially when tenter hooks are driven into the top rail; it is also neat, but for durability is not to be recommended, as the stumps being young, and all inserted in the ground, soon decay. In the vicinity of plantations it may be fairly cheap; but if there be a demand of the suitable material for hop-poles, it will be too expensive for general adoption. Its average cost may be placed at from 1s. 6d. to 2s. per yard. There are other varieties of timber fencing, as open paling for gardens, diagonal larch, for the same purpose, and the simple stump and rail fence in which the stumps being driven and the rails simply nailed. These all vary in expense, but may be calculated at from 6d. to 1s. per lineal yard.

Chap. V. Sect. 1. Their Varieties and General Management.

Other kinds of wooden fences.

We have also fences of a still more temporary kind, namely rod, wattle or basket fences, which are made from hazel rods with uprights of the same material, but somewhat larger in size, driven in about every 15 inches. The rods, split or not as preferred, are interwoven through the uprights. This kind of fence, however, will last but a short time, and consequently is not economical. It is useful for purposes where shelter is required, and may be therefore recommended for nurseries and young plantations; but it cannot be depended upon, for a period exceeding two years, when more than ordinary pressure is put upon it.

Next in order is *wire;* and this, perhaps, is the cheapest and most durable of all, especially at the present time when wire, composed of a series of smaller wires and galvanised, is obtainable at so reasonable a figure. It is necessary that

Wire fencing

CHAP. V.
Sect. 1.
Their Varieties and General Management.

the gauge of the top wire be of considerable size, but it may be decreased in the lower strands; this is important, as the cost is then materially reduced.

Wire may be strained on iron strainers and uprights, or on wood as preferred. Where wood is plentiful, it is perhaps cheaper, and has this advantage, that where breakages occur, a new stump may be driven in, and the wire stapled on. Immense stress is exerted by the screw used straining the wire, and care must be taken to sink the straining posts deeply, to have them well rammed, and a strong stay placed against them on the inner sides; if this is neglected a post may be drawn from the ground. Stumps are driven in either before the straining or after, and the wire stapled to them. There are now, however, a number of iron straining posts, all possessing, more or less, merit, which cannot fail to diminish the use of wood. A fence of this character is rapidly put up, and costs about sixpence or ninepence per yard.

Continuous iron fence.

Another most excellent fence is the *continuous iron;* and for appearance and usefulness there is perhaps none better. It may be obtained of any size and height, and costs from 3s. to 4s. a yard.

Walls.

Next, and finally, we come to *walls*. In certain districts stones abound, as for instance, in soils on the oolitic formation. Here they are of a flat and shaly nature, and well adapted to the purpose of walls; particularly where, as in many localities, they lie scattered on the surface, and need only collecting. There are men who make this building of walls their principal occupation, and it is to them we must look for success, as a wall built by an inexperienced hand will soon crumble down. The process is to bind the work together at various intervals by whole stones running through the wall. On the top, mortar or mud is placed, and the coping stones laid on, whereupon the wall is complete. Such walls suffer a good deal in the hunting season, but otherwise remain, with slight repair, for years. The cost varies of course in different localities, but it may be stated at 1s. to 1s. 6d. per yard.

Sod walls are seldom resorted to in this country, nevertheless in some districts a cheap and durable fence is procured by such means. In the colonies we have seen most complete and durable fences built entirely with sods. The sods are cut with sharp spades, ground on the grindstone until they have an edge like a knife. The cuts are made with great precision and regularity, and the sods when cut are placed in position by the builder and fit like joiner's work. At the bottom, in order to obtain a base, a space is left between the first few lines of sods, which is filled up with the earth taken from the ditch, and this base must correspond to the height. The cost of such walls is of course for labour only, and may be reckoned about 4*d*. or 9*d*. per lineal yard, according to height. It is only, however, where sods can be cut that such walls can be profitably built; on arable land, for instance, it is a matter of impossibility, as a turf of some kind is indispensable.

These, then, are the most important varieties of fences in use in Great Britain, and will be resorted to in accordance with the material most easily obtainable in each district. We now proceed to enumerate and describe the various plants most suitable for live fences.

CHAP. V.
Sect. 1.
Their Varieties and General Management.

ESTATE MANAGEMENT.

Chap. V. Sect. 1. *Their Varieties and General Management.*

TABLE FOR CALCULATING THE NUMBER OF PLANTS AT ANY DISTANCE FROM 6IN. TO 3FT. APART, REQUIRED FOR ANY LENGTH OF HEDGE, IN YARDS.

Distance Apart.	Length of Hedge in Yards.								
ft. in.	1	2	3	4	5	6	7	8	9
0 6	6·0000	12·0000	18·0000	24·0000	30·0000	36·0000	42·0000	48·0000	54·0000
0 7	5·1429	10·2858	15·4287	20·5716	25·7145	30·8574	36·0000	41·1432	46·2861
0 8	4·5000	9·0000	13·5000	18·0000	22·5000	27·0000	31·5000	36·0000	40·5000
0 9	4·0000	8·0000	12·0000	16·0000	20·0000	24·0000	28·0000	32·0000	36·0000
0 10	3·6000	7·2000	10·8000	14·4000	18·0000	21·6000	25·2000	28·8000	32·4000
0 11	3·2727	6·5454	9·8181	13·0909	16·3636	19·6363	22·9090	26·1818	29·4545
1 0	3·0000	6·0000	9·0000	12·0000	15·0000	18·0000	21·0000	24·0000	27·0000
1 1	2·7692	5·5384	8·3076	11·0768	13·8960	16·6152	19·3844	22·1538	24·9228
1 2	2·5714	5·1428	7·7142	10·2860	12·8570	15·4284	18·0000	20·5720	23·1426
1 3	2·4000	4·8000	7·2000	9·6000	12·0000	14·4000	16·8000	19·2000	21·6000
1 4	2·2500	4·5000	6·7500	9·0000	11·2500	13·5000	15·7500	18·0000	20·2500
1 5	2·1177	4·2254	6·3531	8·4708	10·5880	12·7062	14·8236	16·9416	19·0593
1 6	2·0000	4·0000	6·0000	8·0000	10·0000	12·0000	14·0000	16·0000	18·0000
1 7	1·8947	3·7894	5·6841	7·5788	9·4735	11·3602	13·2629	15·1576	17·0523
1 8	1·8000	3·6000	5·4000	7·2000	9·0000	10·8000	12·6000	14·4000	16·2000
1 9	1·7143	3·4286	5·1429	6·8572	8·5715	10·2858	12·0000	13·7144	15·4287
1 10	1·6363	3·2727	4·8080	6·5454	8·1818	9·6161	11·4545	13·0909	14·4242
1 11	1·5652	3·1304	4·6956	6·2608	7·8760	9·3912	10·9564	12·5216	14·0868
2 0	1·5000	3·0000	4·5000	6·0000	7·5000	9·0000	10·5000	12·0000	13·5000
2 1	1·4400	2·6800	4·3200	5·7600	7·2000	8·6400	10·0800	11·5200	12·9600
2 2	1·3846	2·7692	4·1538	5·5384	6·9230	8·3076	9·6922	11·0768	12·4614
2 3	1·3333	2·6666	4·0000	5·3333	6·6666	8·0000	9·3333	10·6666	12·0000
2 4	1·2857	2·5714	3·8571	5·1428	6·4285	7·7142	9·0000	10·2856	11·5733
2 5	1·2414	2·4828	3·7242	4·9656	6·2070	7·4484	8·6898	9·9312	11·1726
2 6	1·2000	2·4000	3·6000	4·8000	6·0000	7·2000	8·4000	9·6000	10·8000
2 7	1·1613	2·3226	3·4839	4·6452	5·8565	6·9678	8·1291	9·2904	10·4517
2 8	1·1250	2·2500	3·3750	4·5000	5·6250	6·7500	7·8750	9·0000	10·1250
2 9	1·0909	2·1818	3·2727	4·3636	5·4545	6·5454	7·6363	8·7272	9·8181
2 10	1·0588	2·1177	3·1764	4·2352	5·2940	6·3528	7·4116	8·4704	9·5291
2 11	1·0288	2·0577	3·0866	4·1155	5·1444	6·1733	7·2022	8·2311	9·2600
3 0	1·0000	2·0000	3·0000	4·0000	5·0000	6·0000	7·0000	8·0000	9·0000

SECTION II.

Plants Suitable for Fences.

COMMON THORN—BEECH—HORNBEAM—HOLLY—FURZE.

The Common Thorn or Hawthorn (*Cratægus oxyacantha*) is the most universal of our hedge plants, and deservedly so. By nature it is a tree, but it is not only one of those which bear, but also thrive under repeated cuttings. It bears a pretty and sweet-scented white flower, and blooms freely in May and June, hence its common name of May.

Some proprietors like óne plant left at intervals to attain full growth, the rest being trimmed closely. This, when in flower, adds greatly to the beauty of an estate, but it injures the hedge underneath and cannot be recommended.

The thorn is better adapted than any other plant for fencing, owing to its thorny nature, making it, when well grown, absolutely impenetrable; and by repeated cuttings it becomes exceedingly tough and durable. As to its treatment it is almost impossible to lay down absolute rules; indeed, there is more difference of opinion with regard to the treatment of hedges generally than in any other matter relating to estate management. We are, however, of opinion that when a thorn hedge is planted, it is best to cut all the plants to about three inches from the bottom, then to keep the ground clear of weeds and frequently moved with the hoe or beck, and to leave the plants uncut for two years; the wood by this process becomes larger and better able to stand against the knife. It may then be cut down to a height of a foot or a foot and a half, and thinned, leaving as good a base as possible. The form of the hedge should be slightly wedge-shaped; this gives it strength, and also keeps the bottom thick and close, which is desirable where sheep are grazed. If kept very round, the top

CHAP. V.
Sect. 2.
Plants Suitable for Fences.

is apt to become covered with moss and lichen, and if straight, the fence is weak where it should be strong. The desirable shape is best attained by the process called "breasting," that is, cutting it, so as to leave the twigs at the bottom on the outside uncut one year and on the inside the following year. The next year the whole may be trimmed together, leaving about three inches growth of the previous year. It must be borne in mind that "breasting" should not be repeated except at intervals of two years.

The process of reclaiming an old hedge has been already noticed; another plan, however, is sometimes resorted to in the case of a thorn hedge, and that is, by laying, similar to that of a hazel hedge. Quick or hawthorn will in fact bear any treatment except neglect, and man may use his own devices, no matter how peculiar, as long as judicious prunning accompanies them. If left to itself it resumes its natural form of tree-growth, which of course makes the fence open and bare at the bottom.

Propagation.

Hawthorn is propagated from seed, and as its treatment is somewhat peculiar, a few words are necessary with regard to it. The seed ripens in autumn, and may be gathered during the winter months. It is then covered with sand or light dry earth, and left for a year. It should at first be laid out thinly, as it may otherwise heat; and then be placed in a heap, being mixed with more sand and covered over with earth, like potatoes. This rots the outer fleshy cuticle. If planted the same year it would lie dormant for one season. In the nursery it must be kept clear of weeds, and where too thick, be thinned, the thinnings being transplanted into lines about one foot apart, the plants being placed about five or six inches from each other. The following year the whole will be transplanted into rows and kept well hoed, and there the plants may remain one or two years, according to circumstances, when they may be planted out. When transplanted the root may be slightly cut back. Seed is nearly always plentiful, and the treatment simple, so there is no reason why every estate should not be well supplied with plants. In one instance, however, this is not the case, and that is on light sandy soils; under these conditions it is best to buy strong plants from other districts. A fence of this plant, with judicious care and treatment, may be formed in eight years—*i.e.*, on suitable soils.

CHAP. V.
Sect. 2.
Plants suitable for Fences.

BEECH (*Fagus Sylvatica*) forms a good hedge, and perhaps its use for the purpose is too little regarded. By repeated cuttings it becomes tough and pliable, and, on account of the retention of the leaf well into the following spring, forms, like the hornbeam, an excellent shelter in winter. Unlike the hornbeam, it thrives well on the chalk. The plants are obtained from seed. The nuts should be collected when fallen from the trees, and kept in a room until spring, when they may be planted in the nursery; their after treatment is similar to that already described, except that no root pruning should take place after the first year. The plants must be allowed to remain in the bed until the following winter, when they may be lifted and their tops cut, which latter operation tends to develop the root-fibres. They should then be placed in rows and so left for two years, being kept hoed. At the end of this time they may be either transplanted or left again for two years, and planted out direct according to requirement.

Beech.

Propagation.

In the former case the plants will be about one and a half feet high, and in the latter about three feet. They should be planted 1ft. apart, and sloped (*i.e.*, planted at an angle) so as to cross one another, forming by this plan a trellis-like fence, really impenetrable.

The side shoots may be cut off the first year; and the second year the hedge may be cut in the usual way. A hedge of this kind will often attain great height, and is very beautiful.

The best season for trimming this plant is in July, as it then throws out more summer shoots and becomes more dense. A good plan when planting is to tie the cross plants, taking care first to bark the place where they cross, they

CHAP. V.
Sect. 2.
Plants suitable for Fences.

Hornbeam.

will then unite and form a trellis work quite impervious to sheep and cattle.

The HORNBEAM (*Carpinus Betula*) is a native of Great Britain, and perhaps, next to the hawthorn, is our most valuable hedge-plant. It resembles the beech, but may be distinguished by the feathery leaves and the absence of the varnish seen on the former. It will not form a hedge so rapidly as the beech, but bears cutting better, and is also more hardy. The flowers are unisexual, the sexes being on distinct catkins on the same plant. The seed is a small nut which may be planted in the spring, but will lie dormant one year, or it may be treated as a thorn (see page 160). As a timber tree it is but little grown, though the wood is exceedingly strong, and will bear a greater strain than any other English timber. It is white in colour and of fine texture. It is used in rural districts for handles to tools, &c. The plant retains its leaves late into the year—in fact they often remain till after the new leaves have burst—and on this account it forms good shelter in exposed situations. It is often planted with the hawthorn, and forms in this way a very valuable hedge; the proportion may be one plant of hornbeam to six of hawthorn. As a fire wood it is the best, yielding great heat and a clear flame. It roots deeper than the beech and consequently is less injurious as a hedge plant to surrounding crops. It is very hardy and free from nearly all diseases. It requires, however, fairly good soil and does not thrive on chalk.

Holly.

The HOLLY (*Ilex aquifolium*).—The treatment of holly is very similar to that of the hawthorn, as far as regards propagation. Some, however, are of opinion that it requires to be two years in the pit before sowing; whether this be the case or not it is often eighteen months in the seed bed before it shows itself. When the bed is too stiff and adhesive it will often rot in the ground. The berry contains several seeds, and when collected from the tree in the autumn they should be mixed with double the amount of dry earth or sand, and kept turned occasionally for six weeks and then pitted as already described. In the following year they are sown in beds (which may be three and a-half or four feet wide) and covered with half an inch of earth—one bushel, half sand and half seed, being sufficient to sow such a bed to a length of eight or ten yards. Transplant every other year to develope growth of root fibre, keeping the rows free from weeds and well hoed, as circulation of air through the root is very necessary; a well rooted plant being absolutely necessary to future growth.

This plant is indigenous to Great Britain and attains considerable size. Its value as a hedge plant consists in its love of shade, and in its capacity for development under drip of trees. It is, with the exception of the yew, the only plant we can depend upon under these circumstances. It is also an excellent "fill-gap" and will grow under the shade of a hawthorn hedge and rapidly fill a gap which has defied other processes. In hard winters sheep will often bark the lower branches, and, as it does not throw out lateral branches readily, it is apt to suffer greatly from their attack; it is not, therefore, a good plant for the division of fields, except, as already stated, for filling gaps. For a garden fence, however, it is invaluable, from its glossy evergreen leaf and thick foliage. As a timber it is hard, and capable of taking a high polish, which fits it for furniture-making and other cabinet-maker's work. One peculiarity of this plant is, that it transplants best in June and July; winter planting generally ends in failure.

FURZE or WHIN (*Ilex Europœa*), called by the former name in England and the latter in Scotland. It forms a valuable hedge plant in poor districts possessing clay subsoils. Its growth is rapid, and requires early switching, or it quickly assumes an irregular growth. It will not stand severe frosts, and, after attaining full size, it rapidly dies out; it cannot therefore be recommended as a permanent hedge-

Chap. V.
Sect. 2.
Plants suitable for Fences.

Uses.

plant. It is, however, a cheap kind of fence, as it is only necessary to form a trench on the top of a turf mound in which to sow the seed, and, if kept from bite of cattle, it will form a fence not easily broken through, owing to its spiny nature. When cut at certain intervals, as is the case in plantations and covers, it retains its vitality for unknown periods; it is only when allowed to attain its full growth without switching that it becomes weak and useless. After cutting, the young shoots soon appear, and in a few years it is ready to cut again. It is, also, in its fully developed state very inflammable, and should not be grown near buildings. When cut, it forms a valuable fuel, especially for brick-burning, as it yields immense heat. It should be tied in faggots when cut and stacked when green; the stack being so built as to keep out rain, as, if exposed to wet, it soon becomes rotten, and the steam given off when placed in the furnace injures the bricks. When young, it forms a valuable feed for all kinds of stock, but is seldom used except where it abounds naturally on commons, where other food is often scarce. When used in this way, it is bruised with hammers or passed through rollers made for the purpose. As a cover it is invaluable, and when in flower it is very beautiful and it yields a plentiful supply of seed. For covers about ten pounds per acre will be found sufficient, and may be sown with oats, or by itself. It will show but little for the first year or two, but afterwards becomes most vigorous. It forms an excellent shelter in wet weather, as, from the peculiar nature of the spines, the rain follows the course of the plant and does not drip.

The foregoing are better adapted than any other class of plants to purposes of field fencing; nevertheless all plants which will bear constant pruning are capable of conversion to this purpose. For garden fences, where ornament alone is required, privet, box, laurel, the various cupressus, yew, briar, broom, and berberis are all useful.

CHAPTER VI.
GRASSES SUITABLE FOR WOODS AND PLANTATIONS.

SELECTION OF SEEDS—LIST OF USEFUL GRASSES—MODE OF SOWING—TREATMENT OF RIDES IN WOOD.

It would be outside the limits of the present work to attempt to describe minutely the particular species of grass best adapted to every variety of soil. In practice the best plan will be found to apply to some firm of reputation, such as Messrs. Sutton and Sons, of Reading, or Messrs. Carter and Co., of High Holborn, London, giving full information as to the geological formation, the situation and nature of soil, and the purposes for which the seeds are required, and they will forward them either mixed or separate as may be desired. The practice of sowing seeds so selected will give more satisfaction than allowing the natural grasses of the district to grow without interference; and if sown when plantations are made, the grasses get fully established before the shade is sufficient to retard their growth.

The seeds most useful for the purpose may be enumerated as follows:

1. *Agrostis Stolonifera.*—Fiorin or Creeping Bent.
2. *Aira Cæspitosa.*—Tufted Hair-Grass or Hassock.
3. *Arrhenatherum Avenaceum.*—Tall, oat-like Grass.
4. *Brachypodium Sylvaticum.*—Wood Fescue Grass.
5. *Bromus* or *Festuca Giganteus.*—Giant Wood Fescue.

CHAP. VI.
Grasses.

6. *Bromus Arvensis.*—Field Brome Grass.
7. *Dactylis Glomerata.*—Cock's Foot Grass.
8. *Elymus Arenarius.*—Upright Sea Lyme Grass.
9. *Elymus Giganteus.*—Giant Lyme Grass.
10. *Festuca Duriuscula.*—Hard Fescue.
11. *Festuca Elatior.*—Tall Fescue.
12. *Glyceria Aquatica.*—Water sweet Grass.
13. *Glyceria Fluitans.*—Floating Grass.
14. *Holcus Lanatus.*—Yorkshire Fog Grass.
15. *Millium Effusum.*—Wood Millet Grass.
16. *Poa Nemoralis.*—Wood Meadow Grass.
17. *Poa Nemoralis Sempervirens.*—Evergreen Grass.

The abovenamed grasses are all more or less fitted for covers, thriving for the most part in shady places, being coarse in growth, giving excellent cover, and, as they are bearers of large seeds, are much liked by birds. Many of them are unfit for pastures, being bitter and acrid. The list of course comprises those fitted for various localities, from light dry soil to the rich soil in the neighbourhood of streams and ponds. Nos. 8 and 9 are those specially adapted to sandy situations, especially near the sea, and Nos. 12 and 13 to situations near watercourses and ponds.

Mode of sowing.

The best method of sowing the seeds of Nos. 2, 3, 4, and 6 is the following: Mix equal quantities of each, and give this mixture to the woodman, with instructions to fork the soil in those places through the woods and plantations where grass is required, and to sow a few handfuls of seed, covering and treading it in. The large seeds of the *Bromus giganteus*, No. 5, may be sown separately, and should be covered one inch with soil, or it may be sown in nurseries and planted out. The ordinary pasture grasses may be sown in the rides, adding also Nos. 1, 7, 10, 11, 14, 16, 17, mixed with a little *Trifolium repens* (Dutch clover), and *Medicago lupulina* (trefoil). In open woods No. 2 is recommended; this grass is not only propagated by seed, but it throws off sprouts or small joints from the roots, which become after a while separate tufts.

It may be well in passing to notice the *Tritoma grandi-*

flora, which, though not a grass, is a very suitable plant for covers, and very ornamental. It is a hardy perennial, and easily propagated.

Keeping the rides through woods and plantations in order is part of the duty of the forester. This is best done in September or October. At an earlier period the gamekeeper dislikes much movement in the woods on account of the young birds, and if done whilst growth is still taking place a second growth sets in, and gives an untidy appearance when shooting commences. It is necessary to trim the sides of the underwood, mow the grass, clear out old ditches and watercourses; and, where needed, cut new ones to carry off surface water, taking care to slope the sides to prevent falling in, and so causing stoppage and overflow. It may be repeated here that all drains in woods and plantations should be open, as pipe drains quickly become choked with the roots and fibres of the stuff. It will also be well during this period to see to the fences and gates, and have all secure and in good order for the winter.

CHAPTER VII.
THE "HOME FARM."

LAND STEWARD'S RELATION TO THE HOME FARM — EXPERIMENTS ON THE HOME FARM — THE BAILIFF AND HIS DUTIES — LABOURERS — ANNUAL VALUATION — SUPPLY OF PRODUCE TO THE HOUSE — LIVE STOCK — DAIRY COWS — FAT STOCK — STORE AND YOUNG STOCK — SHEEP — LAMBING — SHEEP FOOD — HORSES — PIGS — POULTRY — FARM YARD MANURE — SEEDS — HAY — HARVEST — IMPLEMENTS — EARMARKING CATTLE FOR PURPOSES OF REGISTRATION — TOP DRESSING EXPERIMENTS ON GRASS LAND.

Chap. VII.
The Home Farm.

The subject of the "Home Farm" will be treated as it bears upon estate management, rather than from a purely agricultural point of view. The works upon agriculture are so numerous, as to make many remarks upon the subject unnecessary. The treatment, however, of a home farm bears directly upon estate management, consequently we cannot pass it by.

Land steward's relation to the home farm.

The land steward must, to fill his position thoroughly, be a practical and scientific agriculturist. He is not often called upon to act as bailiff, and ought not to be on large estates, but he must retain, as his right, the power of oversight over the home farm, without unnecessarily interfering with the bailiff in charge. He must also check expenditure, audit accounts, and prepare the yearly balance-sheet for presentation to the proprietors. He will also be expected to be ready to render advice on points connected with agriculture, and the feeding of stock, both as regards the conduct of the home farm, and in matters relating to the tenants. We take this opportunity, therefore, of impressing upon the pupil the necessity of thoroughly acquainting himself with agriculture in all its branches. He can never consider himself fully qualified until he has recognised and obtained this knowledge. We are led the more to give this advice, as many gentlemen who have presented themselves to the writer for education have informed him " that they only wish to learn estate management, not agriculture." But the two are inseparable.

The " home farm," as its name implies, is that portion of the estate set apart for the use of the proprietor, to supply his house with produce, and to satisfy his tastes in agriculture, if he possesses any. If it be only required for the former purpose, its acreage will depend in some degree upon the size of his establishment, but one or two hundred acres of arable and grass land will probably amply suffice.

Home farms, as a rule, do not pay, in a strictly pecuniary sense. If they can be made to pay their rent, it is all that can be expected; in fact, if they do this, the result ought to be looked upon as satisfactory.

Many landed proprietors, whose tastes tend to agricultural and pastoral pursuits, often ride hobbies very hard—hobbies which cost money, and the expense of which should not be debited to the farms they occupy. They may be, and often are, decidedly useful and beneficial, and tend greatly to promote the interests of agriculture, but they do not constitute a part of the economical and prudent management of the home farm. Many a theory has been verified by such hobbies, and many a useful agricultural fact ascertained.

Experiments, the trial of new implements, the testing of new feeding stuffs and manures, are essential to the advancement of agriculture; and if wealthy proprietors will not indulge in these experiments, who will or can? Land stewards, therefore, do well to forward and promote such

CHAP. VII.
The Home Farm.

experiments within the limits which their experience may suggest to them as prudent and reasonable. It can scarcely be doubted that our English landlords do more for agriculture than any other class, and this reputation they should certainly be encouraged to maintain. But these experiments should be distinctly conducted as matters affecting the private purse of the landlord, and not the accounts of the home farm. If, for instance, cattle are fed for prize purposes, the farm should not be debited with more than the amount of food required for ordinary purposes, otherwise it will be impossible to discover from the accounts how far the farm is worked on prudent and business-like principles.

The bailiff and his duties.

The home farm is presided over by the bailiff. He will be selected in accordance with what is required of him. If the holding is small, sufficient only for purposes of supply, a bailiff may be selected from the intelligent class of labourers, more especially where the landlord himself or his steward take an active oversight of the operations. Where, however, a large acreage is held in hand, and extensive operations are carried on, a man of a different stamp will be required. A man must then be sought for who has already held position upon a large farm, or under good and well-known agriculturists, who is able not merely to carry out orders, but to originate an opinion and act upon it.

Bailiffs should be required to keep carefully and neatly a set of books supplied them by the steward, but the books should be as simple as possible. To expect a complicated set of books to be kept by any bailiff is not only unnecessary, but unreasonable. They should be such as will enable the steward to produce from them a *cash statement* when required, and also produce at the end of the year a balance sheet.

If a man of the latter class is employed, he should be allowed the privilege of selling and buying, as it gives him an extra interest in his work. A constant attendance at

markets is neither necessary nor wise, but a reasonable
intercourse with others in like situation is salutary, and
gives room for interchange of ideas. With reference
to buying and selling, however, one great failing of bailiffs
may here be noted, namely, their tendency to encourage
"Middlemen." They believe that, by selling here and
selling there, they are in a better position to buy of the
same parties. They believe that, if they offer samples to
Mr. A., and buy their manures, seed, or food of Mr. B.,
Mr. A. will not treat them with the same liberality as if he
had a share of their custom. Our opinion is, that to sell to
the consumer or miller direct, and buy of the manufacturer,
is the true essence of success. The profit attaching to
agriculture is so small, that it admits of no division. All
trades are, of course, subject to this class of men, but none
to such an extent as agriculture.

The bailiff should, at least once a week, attend upon the
landlord or steward, and give him some idea of the work of
the coming week (*i.e.*, as far as weather will permit). If
this is impossible, regular communications from the bailiff
through the post should be insisted upon, giving every
important detail connected with the farm.

He should keep a journal in which all casualties—deaths,
with their causes, and births of live stock—should be
entered, as well as every other matter of importance.

The economy which must be exercised in every department, not only as an act of justice to the employer, but as
the only means of making the farm pay; and also as an
example to the tenants, must depend in great degree upon
the capacity and care of the bailiff. Extravagance is the
common order of the day on most farms. Hay that would sell
for 4*l.* or 5*l.* a ton is given in profuse quantities and trodden
under foot; straw, now so valuable, is rotted in open yards,
the manurial matter running into the gutters.

Three horses are used in place of two. Two men are
employed to do the work of one. And this kind of extravagance often goes hand in hand with slovenliness of every

CHAP. VII.
The Home Farm.

The bailiff and his duties.

description. Cattle and sheep, by inattention, are allowed to go back in condition; young stock are kept shivering in open fields or cold yards, " living " upon the food they receive, instead of growing. Horses stand on filthy litter, and ventilation is stopped by plugs of straw. Teams sent to market are kept shivering outside public-houses, whilst the men in charge drink and chat. Disease is promoted, and a veterinary is called in, whose visits are accompanied by long bills.

In all these matters a wise and judicious bailiff may exercise much control, and he should always consider that the responsibility with regard to them rests with him.

The bailiff should carry out orders promptly, and not allow his own ideas to supersede his employer's wishes; at the same time a fear of speech on the part of the bailiff is much to be deprecated. He should be ready with practical advice when he feels it necessary. His authority over the men should be never interfered with, either by the landlord or steward. On the farm he should be supreme, and all orders emanating from any quarter should come through him.

He occupies a place which needs great tact and judgment. He is called upon for help from all quarters of the estate, and often when he feels it impossible to render it. He must, nevertheless, do his best to meet all demands upon him, and he should be allowed such an extra number of horses as may fairly enable him to do so, or be allowed to hire steam for purposes of cultivation, to make up for loss of time.

Labourers.

The labourers upon a home farm should receive the same wages as are paid by the tenants on the estate, and as much work should be expected of them. We do not, of course, imply that, if tenants underpay or in any way oppress their labourers, the landlord should do the same; but there should be as far as possible a reciprocal feeling in this matter. Good labourers should not be attracted by an extra one shilling a week, or by any other additional advantage, if the landlord desires to avoid giving ground of unpleasantness between himself and his tenants. They should be well housed, and overcrowding should be strictly forbidden. No lodgers, without permission, should be allowed. At the same time, the labourers' home should, as far as possible, be as free from intrusion as his employer's. He should have a plot of garden-ground, not exceeding a quarter of an acre; an allotment for this purpose should in no case be denied.

CHAP. VII.
The Home Farm.

Allotments.

Subject to the qualification that the landlord, in providing decent house accommodation, should not press for a rent disproportionate to the labourer's income, the labourer should receive no part of his wages " in kind;" his whole income should be in "money."

With regard to beer in harvest, our opinion is against giving it. Give money, and let the men supply themselves in accordance with their tastes. Make this proviso, however, if the men club together for the purchase of beer, that the allowance must be under the control of the bailiff.

Beer.

As much work as possible should be done by "piece or task work," so that the industrious may have an opportunity of making more money than the idle. This is too often lost sight of. Many a pound is lost by the habit of day pay. Self-interest, so absorbing in all of us, is altogether ignored in our dealings with the labourers. Almost every operation on the farm may be performed by contract, if the bailiff will but give it consideration.

Taskwork.

Each year, either at Michaelmas or Lady-day, a strict valuation should be made, in accordance with the foregoing section. The landlord must be looked upon, *pro tem.*, as outgoing tenant. The valuation should be made by the steward in conjunction with the bailiff. By it, an accurate balance for the year can be arrived at, as will be hereafter explained. At the same time it will serve as a check, more especially as relates to live stock. For instance, if 500 sheep are valued in one year, and during the following year 200 lambs are produced, and 150 of one kind and another

Annual valuation.

sold, there should be, at the time of the next valuation, 550 sheep in the flock. If in the valuation this is not the case, a reason must be given, and the skins produced.

A system of farm accounts will be given, but we may here mention that a detailed inventory and valuation should be rendered to the landlord, so that he may himself check the figures.

All farm produce supplied to the house should be charged as if sold in the market. Horse labour to the estate must also be charged at so much per horse, say 5s. or 6s. a horse per day.

Dairy produce should be supplied as "milk," at so much per gallon, say 10d. This is generally a better practice than selling to the house milk, cream, and butter. If it is adopted the house itself can sell any surplus quantity.

The cows should be milked into graduated buckets, and an average taken each week by the bailiff, and entered quarterly in his journal for inspection by the steward.

Corn, hay, and straw for the private stables, mutton, pork, bacon, poultry, and eggs, and any other produce that may be supplied, should be duly entered and charged.

We will now proceed to the consideration, in detail, of those departments which are most prominent. First in importance is:

The dairy buildings should be near the residence, for two reasons, first, in order that the milk may be delivered with comparatively little trouble, and secondly, that the landlord and his friends may visit it when they feel so disposed. The attendant should be a man thoroughly acquainted with his work, and should not be changed where it is possible to avoid it, as cows do not like strangers about them. The buildings, especially the milking stalls, should be kept sweet and clean; the walls should be repeatedly lime-washed, as nothing tends more to create purity. Calf-pens especially should be cleansed in this way.

The food should be regulated by the bailiff, and the supply be regularly sent to the buildings. The bailiff should inspect the cows and buildings at least once a day. The hours of milking should be regularly kept, and the cows milked in rotation. The date of taking bull, date of calving, sex of calf, &c., should be duly noted in the cowman's note-book, and a memorandum taken of such events by the bailiff. Registration for such purposes will be remarked upon hereafter. CHAP. VII.
The Home Farm.

When calving, the cows should be carefully watched, and left as much as possible to the care of the cowman. Let nature have its own way wherever practicable. When necessary, however, to interfere, the cowman should, if possible, communicate with the bailiff. In the event of any illness, apart from this, he must also at once let the bailiff know, who should, if he is fit for his position, be capable of treating all common complaints. Calling in professional aid in every case is to be discouraged. In the event of the bailiff being unable to treat any malady, he should apply either to the landlord or the steward. The immediate resort to violent medicines is, as a rule, an error: Nature will often, if left to herself, do more than physic. Dietary also is much to be regarded. Many animals no doubt die from the use of medicines injudiciously applied when simple treatment might have saved them. Calving.

Illness and its treatment.

The best winter food, in our opinion, for dairy cows is good hay (the best that the farm can produce) and crushed oats. The best cream and butter will be produced from this diet. Opinions differ, however, upon this point. Regular food of good quality, ample supply of water, exercise and cleanliness, with regular milking, are the great points necessary in dairy management. Food.

Fat stock will need the constant care of the bailiff, more especially in the winter. A good stockman is all-important. He should reside as near as possible to the stalls or boxes, in order that he may visit the beasts the last thing at night. The quantity and quality of the food given are scarcely more important than the regularity and the periods of feeding. A full manger now and an empty one by-and-by, Fat stock.

CHAP. VII.
The Home
Farm.

Care and
treatment of
fat stock.

will not fatten a bullock. When the bullocks are tied up they will need regular grooming; they cannot get at themselves to lick as they would do in yards or boxes. Before each meal the manger should be emptied and swept, the refuse being carried direct to the pigs, or to other stock, who are less particular. No food should be allowed to accumulate, as it is apt to get sour and distasteful. A constant supply of water must be given. If not supplied to each stall or box, a supply by bucket should be given at least twice a day.

In the event of any sickness the bailiff should have notice, and after this should be responsible. He should visit the stalls, when in full season, at least twice a day. The supply of food should be regular, and the diet an increasing one, according to the condition of each beast. There must be no set allowance, as bullocks differ much in constitution. The first supply of food should be given about six o'clock in the morning, again at eight or nine; then from twelve to one, four to five, or from that to six, and, finally, about eight or nine o'clock at night. The cake should be given separately, but meal and chaff should be mixed with pulped roots. No whole fodder should be allowed, as no process is more wasteful. Two-thirds hay and one-third straw make a good chaff, and should be cut about $1\frac{1}{2}$ or 2 inches long. Sugar, or molasses and water, poured on the mixture and well mixed, makes a palatable diet. It is well to prepare the food a day or two in advance, as slight fermentation is by no means an objection.

Hours of
feeding.

Selling of fat
stock.

As to the time for selling, it is well to remember that when they reach fair condition they begin to pay for what they eat. A fat beast eats very much less than a lean one. We think the practice of clearing out the stalls early is too often resorted to. A month's feeding towards the end is equal to six weeks at the commencement.

Good ventilation is very important, but the beasts should nevertheless be warm. The use of limewash may be profitably resorted to whenever practicable, and may be applied even to the manger.

When on pastures in summer, they will require little attention, beyond a visit once a day. If they are receiving cake, care should be taken to prevent the strongest getting the greater share. This can be done best by allowing a feeding trough to each beast. The feeding place should be changed each day, so as to distribute the manure regularly.

Store and young stock.

When in the yard in winter, they should have an ample supply of water, and a liberal allowance of food. They will thrive on oat or barley straw and cotton cake, if there is nothing else for them, but a more nutritious diet is better if procurable, especially for very young stock. A fair diet will be 3lb. of best oil cake, hay and straw chaff without limit, and plenty of water. If possible they should run out once a day, even in winter. Beasts in yards should be carefully selected according to temper and strength. If this is not done, the weak ones are driven off from the mangers, and cannot feed. They should not be turned on to the pastures in spring until the growth of grass has fairly started, and should be for the first week or two brought into the yard at night.

Cattle of this kind are not generally subject to much illness. Their maladies are often simple, and will give way to simple remedies. Change of diet will do more perhaps than anything else. The most prevalent source of disease is cold or chill brought on by exposure and irregular feeding.

It is impossible in a work of this nature to consider so important a subject as this with the detail it deserves. We shall simply refer to it in its general bearing upon the management of the "Home Farm."

Sheep.

A thoroughly good shepherd is indispensable, one who will not only carry out instructions, but take an interest in his flock. A shepherd, it will be found, considers his sheep, a bailiff considers his land as well; consequently there is often some slight antagonism between the two. The bailiff

CHAP. VII.
The Home Farm.
—

looks to the general welfare of the farm, and is often obliged to limit the amount of feed, and prevent the shepherd from moving too fast over roots or other feed. A shepherd cannot look beyond his flock, and thinks but little of the future.

On home farms, as a rule, a considerable flock of fat sheep is required. The supply to the house will vary according to seasons and the number of visitors; but there must always be a supply. When the supply exceeds the demand, a few may easily be sold to a neighbouring butcher, owing to the nature of the case; therefore, a smaller breeding flock than on other farms of the same size must be kept. Wether lambs also must be kept each season, in addition to the ewe and lambs for stock purposes. If the landlord's

Ram breeding. inclination is for ram breeding, the ram must be put early to the ewes, as early lambs are desirable in order to obtain the necessary growth for service. They must be ready for use in September, so that a month makes a considerable difference in their size and strength.

A selection of ewes should be made from the whole flock, and a ram be placed with them, carefully chosen to make good any marked defect in the flock. It is a good plan to mark the ewes according to the time they take the ram with a No. 1, 2, or 3, in pitch or paint. When the time of lambing arrives, those marked "1" can be taken to the fold at night, and not the whole flock, as must otherwise be the case.

Selection and treatment for exhibition purposes.

The ram and ewe lambs for show, or for any other particular purpose, should be selected early, and separated from the flock and fed highly, as early maturity is all important. As early as possible they should be "trimmed;" this should be done by an experienced lamb trimmer. The wool must be cut closely off the face and back, and snipped more or less all over. This, to gain the necessary show "touch," must be repeated every fortnight. When very high condition is required they must be kept under cover; this has a very marked effect upon the wool. More than the necessary number must be selected in case of deaths, or bad points exhibiting themselves further on. Great care in selection is needed, and an experienced man, acquainted with the special breed, should perform this duty.

For ordinary purposes, the lambing should take place in January or February, and in a fold in the open field. The place for the lambing fold should be selected before harvest, and one or two stacks of corn be made on the spot. When these are threshed, they not only form a shelter, but afford the litter requisite for the fold, and thereby double cartage is saved. The food necessary for the flock should be supplied by the bailiff at regular intervals.

The shepherd should be supplied with a comfortable portable house, fitted with a stove, so that he can prepare gruel or other warm drinks when necessary. It should be fitted with a "bunk," on which he may sleep when he is able. It is a good plan to supply him with coffee or tea. The medicines should be simple and few; a little port wine and tincture of opium for scour, cordials for exhausted ewes, and Epsom salts form the chief.

The chief source of disappointment at lambing often arises from the previous treatment of the ewes. Feeding too freely on turnips is a very constant evil. Ewes heavy in lamb should be limited in this respect. If possible, they should be fed on pastures or old lays, and the turnips should be carried to them, and these should be pulled sometime before they are needed. An ample supply of good hay or other dry food is absolutely necessary.

After lambing the ewes should be kept liberally, close attention being paid to their milk supply; when the lamb is weakly, the extra supply should be drawn off; when strong, the diet of the ewe should be increased. The turnips in each fold should be pulled and left to wither for at least a day. The lambs must be allowed free egress to the crop outside the fold, and the ewes should have an ample fold, and be allowed as much as possible to run back. When the lambs can pick they should have trough food outside.

CHAP. VII.
The Home Farm.

Sheep feed.

Weaning of lambs.

Washing and shearing.

It is the bailiff's duty to visit the flock at least once every day throughout the year; he should, however, interfere as little as possible with the shepherd. Sheep, when fat, should be killed or sold immediately, and others brought in, as there is great waste in keeping them when they get beyond a certain condition.

The bailiff must see that there is a constant supply of food, and this will need great foresight and care. The general rotation of sheep-feed upon hill farms is, turnips, swedes, rye, winter-barley, vetches, clover, after-math, stubbles, &c., and so on to turnips again. The interval between the completion of the root crop and the second crop of clover has to be got over by catch-crops, *i.e.*, rye, winter-barley and vetches, and these must be sown in quantities according to the size of the flock, and in accordance also with the rough sheep pasture at hand. Where there are pastures, difficulties connected with a short supply may be sometimes overcome, but, in this case, some night-fold will be necessary. The drawback to catch-crops is in the hindrance to sowing the root crop. It is best, when the last crop of vetches is fed off, if late, to sow a crop of mustard or rape, rather than roots. In all transitions from one class of food to another, care must be taken to accustom the flock to the change, before giving them full allowance. If this is neglected, death will often ensue, or purging will take place, which will need immediate attention.

Mangold may be carted to the crops of rye and vetches, and fed off upon them: they are mellow by this time, and are easily eaten by the sheep, so that slicing or pulping may be dispensed with.

Lambs may be weaned in May and June. They should be weaned gradually, *i.e.*, be separated from the ewes for several hours at a time, each day. The process is easily accomplished, as the lambs have learnt for some time to look after themselves.

The next process is washing and shearing. This takes place in June; it is unnecessary, however, to detail the practice. Soon after the lambs should be dipped, and later on the ewes may pass through the same process.

The shepherd too, at this time, must watch carefully for the attack of the fly. He should carry a "Mercury stone" in his pocket, and rub the place with it immediately a sheep is struck, which he will easily detect by the uneasy state of the sheep. The attack is generally upon the head or flank, and will often prove fatal if the maggots are left undisturbed. In warm, moist weather, and near woods, this attack is most to be dreaded. From this period to September, when the rams are usually placed with ewes, the latter should be kept liberally, as it is a time in which they can hardly be in too high condition. The production of twins is believed to be generally owing to this high condition.

Treatment of sheep, however, will depend upon districts, and upon the breed. Some districts and soils are not adapted to breeding purposes; in those cases sheep are bought in, generally about July, and sold when fat. The bailiff must, of course, consider the plan best adapted to the holding, and act accordingly.

Farm horses are, perhaps, the most valuable portion of a farmer's capital. They are the working power, and if one fails, it cannot but affect the routine of work. Over this department the bailiff will need to exercise great vigilance. The stables and the horses should be carefully inspected each day, and, if possible, morning and night. Where a large number of horses are kept, it is well to have a man responsible for the whole, whose duty it shall be to see that they leave the stable and return to it at the right hour, that they are properly groomed, and the stables perfectly cleansed; to give out the proper amount of food, inspect the harness, and, in fact, take the full charge of the whole stud. Where, however, the numbers will not admit of this, the bailiff himself should act in a similar capacity.

Regular hours for feeding should be strictly adhered to. The food should be of the best, but economy in food is most

CHAP. VII.
The Home Farm.

Food.

important. We recommend three bushels a week of bruised corn, consisting of two bushels of oats (not less than 36lb. to 40lb. per bushel), half a bushel of beans and half a bushel of maize; but the quantity should be *measured after bruising*. Mix with this a full allowance of wheat hulls and hay and straw chaff. No rack food should be allowed, and racks should be altogether dispensed with. The waste of hay in farm stables is beyond all belief.

Health.

The health of the animals depends almost entirely on diet and pure air. When we enter farm stables in the morning and find them reeking with ammonia, until the tears are forced to our eyes, and every hole through which pure air can enter is stuffed with hay or straw, what but disease is to be expected. Greasy heels, from standing in filth, ophthalmia from the foul atmosphere, and other complaints from similar causes, are a result which need not excite surprise.

Ventilation.

Whenever possible, lofts over stables should be avoided; when however this cannot be dispensed with, the "king-posts" should be cased with boards, forming a chimney, as it were, for the passage of the foul air. Cold air should be allowed to enter from below by moderate apertures, but these must not be immediately opposite any horse, as a blast of cold air upon a horse leads to chill. By this constant circulation, caused by the entry of cold air and the exit of hot, the atmosphere is kept pure and unoffensive. The bailiff must, however, see that these wise provisions are not rendered useless by the too frequent plug of hay. Carters, as a rule, dread fresh air and light.

We like to see stables open to the roof, and if the tiles do not fit well, the rafters may be cased for a few feet above the horses. A ridge tile lifted an inch here and there will give perfect ventilation.

Treatment of accidents and diseases.

Accidents and diseases should be at once reported. A horse suffering from any complaint should be removed from the rest. The carter should be allowed under no circumstance to administer any draught or ball, or apply any lotion or liniment, without receiving orders from the bailiff.

The stables should be lime-washed as often as practicable, but the wall in front, by the manger, should be toned down with ochre; a white wall is bad for the eyes. The manger should be swept out every day, and the unconsumed food be carried to the pigs. *Chap. VII. The Home Farm.*

On wet days, the carters can be profitably employed, oiling the harness. If this is done, it saves many pounds at the saddler's in the course of the year. No portion of harness should be taken to the saddler for repair without first submitting it to the bailiff. *Oiling and repairing harness.*

One word on the bearing-rein, for there is nothing more painful than to see a team of willing horses pulling with all their strength and will, but chafing under this instrument of cruelty and torture, their heads forced into an unnatural position in order to obtain what is believed to be effect. The natural position for the head, when pulling, is forward, not tucked into the chest, and this fact is now so generally recognised by all intelligent persons who have taken the trouble to consider the question, that to allow the use of the bearing-rein for heavy draught horses is a sure indication that the owner is a person with whom custom has more influence than reason; therefore make the reins too short to reach the hames, or make it an offence to place them over the collar. But, generally, carters need nothing but enlightenment upon a point of this kind; for, as a rule, they are kind to their horses, and take pride in them, and this is greatly to be encouraged. *Bearing-rein.*

In the treatment of foals, great care is needed from their birth. The mares must be allowed an extra supply of corn, as they have not only to work, but supply milk for the foals. If the mare suffers, the foal will also. *Treatment of foals.*

They should be allowed plenty of exercise, and be taught as early as possible to pick for themselves. They may be allowed a little good meadow hay, bruised oats and linseed. When weaned, they will require constant attention for a while, and their food should be good and nutritious. If allowed to fall off in condition at this period, it will not be

184 ESTATE MANAGEMENT.

CHAP. VII.
The Home Farm.

easy to recover it. Crushed or bruised corn is advisable and economical for all horses, but for foals from the period of weaning to five years of age is indispensable. Whilst shedding their teeth they cannot grind a whole oat.

Pigs

This subject will not need much consideration; not that it is unimportant, but particulars as to breeds, feeding, and general treatment, have been written too often to need repetition. As a home farm stock, pigs are necessary for the supply of pork and bacon to the house; and opportunity should be given to the various officials and servants on the estate to purchase at first price. Carters who may not be allowed to keep pigs should be supplied slightly (say 2s. a score) below the market price.

As a paying stock upon the home farm we do not recommend it; and would encourage only sufficient numbers for the before-mentioned purposes. Our experience has been that 12s. per score is needed to cover the expense of pig-feeding. It is often 10s. and even less, consequently a loss is the general result. Young pigs sold off the sow will, no doubt, pay; and a few breeding sows and a boar are necessary. Sows should be in pig, or with pig, as they will not pay under any other circumstances; and when they prove unprofitable in this respect, they should be at once fatted. The piggery may be under the same roof as the fatting bullocks, and be looked after by the stockman; this saves labour and secures regularity.

Poultry.

A most important stock upon all "home farms." A large supply of eggs and various descriptions of poultry is constantly required in a large country house, and it is the bailiff's duty as well as interest to see that this supply is as regular as possible.

This department, where possible, should be left to the bailiff's wife, or, failing this, to his housekeeper. Poultry thrive better as a rule with women than with men. It is not sufficient to keep a large stock and trust to chance for eggs and chickens. It needs care and attention like all other classes of stock. Fowls like liberty, and should be allowed full range, being shut in at night. If fed regularly before roosting time they will invariably come home, and this prevents to a great extent stolen nests and wild broods.

Careful selection of stock birds should be made, and those not considered good enough for the purpose should be killed for the house or sold. Chickens should be hatched more or less throughout the year, to secure a constant supply, and a few good old hens should be kept for that purpose. For layers, however, a good supply of pullets will be needed. In winter, hens may be induced to lay, if fed on warm food, which may consist of potatoes and bran.

Whatever class of poultry is kept it should be "pure," and if more than one breed is kept they should be kept at different homesteads, so as not to intermingle.

Eggs, when more numerous than are required for immediate consumption, may be kept for a considerable period by simply standing them separately upon a shelf, perforated with holes, sufficiently large to take the end of the egg. The plan of keeping them in a basket or box is bad. The date should be written on each egg, to prevent stale eggs being delivered instead of fresh. If in addition to this plan they are rubbed with fresh butter, they will keep fresh for a length of time.

An account of both eggs and poultry supplied to the house or sold should be rendered quarterly, and duly passed through the books of the farm.

Essential as this substance is, nothing is more wasted or ignored. Farm yards as a rule are made apparently expressly for the purpose of destroying the dung made. The roofs possess no spouting. The yard slopes to the all-important pond. Rain does not simply fall on the dung, but passes through and over it, and then runs full of rich fertilising matter into the said pond. The dung, which has thus become simply rotten straw, is carted at great expense upon the land, the essence being left in the yard or allowed

CHAP. VII.
The Home Farm.

Treatment of farmyard dung and covered yards.

to overflow into the gutter. The tea-leaves, not the tea, have been utilised, and it occurs to no one that this is a wasteful and ridiculous proceeding.

Our enterprising analytical chemists have written and lectured upon the subject until they must be tired. Our press representatives have written "leaders," but the effect of all this is to render a few yards comparatively perfect, but the bulk remain as they were one hundred years ago. Cattle are fed in stalls, and the dung, rich in manurial matter from consumption of cake, is thrown out into the yards to be washed. Ought this state of things to be? On home farms, certainly not. They are held by the proprietors, and to them the tenants naturally look (to a certain extent) for example. We cannot, as stewards, point out defective yards and leaky dung heaps whilst those upon the home farm are in the same condition. It is of no use at audit dinners dilating upon the subject of covered yards and boxes, unless we can point to a special example upon the home farm. Covered yards, though admirable in their way, are not strictly essential. Warm sheds well spouted are considered by some much better. When, however, covered yards are resorted to, the ventilation should be perfect. One span of roof should project over the other, and spouting be attached only to every other span; the drip from one falling on to the other. This secures a circulation of fresh air.

Dung heaps.

Another matter connected with dung, and which causes great waste, is the removal of it into heaps. If possible it should be carted direct from the yard to the fields and be immediately spread. Every removal causes an escape of ammonia, the chief fertilising matter. When, however, it is necessary to resort to this practice, the carts should be drawn "*over*" the heap, so as to consolidate it, and when completed, the top should be covered with mould; a ditch should also be cut round it to prevent the run of surface water, and also to collect the rich liquid which will exude from the heap.

It was considered necessary at one time to turn every heap of dung once or twice before applying it to the land, but this idea is not so general.

Chap. VII. The Home Farm.

When we consider the ingredients which well-made dung contains, we understand at once the loss which it sustains by soakage. As we have already stated, substances must become soluble before they can be utilised as plant food. This solubility is brought about by fermentation. On this account dung should not be used too fresh, but should be allowed to remain sometime in the yard. Nevertheless, if it lies exposed to rain as it must if in open yards, the longer it remains the greater will be the loss of manurial matter. As fermentation proceeds the more soluble the substances become. When covered and unexposed, this process increases its value to a very marked extent, as may be seen by its effect on the crop to which it is applied. Well-rotted farm yard manure contains:

Analysis of rotten and fresh dung.

Water	75·42 per cent.
Soluble organic matter*	3·71 ,,
Soluble inorganic matter (ash), soluble silica, phosphate of lime, lime, magnesia, potash, soda, chloride of sodium, sulphuric acid, carbonic acid, and loss	1·47 ,,
Insoluble organic matter†	12·82 ,,
Insoluble inorganic matter (ash), same as above, with the addition of oxides of iron and alumina, &c.	6·58 ,,
	100·00 ,,

Whereas fresh dung of the same description contains

Water	66·17 per cent.
Soluble organic matter	2·48 ,,
Soluble inorganic matter	1·54 ,,
Insoluble organic matter	25·76 ,,
Insoluble inorganic matter	4·05 ,,
	100·00 ,,

---

* Containing nitrogen, ·297: equal to ammonia, ·360.
† Containing nitrogen, ·309: equal to ammonia, ·375.

CHAP. VII
The Home Farm.

This at once shows the advantage which rotten dung possesses over that newly made.

No manure which we can buy will ever rank with good dung. We may buy this and that ingredient, but cannot purchase the useful combination of substances presented to us in this natural fertiliser. If, therefore, we value the progressive fertility of our soils we must continue to make as much as we possibly can; and our aim must be to make it with as little cost as possible, and after we have obtained it to prevent waste. This is best done by covered yards, boxes, or open yards well spouted. Liquid manure tanks are very useful and advisable under certain conditions, but the liquid is more useful in the dung, and it will hold a great quantity under the foregoing circumstances.

Spreading of dung.

The drawing of manure to the field and leaving it day after day in heaps is also a great source of loss, such fermentation as takes place liberates ammonia, and the rain washes the soluble matter into one spot, instead of equally over the whole field. If possible, dung should be spread as fast as it is deposited from the cart.

To summarise, then, the foregoing remarks: Make dung where, whilst it receives sufficient moisture for the purposes of putrefaction or fermentation, it cannot be washed by every rain that falls. If it is exposed to constant rain wash, fermentation ceases; on the other hand, if kept too dry, as under some covered yards, the process is retarded, and the dung becomes dry and mouldy, whereas healthy, well-fermented dung should be black and moist.

Leave it untouched until required for use, every removal being attended with loss.

Spread it quickly. For land where small seeds are to be sown apply it in autumn, in order that it may become incorporated with the soil. Much good seed, especially swede, is lost by spring application of dung.

If the value of dung wasted annually upon an average sized farm could be reckoned and represented in actual cash, the amount would do more than astonish us.

After a dressing of manure we naturally sow the seeds; therefore the subject of seeds next presents itself.

CHAP. VII.
The Home Farm.

Seeds.

We are apt, whilst eradicating weeds with one hand, to sow them with the other. We undertake a long and expensive process of fallowing to get rid of weeds, and we buy seeds improperly dressed for our next crop. It is better to buy good seeds from well-known seedsmen, even if we pay high for them, than to buy of local men at a low price. As far as vitality goes their seeds are often as good as need be, but they are unable to dress them as carefully as those who make it their special business. These remarks apply principally to small seeds, such as clovers, grasses, and turnips. The two former especially need the greatest care. The latter, if purchased of such firms as Messrs. Sutton and Sons, Carter, or other first-class firms, are known to be from selected bulbs. In the ordinary market, however, they are too often taken from a portion of a whole field laid by for seed indiscriminately. If like produces like, we cannot expect success if we adopt this method of buying seed. Bailiffs, therefore, should, in our opinion, purchase all small seeds of the best firms.

With comparatively little trouble the bailiff may, however, grow his own swedes, mangolds, and turnips. He can select the best bulbs, and transplant them to his garden or elsewhere, and thus secure for his own use the very best seed. By placing the seed in water a short while before use the light seeds and weeds may be skimmed off. This is, perhaps, one of the best home methods. The seed will soon dry sufficiently for drilling, if spread on a barn floor.

Seeds before being bought should be tried in flower pots or saucers, and be examined by a magnifying glass, and the bulk when supplied should be carefully compared with the sample.

In the selection of large seeds, viz., cereals, vetches, &c., more latitude may be allowed. "Seedsmen" proper do not as a rule supply them. They may be bought in the market;

CHAP. VII.
The Home Farm.

Change of seed.

Hay.

Early cutting.

but may to a great extent be grown upon the farm. A change, however, is very desirable; but even this may be effected upon the same farm, where the soil varies in any marked degree.

There is a difference of opinion upon the subject of change of seed; some are of opinion that the change should be from rich to poor soils, some hold the reverse opinion. We, however, believe the best change is effected by the use of seed from soils very similar in character.

Seed in every case should be fully developed, clear and bright in the skin, showing freedom from exposure at harvest time and fermentation in the stack, and of good weight.

This is one of the most important matters connected with the operations of the farm, and demands the exercise of care and thought.

Perhaps of all farm operations, that of hay-making will test the ability of the bailiff more than any other. It is an operation that tries the skill and patience to a marked degree. On home farms, as a rule, a considerable quantity of hay is made, owing principally to the extent of pasture land usually occupied by the proprietor. With regard, however, to excessive hay-making, it is to be observed that it usually comes at a time when every attention on the part of the bailiff is needed to secure a full crop of roots. On most farms the root crop is a most important one, and anything that serves to prevent the attainment of this is to be avoided. It is not an unusual thing to hear, that so-and-so has no root crop, when as a rule good crops are plentiful. Why is this? Simply because he has made too much hay, and the early season so favourable for sowing the root crop was of short duration. The set-off of extra hay is insufficient to cover the loss sustained.

In cutting hay the bailiff had better err on the early, rather than the late side. The grasses contain more nourishment, and if the quantity per acre is less, it is quite balanced by the extra after-math. Moreover, grass, if left too long, will ripen its seeds, which tends to impoverish the soil. The practice of leaving it, however, is often pursued by many bailiffs, upon the false hope of obtaining more bottom.

The best plan is to lay up as much land for hay, both of seeds and meadow, as is needed for home use, allowing a sufficient quantity, of course, for the next year, in case of a bad season.

To detail in a work of this character the various processes of hay-making is unnecessary. It may be observed, however, that not only interest but the credit of the estate make it incumbent on the bailiff of a home farm to conduct the operation with the utmost skill he possesses. He will probably be supplied with the latest machinery, and have the command of a great deal of manual labour. In important seasons of this kind, he can generally command the services of men employed in other departments of the estate, in addition to his usual hands. The principal matter to attend to, to secure a good and sweet crop of hay, is to spread it immediately it is cut, but always at night to get it into wind-rows or cocks. The greatest injury takes place after hay is partly made. Whilst the sap is in the grass, and the culms unbroken, rain will run off like water off a duck's back; but when dry and broken, the rain will penetrate and wash out the nutriment.

Upland hay, or clover and sainfoin, as is well known, must be left in the "swathe," and turned when the top is made. The less it is turned the better. In fact, now that the machines lay the swathes so wide and flat, there is often no necessity to turn at all. Many farmers leave it untouched until ready for carting, when they collect it with the horse-rake.

When the ricks are made (which should be near the homesteads), let them be quickly thatched. It is better to run the risk of spoiling hay in the field, than to carry it when unfit. There is a chance of obtaining a good stack in the former instance, but none at all in the latter.

ESTATE MANAGEMENT.

CHAP. VII.
The Home Farm.

Harvest.

Cutting wheat and oats green.

Cost of harvesting.

After hay time comes harvest, and often the seasons overlap. The bailiff at this season should be well "within himself;" *i.e.*, he must have his work on all sides well forward, his men must be well in hand, he must be constantly on the farm, and he must know by careful observation which field is most fit for the sickle. The operations of harvest are too often delayed. Both wheat and oats may be cut when comparatively green, and advantage derived by the process. In wheat under these conditions, the skin or bran is thinner, the quantity of flour is greater, and the straw is more valuable. In oats, too, the effect is similar. Oat straw when harvested early is as valuable as fair hay. If left until all is ripe together, much injury ensues, as that that is cut last is altogether over-ripe. The skin is thick and opaque, and the straw woody, and free from nutriment; the sap has all been expended in ripening the grain. The land, too, has been too fully scourged by this ripening process. Both wheat and oats may be cut when, by pressing the grain between the finger and thumb, the inside is found thick, not milky. They will ripen in the stook or shock, if left long enough.

As much of this should be performed by task work as possible. Prices, however, will vary in different districts and in accordance with the quality of the crop. Reaping with sickle may be 12*s.* or 13*s.* per acre. Tying behind machine, 4*s.* 6*d.* or 6*s.* Mowing by hand, 3*s.* or 4*s.*, and so on. Carting and stacking may even be contracted for, but no contract of this kind should be entered into without the full inspection of the bailiff throughout the process.

There is an old saying, that "Grain had better spoil in the field than in the stack," and this is perfectly true. As the corn goes into the stack, so it will come out, no matter how long it remains there. Grain often recovers in the field to a very marked extent, when bad weather gives way to sunshine. As a rule, in bad weather the crops are best left alone, only putting up such sheaves as may have been blown down. By constant removal the whole gets exposed to rain instead of only a portion.

Implements.

This is an important item upon all farms, more especially upon home farms, where expensive machinery is often employed. The amount of money required to set up a farm in a complete set of implements is very great, and no portion of the farmer's capital is so exposed to depreciation, not only from wear and tear, but from the fact of old implements being pushed aside by new methods and patents. Fully 15 to 20 per cent. ought to be deducted each year when the valuations are made.

This natural depreciation is often increased and hastened by the carelessness of the bailiff and his men. Expensive machinery is left constantly exposed to all weathers. Sun and wet, one as injurious as the other, are allowed to work their will. Elevators especially suffer much from this neglect; they possess so much surface, lie so exposed, and being very large cannot easily be covered. When not in use they should be drawn at once to a shed or into a barn.

Reaping machines, also, are constantly seen, week after week, in the field where last used.

It answers to keep implements in constant repair. A coat of paint yearly is money and labour well expended.

All repairs should be attended to in their proper seasons. When the wheat is fit to cut or the grass ready for mowing, it is too late to think of sending the machine to be repaired. On estates, all repairs should be, as much as possible, placed in the hands of the clerk of the works, and no machine should be sent away without his sanction.

The following sketch is from an engraving that appeared some time ago in the "Agricultural Gazette," and is inserted here by the kind permission of the editor. Requiring a method for distinguishing cattle for purposes of registration, we applied for the necessary information to the ever-courteous editor of the "Agricultural Gazette," who thereupon published this drawing.

The system is that practised at Aylesby, as slightly altered by Mr. Torr from the original system at Wiseton. By adding together the figures represented by each clip, any number up to 99 may be obtained, except 2 and 7 or 20 and 70; and to form these a second clip is cut by the side of the 1 and the 10, as shown on the pair of ears below.

EAR-MARKING OF CATTLE, FOR PURPOSES OF REGISTRATION.

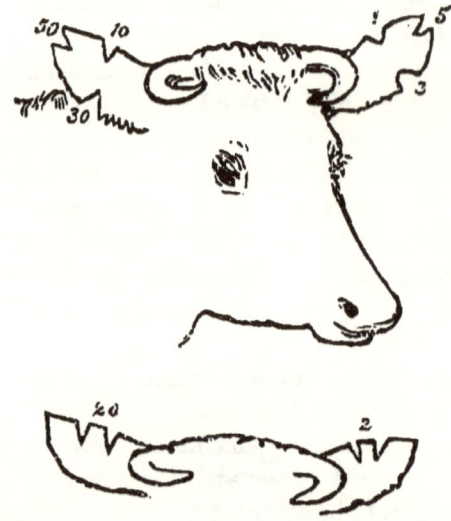

We have found the system an admirable one, and recommend it to those who have the care of a fine herd of cattle.

This matter of registration is better conducted by the steward than by the bailiff, as it requires careful entries and selection. Messrs. Hallifax and Co., of Oxford-street, furnish a very excellent private "Herd Book" for entries, for the sum of 7s. 6d. From this book the forms are filled up for presentation to the secretary of the shorthorn or other herd books.

TOP-DRESSING EXPERIMENTS UPON GRASS LAND.

A table is given below showing the result of some experimental dressings upon grass land, the object of the experiments having been to obtain information concerning the effect, over an extended period, of various artificial and natural manures.

The grass land chosen was a naturally poor one upon the Rotherfield estate, in Hampshire. The soil, which was examined by Dr. Voelcker previously to the experiment, was found to contain no lime, except such as remained from a dressing of chalk applied nearly thirty years before. It was a porous clay resting upon the chalk. Care was taken that each plot should be as nearly as possible of the same quality.

The manures were applied in the month of January, 1875, this month being considered best for the purpose. The results were carefully noticed when the plots were cut in July, the weight of each being taken as soon as cut. All were cut the same day, no rain or other change occurring during the operation. As will be noticed, these results were rather peculiar.

The next year was hot and dry, and the yield of grass was much less than the previous year; nevertheless, there still remained a marked difference in favour of several of the manured plots. The third year again gave a heavy yield of grass, and still the dressings showed a return, and a return in some degree proportionate to the last.

It will be observed that the most effective dressings were Peruvian guano, soluble guano, and farmyard manure. The plots dressed with nitrate of soda exhibited a considerable increase the first year; not, however, to such an extent as the guano; but the following year the effect was not only reduced to a minimum, but in one case to a decrease, showing the transient value of the very soluble nitrate.

Another very peculiar result is the loss upon the plot dressed with ½in. bone the first year, and the very slight increase the second and third.

TOP-DRESSING EXPERIMENTS ON GRASS LAND, SHOWING THE RELATIVE EFFICACY OF VARIOUS ARTIFICIAL AND NATURAL DRESSINGS.

Plots One-tenth of an Acre. Manure applied January 20th, 1875.

No. of Plots	Description of Manure	Quantity of Manure per plot of One-tenth of an Acre.	Cost of Manure per Acre.	GRASS CUT JULY 31ST, 1875, SHOWING THE AMOUNT ATTRIBUTABLE TO THE DRESSINGS AT THE FIRST YEAR'S CUTTING.			GRASS CUT JULY 21ST, 1876, SHOWING THE AMOUNT ATTRIBUTABLE TO THE DRESSINGS AT THE SECOND YEAR'S CUTTING.			GRASS CUT AUGUST 2ND, 1877, SHOWING THE AMOUNT ATTRIBUTABLE TO THE DRESSINGS AT THE THIRD YEAR'S CUTTING.		
				Weight of Grass per Plot.	Increase per Plot over average of Unmanured Plots.	Decrease per Plot.	Weight of Grass per Plot.	Increase per Plot over average of Unmanured Plots.	Decrease per Plot.	Weight of Grass per Plot.	Increase per Plot over average of Unmanured Plots.	Decrease per Plot.
		lbs.	£ s. d.	cwt. qr. lb.	cwt. qr. lb.	cwt. qr. lb.	cwt. qr. lb.	cwt. qr. lb.	cwt. qr. lb.	cwt. qr. lb.	cwt. qr. lb.	cwt. qr. lb.
1	Peruvian Guano	45	3 0 0	18 2 12	7 1 8	...	8 0 2	2 1 8	...	11 2 24	3 3 22	...
2	Soluble Guano	45	2 10 0	17 2 23	6 1 14	...	7 1 7	1 2 13	...	10 2 18	2 3 16	...
3	{Soluble Guano	33¾ }	2 9 6	16 1 8	4 3 22	...	7 2 12	1 3 18	...	9 1 21	1 2 19	...
4	Superphosphate	22½ }										
4	Superphosphate	45	1 4 0	14 2 10	3 1 1	...	6 2 24	1 0 2	...	9 0 26	1 1 24	...
5	Nothing	...	...	11 1 18	...	...	5 2 23	...	...	8 17	...	...
6	Fine Bone Dust	67	2 17 0	12 2 7	1 0 26	...	6 2 9	0 3 15	...	9 0 19	1 1 17	...
7	{Superphosphate	22½ }	2 2 0	14 1 14	3 0 5	...	5 3 24	0 1 2	...	8 0 0	0 0 26	...
7	Nitrate of Soda	22½ }										
8	{Superphosphate	22½ }	2 9 0	15 2 7	4 0 26	...	5 2 9	...	0 0 13	7 3 3	0 0 1	...
8	Kainit	33½ }										
9	{Nitrate of Soda	11 }	2 18 6	15 1 20	4 0 11	...	6 0 14	0 1 20	...	8 0 9	0 1 6	...
9	{Soluble Guano	11 }										
9	Nitrate of Soda	11 }										
9	Superphosphate											
10	Nothing	...	...	11 1 0	...	...	5 2 22	...	...	7 2 16	...	...
11	Dissolved Bones	56	1 17 6	12 2 7	1 0 26	...	6 0 15	0 1 21	...	7 1 0	...	...
12	{Dissolved Bones	60 }	3 8 9	13 1 18	2 0 9	...	5 3 20	0 0 18	...	8 0 0	0 0 26	...
12	{Soluble Guano	26 }										
13	Special Grass Manure	56	2 0 6	13 0 20	1 3 11	...	5 3 2	0 0 20	0 0 20	7 0 14	0 1 12	0 2 2
14	{½ in. Bones	56 }	2 7 0	10 1 27	...	0 3 10	5 3 14	0 0 20	...	8 0 14	0 0 5	...
15	Farmyard Manure	1 load	2 10 0	15 0 18	3 3 9	...	7 2 7	1 3 13	...	11 3 7	4 0 5	0 2 16

. The first Ten of these Experiments were conducted under the directions of Dr. Aug. Voelcker, F.R.S.

The table, however, is clear, and open to criticism; it shows that in plots 1, 2, and 15 there is a decided residuum left even after three successive cuttings. If this residuum could be arrived at, we should obtain the "unexhausted value;" but this is impossible, because such value is that which remains after each successive trial; we can only, therefore, from the results of the preceding years, come to a conclusion as to the amount of grass attributable each year to the various dressings.

With regard to the pecuniary result: if we take, for instance, plot 1, we find Peruvian guano, at a cost of 3*l*. per acre, gives an increased yield of 6½ tons of grass in the three years; say, in rough figures, 1½ tons of hay, which at 70*s*. per ton represents 5*l*. 5*s*. as a return for an outlay of 3*l*., which may be considered a good investment.

It is therefore clear that an incoming tenant should pay a sum of money to the outgoing tenant as an equivalent for money so wisely invested.

These experiments must not, however, be confounded with similar ones conducted upon arable land, as the results would be widely different.

CHAPTER VIII.

REPAIRS, BUILDING, AND MATERIAL.

REPAIRS GENERALLY—CLERK OF THE WORKS—NEW ERECTIONS
—FARM BUILDINGS—TANKS—COTTAGES—MATERIAL—TIMBER
—MINERAL SUBSTANCES—UTILITY OF GEOLOGICAL KNOWLEDGE
—GRANITE—SLATES—TRAP, OR GREENSTONE—SANDSTONE—
LIMESTONE—MALM ROCK—CHALK AND LIME—SAND—MORTAR
—CEMENT—CONCRETE—BRICKS AND BRICKMAKING—TILES.

CHAP. VIII.
Repairs, &c.

Repairs generally.
Clerk of the works.

THE maintenance of farm and other buildings in such repair as will enable a full rental to be secured is the first object of all stewards. The wear and tear and natural decay are so great that, on estates of any magnitude, a complete staff of skilled workmen is required. Those men are under the direction of a foreman, himself a skilled mechanic, styled the "clerk of the works." He should be a man of great ability, able, by a complete training, to undertake anything relating to building and repairs. To thoroughly fill his position he must have passed through an apprenticeship, both at the bench, the mortar-board, and the draughtsman's table. He will be required to provide plans and elevations with their accompanying specifications and estimates, superintend the preparation of the various materials, and be methodical and self-reliant.

The average annual amount of repairs upon an estate will depend upon the description of the buildings. When they are built of permanent material, the necessary repairs will be superficial and easily kept pace with; when, however, they consist of wood, thatch, or other perishable material, the expense will be constant and heavy. So absolutely necessary are repairs, to maintain a regular income from the land, that the matter is recognised in all valuations for purposes of assessment as a subject of deduction.

<small>CHAP. VIII.
Repairs, &c.</small>

We are of opinion that, when an ordinary staff of workmen only is kept, they should be occupied entirely in repairs, especially when they are expected to keep farm implements as well as buildings in repair. When the erection of new buildings is necessary, the work should be entrusted to a local builder. The plans, however, and specifications must be drawn up, or at least examined, by the clerk of the works, and the works also, whilst in progress, be under his inspection. When the building is undertaken by the estate staff, repairs often fall into arrears which it is almost impossible to recover. But this is, of course, a matter of judgment, and the course adopted may depend upon the question whether or not repairs are well in hand at the time the new work is projected.

<small>New erections.</small>

We do not intend to detail the various functions of the clerk of the works, nor to give plans of farm buildings and cottages. Opinions upon the latter subject differ so widely that it would be almost useless to attempt to express a judgment on the matter within the compass of a few pages. We may, however, point out one or two matters of a general practical bearing in the erection of farm buildings and cottages, which are important, not only in their relation to present occupation, but to future stability.

<small>Farm buildings.</small>

The erection of farm buildings should take place upon sites situated as nearly as possible in the centre of the farm, and in proximity to main roads. The buildings should also be grouped with a due regard not only to economy in the cost of erection, but also to the lessening of the cost of labour in the various branches of farm management. The stores for reception of food, for instance, should be situated in a central position, so that their contents may radiate, as

CHAP. VIII.
Repairs, &c.

Water supply.

Tanks.

it were, to all classes of stock. By this centralisation, labour of every description is minimised.

There should be a good water supply, and this can always be obtained where there is a sufficient surface of roof. The supply should be collected in tanks near the centre, and not in open ponds, which are exposed to evaporation and waste. If the buildings are upon an extensive scale, a cistern on the top, supplied by a force pump from the main tank, will facilitate the diffusion of water throughout the whole of the buildings. The allusion to tanks suggests one or two special observations as to their construction. The usual forms are oblong, square, or circular. No set form, however, can be given, as the form must be chosen according to circumstances. Oblong or square tanks it is necessary to build with brick or some other material, and cement thereon; but in the case of circular tanks where the soil is firm, bricks are not needed, as the cement can be applied direct. On the Rotherfield estate this practice has been in use for several years; and those made some years ago are still perfect. When sunk in chalk, or clay resting on chalk or in any firm clay or rocks of harder structure, the plan answers well; but where flints or rubble abound the sides must be puddled, or brick be used. Upon these sides a tolerably thick coating of cement is laid. A ledge should be left near the surface when excavated, which will serve as a foundation for a brick dome, which, when carried up, completes the tank. The plan is exceedingly cheap compared to that of bricks, and bears the test of time, which alone will decide whether the term "cheap" can be legitimately used. When this practice is resorted to, especially in the case of softer formations, it is necessary that the plasterer should follow the excavator immediately, otherwise wet or frosts affect the sides, and cause crumbling and flaws. The sides of an open tank should slope slightly outwards, which allows the ice in winter to float upwards, thus preventing injury by expansion. It is also to be noticed that, where the water is collected off roads, the flow should first enter a dip-hole, where sediment may be collected, the clear water only entering the tank; otherwise the tank will constantly need cleansing, which should be avoided, as likely to injure the cement. It is a good plan to protect the tank by a wall or fence, and to have steps to the bottom at one end.

CHAP. VIII.
Repairs, &c.

In the erection of cottages we must bear in mind situation, water supply, and sanitary arrangements.

Cottages.

The situation should be chosen as far as possible where there is a free circulation of fresh air, on a slope, and with a N.E. aspect. But the locality will, of course, depend to a great extent upon the purpose for which the cottage is to be used. If for a stockman, it should be near his cattle sheds; if for a carter, near his stables; if for a day labourer, in or near the village. Centralisation of cottages, forming villages or hamlets, is a wise provision, as it brings together individual interests, and enables any design for the common good to be carried into better effect. It is better for purposes of education, for attendance at church, and obviates many objections incident to lonely and outlying cottages. Wherever distant cottages are necessary there should always be a pair. When there is but one, great distress or illness or accident may take place, and no one may hear or know of it for days. Domestic calamities are so frequent as to render this objection very plain to all. Again, where a poaching propensity prevails, these lonely cottages form an excellent shelter.

The more, however, we centralise our cottages, the greater will be the attention necessary to insure efficient sanitary measures. The word "sanitary" means "pertaining to or designed to secure health." Therefore, although the term is usually coupled with matters relating to drainage, it properly extends to all measures which are requisite for the securing of health. What is important for one cottage is all the more important when the cottage is situate in a village, as one defective cottage may contaminate the others.

Sanitary arrangements.

The principal sanitary precautions requisite are to secure

CHAP. VIII.
Repairs, &c.

Circulation of air.

Hollow walls.

Drainage.

the full ventilation of pure air, freedom from damp, sufficient drainage, and supply of pure water.

Under every cottage there should be an uninterrupted rush of fresh air, secured by air bricks, one of the many patents now in use. The draught should not be confined beneath the floor of single rooms, but as far as possible it should pass under the whole building. There should be at least a foot, and if possible a foot and a half, between the ground and the top of the joists. This prevents the accumulation of damp, which not only rots the boards at an early period, but is injurious to health, especially to that of children.

The walls should be hollow, *i.e.*, there should be a gap of at least two inches between the outer and inner wall. Any wet driving through the outer wall will then drip down between and pass out below, instead of through to the inside. When this precaution is neglected, much harm is done, especially where no fire is kept up; even in those rooms where there is a fire, the damp and heat combined create a humid atmosphere, which is very unhealthy. These walls are bound together by "ties," made of iron or glazed bricks; if a common porous brick is used, the damp will pass through and show itself on the inside.

Where, as in the erections of rough rock or rubble, this arrangement of the walls is impossible or difficult, it is a good plan to smear the weather sides inside with a thick coat of pitch, and then to lath and plaster over it. We have found this most effective.

Any rush of surface water which may prevail in the neighbourhood should be carried off. Ventilation is best secured by high rooms, and if the upper portion of the window is fitted with a perforated pane, or one of the circular discs which revolve by the current of air, pure air must result. This is an especially important matter in bedrooms where there are no fireplaces, and where many children sleep.

The subject of drainage is perhaps the most important. The results arising from any defect in this matter are often fatal. The dead-well or cesspool should be as far as possible from the cottage, and the pipe communicating with the sink should have a full amount of fall. When connected with the sink there should be a trap, either outside or in. If inside, the lead pipe itself may be turned so as to form a very effective one; if outside, it may be by a glazed pipe made for the purpose, or one may be built of brick. These "traps" are to prevent the inlet of foul air from the pipe or cesspool to the house. Their principle is, to place between the house and the cesspool a "trap" of water constantly full, and through which of course gas cannot pass; it may be at once understood from looking at a common glazed pipe of the "S" form. The "S" being placed horizontally, one end of it points vertically upwards to receive the drainage, and one vertically downwards to discharge it. It is clear that the lower bend of the "S" will be kept continually full of the liquid matter, so that there is never any outlet for the passage of gas. When these cesspools contain only the washings from the sink they need not be very large. They should be lined with cement, as, if loose bricks only are used, which is termed "steaning," the fluid will penetrate through the surrounding soil and be wasted. This is to be avoided, as the substance possesses rich manurial qualities, and should be mixed with soil for use in the garden. The top should be covered with a stone or board, which may be removed for the periodical clearing.

Closets should, in our opinion, be removed from the cottage. They may be erected by themselves, or be under the same roof as the woodsheds. The old-fashioned pit is still the best. It should be bricked up, and the entry to it be from the outside. Earth-closets, admirable though they are, are not suited for the use of the cottager—they need so much constant care.

In those districts where the water supply is obtained from wells, ponds, or rivulets, too great attention to these matters cannot possibly be given.

CHAP. VIII.
Repairs, &c.

Where closets are allowed to overflow or penetrate through the soil, the poisonous fluid must find its way by degrees to some well or stream, and the fact of its having done so is made manifest by the outbreak of the fatal "typhus."

Tanks, supplied from the roofs of the cottages, yield the purest supply of water, and if these are periodically kept cleaned and lime-washed, the quality of the water is excellent—clear, sparkling, and cold. As a rule the roof of an ordinary cottage, slated or tiled (the former is best, as none of the water is absorbed), will supply any reasonable amount of water. The tank may be constructed to hold about 2000 gallons.

Material. Timber and mineral substances.

We now pass on to the question of "Material;" but, as we have fully considered the subject of timber under that head, we shall dwell only upon such substances as we find in the soil, or mineral substances, viz., Rocks, Limestone, Earth, Gravel, and Sand.

Utility of geological knowledge.

We may here remark that a knowledge of geology is a very important branch of estate management. We do not intend to imply that a land steward must be a geologist, but a general knowledge of the nature of the earth's crust may prove very useful to him in its relation to this question of material, and even more so in its bearing upon value; for it may assist him in forming an estimate of the materials —brick-earth, clay, sand, chalk, &c.—which are likely to occur beneath the surface of any estate.

To understand that it must be so, it is only necessary for him to call to mind the way in which the rocks or substances composing this crust have been formed, and how they have attained their present position. The term "stratum," which is applied to each layer of rock, means that it was "spread," the spreading process having been generally due to the action of water, which has deposited the rock as sediment, and subsequently by the upheaval of the earth's surface or otherwise left the deposit high and dry. This is at least the process by which a large portion of the rocks or substances known to us have been formed, although the operation has been assisted or modified by other agencies, such as heat, volcanic action, and subterranean chemical changes. For instance, there are rocks, like granite, in which we can now trace no process of stratification, the whole mass appearing to have been fused together by the combined effect of heat and pressure. There are others, such as the slates, as to which it seems that they were originally stratified rocks, but that their original texture was modified after they were deposited by the effect of subterranean heat. Stratification, however, or the existence of matter in layers, is one leading characteristic of the earth's crust. But, inasmuch as these layers, as due to the action of water, must have been originally deposited horizontally one above another, the existing form of the rocks upon the earth's surface (tipped and tilted as they are in all directions) has to be accounted for by the fact that they have at various times been subjected to an alteration of level by the action of subterranean heat, and disturbance by volcanic agency, whole masses of horizontal strata having been upheaved, and thus exposing their broken edges, just as a book might be tilted and display the edges of its leaves. If it were not for this process of upheaval, we should know nothing of the existence of those rocks which were primarily formed, for we never could have reached them by digging; consequently our knowledge of the nature of the earth's crust would have extended only to those few strata most recently deposited, such as gravel and similar alluvial deposits. But the changes that have taken place have so exposed to view the different kinds of rocks, that geologists, by observations at different places upon the earth's surface, have been able to write a complete history of the rocks and of the time and mode of their formation; and knowledge similarly obtained tells miners of the order in which the several rocks or substances occur, so that they are never working in the dark.

Having regard to these considerations it may be well to General remarks.

CHAP. VIII.
Repairs, &c.

indicate, as briefly as may be, the geological formation of these islands—just remarking that Great Britain and Ireland offer to our observation a wonderful epitome of geological phenomena.

The rocks of igneous formation which have been protruded through the earth's crust, and have been the means of upheaving and raising to various angles the stratified rocks above them, are the granite, greenstone, porphyry, &c. of Cornwall, the Channel Islands, and more extensively of Scotland, the sienite of the Malvern Hills, and Mount Sorrel, near Leicester, the serpentine of Cornwall, and the basalt of Scotland, the North of Ireland, and of the Rowley Hills near Birmingham, where it has burst through the rocks of the coal formation, and risen into a group of small conical hills. These few localities will furnish some of the most striking illustrations of this important fact.

But it is with the stratified rocks that we are most concerned; we will therefore endeavour to set them clearly before the reader in a tabular form before entering upon certain geological and practical remarks.

Tertiary Deposits.

English Crag, shelly, and sandy strata occupying the eastern part of Norfolk, Suffolk, and Essex, in which are the coprolite diggings.

London Clay, on which rest the Bagshot sands and clays. In England these consist chiefly of stiff blue clay, and cover the chalk from North Hants, by Reading and London, to the county of Norfolk, and compose what is called the "London basin." Another portion of these deposits covers the chalk of South Hants and the northern part of the Isle of Wight, and extends along the coast from near Dorchester to Brighton, and is called the "Hampshire basin."

The Plastic Clay and sand of Woolwich, Reading, &c., extend more widely from beneath the London clay, filling in deep excavations in the chalk, and partially overlying its surface. This is mostly a red clay.

Secondary Deposits.

The Chalk and Greensand together form the *Cretaceous System* or *Group*.
1. The Chalk is divided into—
  The Upper Chalk with flints.
  The Lower without flints.

The Gray Chalk and Chalk Marl.
These beds are almost entirely a pure carbonate of lime.
2. Upper Greensand.—Marly stone and sand with green particles—chloritic marl, and layers of green calcareous sandstone.
3. Gault.—Stiff blue clay, always separating the Upper from the Lower Greensand.
4. Lower Greensand, consists of grey, yellow, and green sands, red ferruginous sands, and sandstones (which latter predominate), silicious limestones, &c. The greensand beds follow the chalk of the North Downs, from near Alton to Folkestone, and that of the South Downs from the same point to Beachey Head. It also extends from Dorsetshire in a north-easterly direction into the north-east of Yorkshire with little interruption.

The Wealden Group of deposits consists of—
1. The Weald clay and
2. The Hastings sand, occupying the central parts of Kent, Surrey, and Sussex.
3. The Purbeck Beds.—Various limestones and marls of the Isle of Purbeck.

The Oolite Group—
1. Upper or Portland Oolite.—Coarse shelly, fine-grained, and compact limestones.
2. Kimmeridge Clay.—Blue and yellowish slaty clay, containing gypsum, and lignite, called Kimmeridge coal.
3. Middle Oolite, Coral Rag, or Coralline Oolite.—Shelly freestones, coarse limestone full of corals, yellow sands, &c. Oxfordshire, Berkshire, Calne and Steeple Ashton, Wilts, Somersetshire, and Yorkshire.
4. Oxford Clay.—Dark blue clay with septaria and gypsum. Somersetshire, and Dorsetshire into Yorkshire.

Lower Oolite, composed of the following beds, viz.—
5. Cornbrash.
6. Forest Marble.
7. Great or Bath Oolite.
8. Fuller's Earth. Near Bath, &c.
9. Inferior Oolite. Cotteswold Hills, Dundry Hill, near Bristol.

The Lias Group.
1. Blue Lias.—Shale and sandy marl stone, blue, white and yellow earthy limestone, in beds interstratified with clay. Dorsetshire, Somersetshire, Yorkshire, north of Ireland, &c.
2. Northamptonshire Sandstones.

New Red Sandstone, or variegated sandstone.
Red, white, blue, and green argillaceous sandstones—often micaceous, and containing gypsum and rock salt. Nottinghamshire, Yorkshire, &c., and extensively overlying the coal formation.

CHAP. VIII. *Magnesian Limestone.*
Repairs, &c.
1. Marl slate, variegated marls, yellow magnesia limestone, flexible sandstone. Nottinghamshire, north-east to Durham.
2. Red Conglomerate. Exeter.

The Carboniferous Group.
1. The Coal Formation, or Coal Measures.—Sandstones, conglomerates, clays, ironstone, shales, and limestones, interstratified with beds of coal. Centre and North of England, South Wales, and southern part of Scotland.
2. Mountain Limestone, or Carboniferous Limestone.—The upper part millstone grit, compact crystalline limestone. Devonshire, Mendip Hills, Derbyshire, extending north into Scotland, and widely developed in Ireland. It abounds in lead ore in North of England, and alternates with coal measures in Scotland.
3. Old Red Sandstone.—Coarse and fine silicious sandstones, and conglomerates of various colours—red predominating—extensive in Shropshire and Herefordshire, Devonshire, Brecknock, Dumfries, Forfar, and other localities in Scotland.

The Silurian Group of rocks present a great variety of argillaceous limestones, coralline and shelly limestone, sandy and argillaceous shales, micaceous sandstone, calcareous flags, &c. Many of the beds abound in fossils. These rocks occur in Shropshire, Herefordshire, Worcestershire, Gloucestershire, Radnor, Carmarthen, Denbighshire, &c.

Beneath these we come to the lowermost stratified rocks—viz., the clay slates of Wales and Cumberland, the slates, mica slates, and gneiss of Scotland,—the latter, largely developed in the Grampian range, are highly metamorphosed by the heat of the subjacent igneous rocks.

Now, with this general view of the strata as presented to us in our islands, we may clearly see the source of the wealth of material which is always within our reach for building and other economic purposes, and of the wealth derivable from the variety of soils produced by the decomposition and mixture of so many strata of varying chemical and mechanical characters.

We will now enter into some details respecting the nature and economic uses of some of the natural productions above enumerated, beginning with the lowermost, and working upwards.

Granite.

Granite consists of quartz, felspar, and mica, crystal-

lised together in the act of slowly cooling. When these CHAP. VIII.
substances are equally distributed, and form a fine-grained *Repairs, &c.*
granite it is best for dressing purposes.

We obtain our chief supply from Cornwall and Scotland; but the Channel Islands yield a great variety of fine-grained granites, many of them of delicate colours.

Sienite resembles granite, but its third ingredient is Sienite. hornblende instead of mica. The sienite of Mount Sorrell is much used in its district, at Leicester, for instance, both for building and paving.

There is a large class of igneous rocks grouped under the Trap rocks. term of Trap. They may be broadly stated to have been submarine land streams. In some places they occur in tabular masses or platforms at different heights, so as to form on the sides of hills a succession of terraces or *steps*, and thus called "trap" from "trappa," Swedish for a flight of steps. The chief of these rocks are those called basalt and greenstone. The former is of a black colour, hard and fine grained, but easily broken—some of it is coarser grained, or vesicular, like many more modern lavas. Basalt rocks often have a columnar structure, as is well seen in Fingal's Cave, Staffa, and the Giant's Causeway, and the basaltic cliffs of the North of Ireland.

Greenstone consists of hornblende and felspar, and is Greenstone. either crystallised like granite, distinctly exhibiting the two ingredients, or these are more intimately blended, when the stone is of a greener colour. Greenstone is a hard and durable rock, tougher, or more difficult to break, than granite. It is often used for kerb-stones, and much of it is conveyed great distances to be broken up for metaling roads; otherwise its use is for the most part confined to the districts in which it occurs.

The slate rock is called clay slate, in consequence of Slate. argillaceous earth, the base of all clays, entering largely into its composition. It is a stratified rock, but the lines indicating this fact are in a great measure obliterated by the action of heat. It derives its greatest value from the

P

CHAP. VIII.
Repairs, &c.

peculiarity of its structure admitting of its being cleaved into thin laminæ. The lines of cleavage do not correspond with those of stratification, but stand in regard to them at varying angles. The best slates are obtained from Carnarvonshire, but useful ones are found in Westmoreland and Ireland. The slabs are taken from the quarry, split with iron wedges, and trimmed with knives. Slates are cut to various sizes, and are distinguished by various names as Imperials, Duchesses, Rags, Queens, Countesses and others. They will of course be selected in accordance with the purposes for which they are required, and the cost may be estimated at from thirty to fifty shillings per square.

Passing from the igneous and primary to the ordinary stratified formations or secondary rocks, we must endeavour to generalise our remarks as much as possible, or we shall be led into a larger geological essay than would be suitable for the present work. To begin with sandstones.

Sandstone.

Sandstone consists of siliceous grains, or sand, naturally cemented together by a base of silex, argillaceous earth, carbonate of lime, or iron, and are thence called siliceous, argillaceous, calcareous, or ferruginous sandstones. From this circumstance and others affecting the quantity and nature of the base, they differ in character from a hard rock, to one which can be readily broken up in the hand. The sand is often destitute of base and has no cohesion.

Testing of sandstones.

It may be seen from this that the durability and other qualities of sandstone must vary considerably. Before using sandstone, the character of which is not well known, it may be tested by weighing a mass when dry, and again after immersion in water. If the weight is much increased by the absorption of water it cannot be considered a good material. The best sandstone known in use for building is that universally used in Edinburgh for architectural purposes. It is a fine white freestone belonging to the rocks of the coal formation, and is obtained from Craigleith quarry in the neighbourhood of the city. The common York paving stone also belongs to that formation, and also the hard Pennant sandstone of Gloucestershire and South Wales. Many other kinds are used, more or less locally, derived from the Silurians, old red sandstone—the new red, used much at Liverpool, the Hastings sand, the green sand, lower and upper—the latter largely quarried at Ventnor and Shanklin. Escaping from beneath the chalk surrounding the Weald of Hants, Sussex, and Kent, is a grey variety of sandstone called firestone, belonging to the upper green sand. It is soft and readily worked, but is very durable; so little affected by the weather, that in some old monastic buildings the tool marks can still be distinguished.

The limestone rocks perhaps possess more interest than any others, as they exhibit to us most remarkably the records of life in the early ages of the world. Some of them are almost entirely built up by the remains of corals, encrinites, and shells; indeed their very existence appears to have depended upon animal life. They are all a more or less pure carbonate of lime, and may be converted by heat into the state of quick or caustic lime for building and agricultural purposes.

These formations provide the building materials which will, more frequently than any other, come under the notice of the land steward. Under the present head we shall allude to them only as building stone, and shall consider them in their aspect of lime when we come to speak of mortar and cements.

From the Silurian group of formations, and the mountain limestone beds are obtained some of the most durable building stone, hard enough to make good roads. They yield also black and variously coloured marbles. Marble is the term applied to limestones which have been brought to a more or less crystalline state by the action of subterranean heat under pressure, and capable of taking a high polish. Even so soft a limestone as chalk may be seen in the north of Ireland in contact with basalt rendered quite hard and brittle, though not visibly crystallized. Many beautiful marbles of similar age to the above are obtained in Ireland.

CHAP. VIII.
Repairs, &c.

Some of them are perfectly black and contain shells and corals which are of a pure white; others are green, yellow, brown, dove-coloured, &c. It is a great pity these marbles are not brought more into use. All limestones consist of carbonate of lime; the various impurities they contain giving the various colours which we meet with amongst them.

Adhesive and absorbent powers of limestones.

The value of limestones used for building is determined by reference to their adhesive and absorbent powers. When required for buildings of importance the various kinds procurable should be thoroughly tested. This is done by immersion of small blocks in water to ascertain their absorbent power, as stated in speaking of sandstones, and also by determining the force necessary to crush blocks, say cubes of two inches. The action of frost we may presume must be greatest on the most absorbent specimens. But it would be, perhaps, impossible to determine the amount of chemical action exerted by the atmosphere. We get some illustration of this by contrasting the climatic influences of Egypt and London.

Freestone.

We would here allude to the term freestone. It appears to be usually applied to the softer limestones, but we are disposed to use it as a general technical term applicable to all building stones which are soft enough to be readily squared for use, and not as possessing any geological significance.

Dolomite or magnesian limestone.

Passing to the stratified rocks above the coal measures, we find the dolomite or magnesian limestone, between them and the new red sandstone. This formation yields a valuable building stone. Above the new red we have the argillaceous limestones, and the clays of the blue lias system which do not provide us with building materials of special or general importance.

Oolites.

The lias rocks are generally regarded as the base of the next great range of deposits—that of the oolites. These constitute an extensive series of strata, geologically most interesting and economically important. The term

REPAIRS, BUILDING, AND MATERIAL. 213

oolite, or stone-egg, is applied to the limestones of this series from their prevailing character, being, that they are made up by a multitude of minute spherical concretions resembling the roe of a fish—and sometimes called roe-stone. This peculiarity is strongly marked in some strata, but obscurely in others. Sometimes the concretions are so large that the stone is called pisolite or pea-stone. This formation occurs in England on a line extending from the Island of Portland to Whitby on the Yorkshire coast. CHAP. VIII.
Repairs, &c.

This whole series of limestones, with a few accompanying subordinate beds (see tabular view), are separated one from another by two principal intervening beds of clay, each several hundred feet thick. The entire group based upon the lias clays—the lower oolites are separated from the middle by the Oxford clay, and the middle from the upper by the Kimmeridge clay. The great or Bath oolite, and the upper or Portland oolite, as is well known, yield the finest freestones England produces—as pre-eminent amongst limestones, as the produce of the Craigleith quarry near Edinburgh is amongst sandstones.

Immediately above the Portland oolite commences the wealden formation, so called from one of its chief members occupying the Weald of Kent. It begins with the limestones and marls of Purbeck Island. The limestone is the well-known Purbeck stone, some of which, in its upper beds, is called Purbeck marble, and is full of small freshwater shells. The middle portion is the Hastings sand, consisting of soft yellow sandstone and beds of hard shelly limestone. The upper portion is the Weald Clay. This last contains beds of hard limestone, full of potamides —a species of freshwater mollusk. This substance called Sussex or Petworth marble and the Purbeck marble were both formerly much used—the former for monumental purposes, the latter in the construction of the small dark-coloured columns in clustered Gothic architecture. Wealden.

Petworth and Purbeck marbles.

Above the wealden commences the cretaceous system, consisting of the greensand and chalk formations. The

CHAP. VIII.
Repairs, &c.

Malm rock.

Chalk.

Flints.

former has been alluded to under the head of sandstones, but we may here remark further on the grey sandstone or fire stone, that with other marly and argillaceous beds it constitutes a peculiar development of the upper greensand in East Hants and Sussex, called the malm rock. It has no green bed except one of chloritic marl, from about five to ten feet thick, in contact with the chalk marl above it. Some of the upper beds consist of a hard blue argillaceous rock, combined with silex, but with little or no lime. It is a capital building stone, but not easily worked, and, besides for building walls, it is used for lining lime kilns, in which case it is often glazed by the melting of the silex. The grey sandstone beds are called fire stone, because it is used for hearth stones, and for flooring ovens. (See Gil. White's Natural History of Selborne; Letter 4. Bell's edition.)

With the Chalk we come to the end of the secondary strata. Like all other limestones, it is an almost pure carbonate of lime. It is of great extent, occupying a line of country from the Isle of Wight and the Dorsetshire coast to Flamborough Head, often rising into high sheep downs. A large portion of it is concealed by the tertiary beds of clay and sand of the London and Hampshire basins. It is more used for dressing land either burnt into lime or not, and for the manufacture of lime for building or agricultural purposes, than it is as a building stone. It is, however, employed to a small extent for building barns, stables, and other erections on a farm, care being taken to place the stone in the position it occupied in the pit, i.e., keeping the natural bedding planes in their original horizontal position. The bottom of the lower or grey chalk makes good hydraulic lime.

The flints of the upper chalk are used both for building and road making. When faced, they make a beautiful wall. The church at Westmeon, in Hampshire, is a very striking piece of flint work, being constructed entirely of faced and squared flints. But this work is very costly.

For ordinary erections they are used in the rough state, and form dry and pretty walls. Broken flint makes a better concrete than rounded gravel.

Chap. VIII. Repairs, &c.

The tertiary formations in England rest entirely on the chalk. They occupy two large areas called the London and the Hampshire basins. (See the tabular view.)

Tertiary formations.

The plastic clay and sand lie immediately on the chalk, and fill up deep pits and fissures in its surface. In Hampshire, and parts of other counties, this clay in the form of a red brick earth partially, and in varying depth, according to the inequalities of the surface it rests upon, overlies the chalk far beyond the limits of the London clay above. The clay is too sandy, and makes rather porous bricks.

The plastic clay and sand.

The London clay and the Bagshot beds above it are of great thickness. They yield brick earth and much of the septaria from which Roman cement is made. Cement stone is also dredged from the sea off Bognor and Harwich. The Bagshot Sands are beautifully exposed in the cliffs and chines of Bournemouth and Boscomb.

London clay and Bagshot beds. Septaria.

Above the tertiary beds already spoken of, we have, in the Isle of Wight, a number of others, extremely interesting to the geologist, consisting of marls, limestones, and clays, and presenting alternations of marine and freshwater deposits. Amongst these, almost the only building material is a freshwater limestone, not much used far from the localities where it is quarried. The best known quarry is at Binsted, near Ryde. It was, to some extent, employed in the erection of Chichester Cathedral, but it cannot be considered as a good building material. It consists of a mass of shell, not well cemented together by the calcareous matrix.

Freshwater limestone.

It may not be out of place to mention here that the siliceous French millstones are obtained from the tertiary strata of the Paris basin, and also the gypsum from which the plaster named plaster of Paris, from that circumstance, was originally made.

Gypsum.

All the formations above the chalk we have now spoken

CHAP. VIII.
Repairs, &c.

of are the eocene or older tertiaries. The miocene, less recent, or middle tertiaries are scarcely to be distinguished in this country. The pliocene, or more recent, are only represented in England by the crag. Finally the term pleistocene, newer pliocene, or most recent, embraces the superficial beds of gravel, clay, and sand, in which are found the bones and teeth of living species of terrestrial mammalia—depositions of lime still in operation, as the formation of Travertine (the building stone of Rome), the production of calcareous tufa as in Derbyshire, by the action of what are called petrifying springs, and the lining and filling up of caverns with stalactite—the growth of coral,—and the formations by recent volcanic action.

Quick or caustic lime.

After these general remarks on the building stones derived from the rock formations of this country, we will enter into a few practical details respecting methods employed for utilising some of these natural products chiefly in relation to those which are used for making mortar, bricks, and cements.

We may first observe that all limestones when burnt in kilns loose the water which they contain, and also one of their essential elements, namely, the carbonic acid. This changes the stone from a carbonate to the "quick" or caustic condition of pure lime or oxide of calcium. Some limestones, for instance, those of the lias formation, contain a proportion of argillaceous earth, and consequently produce lime all the more valuable in the manufacture of cements.

Cements.

Lime differs much in quality—those that increase in bulk on application of water are called "fat limes," those which do not are called "poor" or "meagre" limes. The former are most useful for mortar, the latter for cements.

Lime-burning kilns.

Lime is burnt in kilns, and when this is done on the estate the "flare" kiln is generally used. This class of kiln has the economical advantage of being adapted to the employment as fuel of wood, hedge trimmings, heath, or any combustible refuse.

Cost.

Lime is generally burnt by the "kiln," the price, of

course, depending on the size of the kiln—but, including the digging of the chalk, filling, and burning, it will run from 21s. CHAP. VIII. *Repairs, &c.*

The process of filling a flare-kiln requires considerable skill. A ledge of brickwork at the bottom of the wall of the kiln is arranged on which to build up a chalk dome. Upon this is thrown the whole mass of chalk, and below it is placed the fire. When burnt the lime is taken out from the furnace hole. Filling.

Well-burnt lime should come out very much in appearance as it goes in, but in the "quick" or caustic state. The object of course of the operation is to drive off by heat the carbonic acid and water, for lime in the form of a carbonate is useless for mortar. When burnt it becomes, as before observed, an oxide of calcium which has a powerful affinity for water. When water is added to it it becomes a hydrate of lime, and great heat is evolved by so much of the water entering the solid state and parting with its caloric of fluidity. Whilst the lime is hot from the process of slacking a certain proportion of sand is mixed with it and a silicate of lime is formed. The particles of sand act as nuclei around which the carbonate and silicate of lime can crystalize. Object of burning.

Use of sand in mortar.

It is, however, better to purchase lime for mortar; and not too much at once, for if kept long it becomes "dead," *i.e.*, slacked by the slow absorption of water from the atmosphere. If any quantity, however, is kept, it must, to secure its properties, be well covered with sods. It should never be kept in wooden sheds, or near straw, as, if it becomes damp, great heat is generated, and there is consequently danger of fire. Keeping of lime.

The sand used for making mortar must be either pit or river sand. Sea sand contains salt which renders it unfit for mortar. A mixture of coarse and fine sand is better than sand of an equal degree of fineness. Sand.

The chalk formation contains "bags" of sand of the plastic clay formation; but as a rule this sand is so mixed

CHAP. VIII.
Repairs, &c.

with loam and clay as to render it unfit for anything but rough work. Sand in itself is not an expensive substance, but it is heavy, and the carriage is both costly and damaging to tackle.

Large beds are found in many formations, often red and white lying close together. The lower green sand formation contains a large quantity of both coarse and fine.

Mortar.

Consists of two and a half of sand to one of lime. The lime must be fresh.

A circle of sand is formed and the lumps of lime placed within, these are then slacked and all is worked up together.

Cements.

As already stated, limes are classed as "fat" and "poor," and it is the latter only that, when mixed with silica, alumina, and magnesia, have the power of hardening under water. These are called hydraulic mortars or cements.

There are many kinds of cement—Smeaton's as used at the Eddystone Lighthouse, was composed of equal parts of Aberthaw or lias lime in the state of hydrate in fine powder and pozzuolana, also in powder, well beaten together. Pozzuolana is a vulcanite concrete thrown up from Vesuvius; named from the town where it was discovered. An artificial pozzuolana is prepared by burning clay. The facing of the London Docks was cemented with the following mixture, viz.: four parts of lias lime, six of river sand, one of calcined limestone, and one of pozzuolana.

A good cement may be formed by adding two and a half parts of burnt clay to one of blue lias lime, thoroughly pulverised and mixed.

Roman cement.

This celebrated cement, the use of which has been to a great extent superseded by others, is made by burning spheroidal masses called septaria. They consist of lime and clay, with a small percentage of iron, and are found in the London and Bagshot clays, in the lias clays, and some others. Much of it is dredged off the coast at Bognor and Harwich, where the London clay passes under the sea.

Plaster of Paris is made from gypsum, which is a sulphate of lime. This beautiful mineral is baked with sufficient heat to expel its water of crystallisation, which treatment renders it opaque. It is then ground to a fine powder. It is a cement which hardens rapidly, so as to render it necessary to mix it for use in very small quantities at a time. It is only fitted, however, for stucco work, as if exposed it absorbs moisture and cracks. It is used for the erection of marble mantel-pieces, cornice work, and mouldings. A cement for filling in cracks in iron boilers is made by mixing iron filings with clay and oil.

Chap. VIII. Repairs, &c.

Plaster of Paris.

Portland cement is the most common now in use. It is manufactured in several parts of England, but chiefly on the banks of the Thames and Medway. It is made principally from the river mud. The ingredients are about two and a half parts of mud to one part of chalk, obtained from the same geological formation. The ingredients are brought to a finely pulverised state by passing through rollers and with water, and are then allowed to deposit, after which they are dessicated and burnt, and immediately placed in wooden casks and fastened down, when they are ready for use.

Portland cement.

Concretes are principally used in foundations, but may be also used for walls. When this is the case, however, the tops must be well protected by coping, or the wet will penetrate, and when frosts set in the wall will crumble away by expansion. Concrete is composed of lime finely pulverised (not slacked), gravel, or broken stones, and sand. Broken flints or other stones are better than rounded gravel. The materials must be mixed near the spot where they are to be used, and mixed quickly, as they rapidly set. The proportion of the materials differ, but five parts of stone and sand to one of lime is often used. The sand and lime (or cement if used) must be first thoroughly mixed, and then mixed well with the stones whilst dry. A little water is then added, and the whole worked up with shovels into the consistency of mortar, and then quickly applied. The

Concretes.

CHAP. VIII.
Repairs, &c.

Bricks.

mass, when first mixed, decreases in bulk, but it rapidly increases, or swells, and this to a marked degree. Concrete is valuable as a foundation on account of damp being unable to rise through it; a damp course of slates, nevertheless, above the ground line is very advisable. Where slates, however, are not at hand, a coat of tar over the concrete will be found useful.

Whenever bricks can be made upon the estate a great saving is effected. No matter what stone or other building material is procurable, bricks, to some extent, are indispensable. Brick-earth is not, however, to be found upon every estate; when found, therefore, it considerably enhances the capital and rental value.

The best brick-earth is that consisting of pure clay and sharp sand, free from stones. When clay preponderates sand must be added, and when the clay is too tenacious some of the top soil may be added, but this makes an inferior brick.

To find brick-earth, an auger will be found very useful, as the use of it saves a great deal of heavy digging. It consists of a square iron bar, about ten feet long, and about one inch square, the end is fitted with a shell auger, and a movable handle is attached to it. A hole should be made with a common crowbar, about six inches deep, and filled with water. The auger is then inserted and worked by two men; it must be lifted about every two feet (more or less, according to circumstances), and the point of the auger cleared, and a little water poured into the bore. When a good earth is found, it must not be at once concluded that a "head" has been discovered, as the over-lying clay beds are most eccentric in their course, especially in the chalk formation. More holes must be bored all round at various distances; by this means the extent and direction of the deposit may be correctly ascertained. Satisfactory results having been obtained we may set to work to open a heading and prepare our brick field.

The clay should be dug in autumn or winter, and when this is completed, the necessary buildings must be erected.

Very little preparation of this kind, however, is required; a rough shed for each moulder, a more permanent shed for keeping sand, tools, &c., in, and in which plinth and coping bricks can be laid out to dry; some T sheds, with prepared floor for drying the bricks, and a pug-mill and kiln. *Chap. VIII. Repairs, &c.*

The bricks necessary for the erection of the kiln, say about 30,000, can be burnt in the hole from which the clay has been dug.

Each moulder's shed must be fitted with a bench, upon which he places his mould and box for supply of water. His tools consist of strike, brush, scraper, and clay scoop or shovel, wheelbarrow, and boards for the bricks. *Brickmaker's tools.*

These sheds must be erected near the heap of clay, and in close proximity to the pug-mill. This consists of a vertical iron shaft fitted with blades, the bottom ones being set at such an angle as to squeeze out the clay. This is cased in a wooden cylinder, open at the top, and open on one side at the bottom. The shaft is worked by a horizontal arm, to which a horse is attached. The moulder wheels the clay, which has been previously wetted, to the cylinder, and tips it in, the horse walking round the while, so that the knives or blades inside work up the clay, which when it reaches the bottom is pressed out by the aforesaid blades, and is carried away by another moulder to each shed. This process is called "pugging," and must be done every morning; the quantity required will depend upon the number of moulders and the number of bricks they are each able to make in the day. A good moulder will make from 800 to 900 in the day. When there is no pug-mill (and its use is by no means general) each moulder is expected to temper his own clay before beginning work. This is, however, rather a tedious process. It is worked up with water, like mixing mortar. *Pug-mill.*

Each shed is supplied with a quantity of moulding sand, which must be what is called "silver sand." It must be perfectly dry. With this the moulder sprinkles his mould and plate each time he makes a brick—this is to prevent the *Moulding sand.*

CHAP. VIII.
Repairs, &c.

clay adhering to the wood. He places each brick upon a board and then upon his barrow, and when this is full he wheels it away to the T shed, where he places the bricks in rows, each brick on edge, the next row being placed upon the other alternately. These rows are called "hacks." Here they are left to dry for three or four weeks according to the state of the weather. The bottoms of the hacks require attention. They must be placed on a raised platform so that water may not rest upon them; when it does it will become absorbed by the brick, and the lower tiers giving way will overthrow the whole, and cause loss. Drain-pipes, 3in. in diameter, laid side by side, make a very good bottom.

The kiln generally used upon estates is the kind termed "flare kiln" and is constructed for burning wood. Two advantages are gained by making bricks upon the estate; a brick is produced at cost price, and a home market is procured for rough bavins and timber. A useful-sized kiln is one that will hold 15,000 to 20,000 bricks. As a rule, 1000 bricks will require for drying and burning 100 bavins.

These kilns are usually square, they must be built very strong, and be backed up with earth, and bound round the top with wood and iron, as the expansion caused by the heat is very great. It is best to cover it with an iron roof to keep out wet; there must, however, be plenty of room for the passage of the fumes. The bricks are put in behind, and when completed the door must be closed with bricks and rammed with sand, as, if not air-tight, the bricks are injured.

' The filling of a kiln requires a great amount of practice and cannot be described in a work of this nature. They must however be so placed that a free circulation of heat passes through them, and each one bind the other to prevent warping.

The first process is to dry the bricks with a gentle fire, which will occupy about two days; when this is done, a full fire is put on and they are "burnt;" when once this is commenced the fire must be kept up night and day without ceasing until the operation is completed. When cold, they are removed and piled up for use. *Chap. VIII. Repairs, &c.*

Bricks are made by the thousand. The price of making may be said to range from 13s. to 16s., and includes digging the clay, moulding and burning. The chief moulder finds all labour. *Cost of making bricks.*

White bricks are made by mixing lime with the clay. The lime is mixed in large reservoirs and let in to the clay during the process of tempering.

When bricks are burnt with coal, the kiln is called a "draught kiln." About 3cwt. of coal are required to burn 1000 bricks. *Draught-kiln.*

The bricks known as "stock-bricks" are burnt in the "clamp," *i.e.*, a pile, so erected as to admit of a draught throughout. When this plan is resorted to, it is necessary to mix crushed breeze with the clay. The breeze is laid about six inches in depth upon the top of the undug clay, and with each spit that is taken off the breeze forms a part, all is then mixed and tempered together. When a sufficient number of bricks are got together the fire is started beneath with small coal and cinder, and this igniting the breeze contained in the brick soon sets the whole mass aglow, the fire is carried on by the draught, so that as long as fresh bricks are applied at the far end, away from the fire, the burning will continue; and in about three weeks those first burnt may be removed, whilst the rest are still burning. The breeze however burns out and renders the bricks very porous. Another danger is the running of the silica in the clay by the great heat; when this is the case the bricks become massed together, and are valueless. It is difficult altogether to prevent this calamity. It is caused by the fusion of the silica and alumina. Clamp bricks are not so valuable as others, being about 6s. to 8s. per thousand less. The outside of the clamp must be plastered with clay to prevent escape of heat laterally. *The clamp.*

A good brick should give a clear ringing sound when

Chap. VIII.
Repairs, &c.

struck, and be dark in colour outside, and a rich red when broken, and be free from grit.

The size of a brick is 9in. by 4½in. by 2½in.

Some clays shrink more than others. When this is the case the mould must be rather larger than common. It is necessary to maintain a regularity in the size, in order that they may work well together.

The first-burned bricks are often light in colour and soft, this is owing to the damp in the kiln from its exposed position through the winter. They are used for inside work.

Tiles.

Clay suitable for brick-making is not adapted to tile-making, and *vice versa*. For tiles the clay must be "strong" and tenacious. The process of tempering is also important, and will require different treatment to that already explained. Reservoirs or basins must be formed on the ground with clay, about one foot to one and a half feet deep. In these the clay must be placed, and allowed to soak for some time in water, it must then be hand tempered.

If any stones are present they must be either extracted or crushed, as if allowed to remain, the heat will burst them, causing a flaw or breakage in the tile.

They are moulded in a similar to way bricks; before being taken off the moulding-plate two holes are pierced through them to receive the pegs, they are then laid to dry like bricks, only they lie flat in lots of three or four, tier upon tier.

They require great care in packing into the kiln, as if improperly done they will twist and warp. The heat too must be uniform throughout. A good tile clay will, when lifted off the mould-plate, remain stiff in the hand; a clay fit for bricks only, will under the same circumstances, fold up in the hand like paper.

For further information upon materials we may refer the reader to, amongst other useful works now in circulation, the "Book of Farm Implements," by Slight and Burns.

The various measurements required in this department will be found in the next chapter.

CHAPTER IX.
REPAIRS, BUILDING, AND MATERIAL
(*Continued*).

RULES FOR ESTIMATING AREAS AND CAPACITIES.
AREA OF BARGE ROOF, HIPPED ROOF, CIRCULAR ROOF—AREA OF BRICKWORK—CAPACITIES OF TANKS—EXAMPLES.

It will be useful to supplement the observations contained in the last chapter, by stating the rules of most frequent application for determining the quantity of material, and consequently the cost involved in effecting new roofing and some other equally common operations.

TO ASCERTAIN SURFACE OF THATCHING, TILING, AND BRICKWORK.

The usual practice is to reckon the two former by the *square* of 100 square feet, and the latter by the *rod* of 272 square feet. Thatching, tiling, and slating are all contracted for by the square, and brickwork by the rod; and, if not contracted for in the real sense of the word, the estimates are based upon such calculations.

1. To find the surface of a common *barge* roof (a roof in the form of a partially-opened book)—

Take the length and breadth in feet, and multiply together: this gives the surface of one side. Multiply by 2, and divide the product by 100, which will give the number of squares contained.

2. To find the surface of a *hipped* roof (a roof in the form of a partially-opened book, but with the topmost corners

CHAP. IX.
Repairs, &c.

sliced off, so that a further triangular roof is needed at the ends)—

Take the mean length and multiply by the breadth: this will give the surface of one side. Then take the length of the end, multiply by the length of the perpendicular distance, from the eave of the end to the ridge, and divide by 2 (see rule of "Triangles"): this will give the surface of the end. Add the two products together, multiply by 2, and divide by 100, and we have the area required.

3. To find the surface of a *circular* roof. We may first show, by way of explanation, that the roof will represent half a circle, of which the radius, or half diameter, will equal the height from eave to ridge, and the circumference twice the circumference of the roof. To show this—take a piece of paper, cut out a half circle; if the two halves of the diameter are brought together a cone is formed, the circumference of which equals the arc of the semicircle, and the sloped height its radius. Hence we get this rule—

Take the length round the eaves, or the distance from eave to point: either will form a sufficient basis for calculation. Then, proceeding under rules for "Circles" we have the distance from eave to point = radius of semicircle and circumference of roof = arc of semicircle, then the radius × ½ circumference, gives the area of the circle, and half of this will be the area of the roof.

N.B.—The distance from eave to point × 2 × 3·1416 (or 3⅐) = circumference of a circle, whose area will be twice the area of the roof.

4. To find the area of *brick-work*—

Take the length and breadth in feet, multiply together, and divide by 272, and we get the area in rods. A rod of brick-work, however, is always calculated to be 14 inches thick (or the breadth of three bricks laid side by side with their accompanying mortar); therefore, supposing the wall measured only 9 inches thick, proceed as follows: Multiply the area by 2, and divide by 3, and we have the area in rods, 14 inches thick; or, if 4½ inches thick, divide by 3.

5. To ascertain the capacity of tanks. Measurements must be taken as follows—

For oblong or square tanks take length, breadth, and depth. For circular take depth and diameter. Then proceed, according to rule, and multiply the sum obtained, which will be in cubic feet and fractions of a foot, by 6, the number of gallons in a cubic foot, and we have the required contents in gallons.

REPAIRS, BUILDING, AND MATERIAL. 227

1. Example of measurement of *barge* roof—
A roof measures $20\frac{1}{4}$ feet in length by $9\frac{1}{4}$ feet in width; required the number of squares.

By fractions—
$20\frac{1}{4} \times 9\frac{1}{4} = \frac{81}{4} \times \frac{37}{4} = \frac{2997}{16} = 189\frac{5}{8}$; $189\frac{5}{8}$ reduced to decimals = 189·625. Then 189·625 × 2 = 379·25 feet, which represents superficial area of the two sides of the roof, which divided by 100 = $3\frac{3}{4}$ squares.

2. Example of *hipped* roof—
A roof measures 25 feet in length at the eaves, 18 feet at the ridge, 12 feet from ridge to eave, and the end measures 16 feet in length at the eaves, with a perpendicular of 10 feet; required the number of squares.

By fractions—
25 + 18 = 43; 43 ÷ 2 = $21\frac{1}{2}$ mean length; $21\frac{1}{2}$ × 12 = 258 superficial feet: area of one side.

Next we have the end (see " Triangles ")—
  16 × 10 ÷ 2 = 80 feet: area of one end;
then—
80 + 258 = 338 × 2 = 676, area of whole roof; 676 ÷ 100 = 6.76 squares, or $6\frac{3}{4}$—*answer required.*

3. Example of *circular* roof—
Required the number of squares of thatch on a wheat rick measuring 20 feet from eave to point (see " Circles "):
20 feet represents the radius; therefore twice that distance, or 40 feet, equals diameter: 40 feet × 3·1416 (or $3\frac{1}{7}$) = 125 = circumference.
Half the diameter × half the circumference equals the area of the circle; therefore 20 × 62·5 = 1250, which is the area of the circle or double the area of the roof;
then—
  1250 ÷ 2 = 625, or $6\frac{1}{4}$, or 6 squares of thatch.

4. Examples of brick-work—
A brick wall 70 feet long by 12 feet high and 14 inches thick; required the number of rods:
  70 × 12 = 840; 840 ÷ 272 = $3\frac{8}{34}$ rods.
The same 9 inches thick; required the number of rods:
  840 × 2 = 1680; 1680 ÷ 3 = 560; 560 ÷ 272 = $2\frac{1}{17}$ rods.
The same $4\frac{1}{2}$ inches thick; required the area:
  840 ÷ 3 = 280; 280 ÷ 272 = $1\frac{3}{34}$ rods.

CHAP. IX.
Repairs, &c.

Examples of capacity of tanks—

An oblong tank measures 20 feet long, 10 feet wide, and 9 feet deep; what does it contain?

$20 \times 10 \times 9 \times 6 =$ contents in gallons.

$$\begin{array}{r} 20 \\ 10 \\ \hline 200 \\ 9 \\ \hline 1800 \\ 6 \\ \hline \end{array}$$

Answer 10,800 gallons—the contents required.

A circular tank measures 15 feet in depth, and has a diameter of 9 feet; what does it contain?

Take either of the rules given and ascertain the area of the bottom. By rule 1, for instance:

$9 \times 3\cdot1416 = 28\cdot2744 =$ circumference;

therefore—

$28\cdot2744 \times 9 \div 4 =$ area.

$$\begin{array}{r} 28\cdot2744 \\ 9 \\ \hline 4\overline{)254\cdot4696} \\ \hline 63\cdot6174 \text{ feet} = \text{area of bottom.} \end{array}$$

Multiply this by the depth, viz. 15, and we have 954 cubic feet as contents, which multiplied by 6 gives 5724 gallons—*the answer required.*

CHAPTER X.
BLIGHTS OF WHEAT AND OTHER CEREALS.

VIBRIO TRITICI ("BURNT CORN" OR "EARCOCKLES")—CECIDOMYIA TRITICI ("WHEAT MIDGE") — UREDO SEGETUM ("BLACK HEAD")—UREDO CARIES ("SMUT")—UREDO RUBIGO ("RED GUM")—PUCCINIA GRAMINIS ("MILDEW")—SECALE CORNUTUM ("ERGOT OF RYE").

WE propose to treat this subject rather from a practical than a scientific point of view. It must in some form present tself to the valuer when settling values upon growing corn, as there are few crops of cereals that are not more or less affected by some of the following blights; and it is in its effect upon value that it is for us most important and that some knowledge of the subject is necessary.

When valuing we have examined superficially crops of wheat, and set a quantity upon them, but on a more minute examination we have found blights of various kinds, to such an extent as to materially affect the award.

The following are some of the most common blights:

The *Vibrio Tritici*, or wheat eel, is one of the infusoria causing the disease known in some districts as "burnt corn" or "ear cockles."

It is an animal blight. The minute eggs are introduced into the sap from the infected grains and hatch in the germen or seed-bud.

CHAP. X.
Blights of
Wheat, &c.

The worms are transparent when young, but become yellowish as they grow older. They attain one quarter of an inch in length. They possess wonderful vitality; if the infected seed is kept dried for a year, the worms will be found alive when put in water and examined by the microscope.

An ear of wheat infected with this pest presents a somewhat peculiar appearance. The glumes or husks are bleared and blackened near the stalk, and the grains are deformed, being puckered at the bottom and flattened at the top, and when ripe are of a dark brown colour, approaching black. If broken open, the inside will be found full of a white substance like cotton; these are the eels.

This is often a great source of loss, as the infected ears are not only lost to the crop, but the whole sample is deteriorated in value by their presence.

The best method of eradicating it is to place the seed in water before sowing, and skim off the infected grains, which will float to the top.

Cecidomyia Tritici ("Wheat-midge").

Oecidomyia, a genus of gnats, attacks both barley and wheat. It seldom however attacks the former in this country. The most important is the *Oecidomyia Tritici*. The British wheat midge is a species that causes great loss in some seasons. The eggs are conveyed into the culms whilst the wheat is in flower, and when they hatch, the little lemon-coloured larvæ abstract the juices, and cause the grain to shrivel. When fully grown they enter the earth and become pupæ, and finally develope into the perfect insect.

We now come to the vegetable blights or fungi, a large class of parasites, called "Uredineæ." They are the lowest order of plants and are called "Cellular" or "one-celled."

Uredo Segetum ("Black-head").

Uredo Segetum, or "Blackhead," is one of these and attacks all the cereals. The attack, however, takes place early, before the ear leaves the sheath. About June the attack is most visible, in some seasons giving quite a black appearance to the crop. It consists of a black powder, and when fully ripe, is dispersed by the wind, and nothing is left but the bare culm.

The damage consists in the loss of the ear, the remaining rs being unaffected.

Uredo Caries, "Smut" or "Bunt," is the most to be dreaded. It is to eradicate this that we pickle our seed-corn.

It is more readily propagated than any other of the Uredines. The spores (seed) are of an oily nature and adhere closely to the grains. The blue-stone or vitriol destroys the vitality of these, hence its use.

An ear infected with this pest presents a diseased appearance. The grains are transformed into a kind of black ball; when these are broken they present a mass of brown powder, which emits a most fetid odour. These are the spores, and will adhere closely to every grain with which they come in contact. The injury caused is sometimes very great, as the fetid smell is transmitted to the whole sample.

Uredo Rubigo, or "Redgum," affects the young wheat plants. Its attacks are most visible in April, when the young roots are beginning to spread after the long winter. Its ravages are most marked upon undrained and badly-cultivated lands. It attacks the leaf in lines, and when fully developed gives off a red or yellow powder like brick-dust.

Puccinia Graminis, "Mildew" or "Mould," is a kind of blight closely allied to the uredines. Few plants ercape the ravages of mildew in some form, but the "wheat mildew" differs greatly from the other varieties in structure. A parasitic fungus is developed beneath the surface of the straw from a branched mycelium or root, and makes its way through the cuticle in the form of black sori. Though rare

CHAP. X.
Blights of
Wheat, &c.

in other cereals, it is always present in wheat and many of our grasses, but it becomes injurious only under certain atmospheric influences. Heavy and flaggy crops are most liable to attack on account of the stagnation from want of a full circulation of air.

This blight attacks the straw, the grain only indirectly, through the injury to the straw and leaf. When very bad, the grain shrivels, and the straw becomes comparatively useless. In 1850 great damage was done; in some cases fully half the crop being lost.

We have no remedy, but to attend to the growth of the crop. If anything happens to check or hinder growth, or to otherwise affect the health of the plant, it is very liable to this attack. The fungus acts as Nature's scavenger, for when disease takes place the decaying vegetable matter, but for this, would yield a most offensive odour.

It is a matter of dispute amongst botanists whether th blight found upon the barberry has anything to do with this blight of wheat. Some affirm that the two are different in character, others that they are identical; the followin extract therefore from a local paper may be interesting:

"*The Barberry and Smut.*—Wm. Carruthers, F.R.S., consulting botanist to the Royal Agricultural Society, writing to the *Mark Lane Express* says: 'The intelligent account of the parasitic fungi found on the barberry and on our cereals, given by your correspondent in a recent issue, is in accordance with the views accepted by botanists until quite lately. See *Treasury of Botany*, new edition, 1876, page 22. But your correspondent is unaware of the very remarkable observations and discoveries made by Professor De Bary in relation to these parasites, which completely confirm the widespread opinion of farmers that the presence of the barberry had somehow to do with the production of the disease in wheat. The important results of the researches carried on in Professor De Bary's laboratory have disclosed a wonderful life history of this fungus, which

I will try to place before your readers in a few sentences, without the unnecessary use of technical or scientific terms. The black spots of the parasite which appear on the straw and leaves of grasses during the autumn and persist on the plants through the winter consist of spores, as the "seeds" of fungi and such plants are called. The spores retain their vitality and are ready for germination in the spring. When they fall on the leaves of the barberry they push out a little root (*mycelium*), which has the power of penetrating the skin of the leaf and reaching its interior. Having secured its position it rapidly grows and soon produces the fruit which bursts through the skin and forms the little rounded cups so well known on the barberry leaf. The minute spores of the barberry fungus do not grow unless they fall on the leaf or stem of wheat or other grass plant. When thus placed and provided with suitable moisture they push out their slender mycelium root. This finds its way through one of the minute stomates or breathing pores into the interior of the leaf or stem. Here the mycelium grows, and within a week or so produces spores which germinate freely throughout the summer on leaves and stems of cereals and grasses, until in the autumn their life terminates in the production of the kind of spore with which we began, which are able to endure through the winter and to reproduce the parasites in the following year to pass again through its remarkable "alternation of generations." For the important discovery and elucidation of the life history of this farmers' pest we are entirely indebted to De Bary. His labours are well known to students of botany, and your readers may remember that under the auspices of the Royal Agricultural Society he has been prosecuting investigations into the life history of the potato fungus, which still requires elucidation. It need scarcely be pointed out, as a practical result of these discoveries, that the farmer must look carefully after the barberry, and avoid as much as possible its growth.'"

Finally we have the fungus known as

CHAP. X.
Blights of
Wheat, &c.

Secale
Cornutum
("Ergot of
rye").

Secale Cornutum, "Ergot of Rye," which it is only necessary to mention, as it will seldom come practically under the notice of the valuer. It will in fact come more often under the notice of the bailiff. It seldom attacks cereals, except rye, and this is a crop little grown in this country. It, however, attacks the grasses, especially the rye-grass, to such an extent in some seasons as to render it a matter of importance. This importance is on account of its possessing the power of causing abortion. There is no doubt that much more loss is sustained through this than is supposed. Long grass under hedgerows and in damp low bottoms is particularly liable to this attack in autumn, and though cattle will not from choice eat these dry culms, much will be consumed accidentally; much of the fungus, too, that has fallen will be taken up from the sward upon which it falls.

The appearance of the fungus is a long black horn, growing from the grain, something similar to a cock's spur. The length varies, but may be from one-eighth of an inch to one inch.

Where very prevalent, the grass should be cut and burned. It is, however, a good plan, whether this fungus is present or not, to cut all long grass about the month of August or September under hedges and other places.

CHAPTER XI.
ACCOUNTS.

SECTION I.
FARM ACCOUNTS.

ACCOUNTS KEPT BY BAILIFF—JOURNAL—CASH BOOK—LABOUR BOOK—INSPECTION BY STEWARD—STEWARD'S LEDGER—FARM BALANCE SHEET.

ALTHOUGH an ordinary knowledge of book-keeping will enable the steward to frame his own system of accounts, or to adapt himself to that approved by his principal, it will be useful to the pupil to have the matter explained by reference to some system, and we accordingly lay before him an outline of the one which we have found useful and sufficient in practice.

The books supplied to the bailiff consist of Journal or Day-book, Cash-book, and Labour-book. In the Journal he enters the amount of farm produce sold to the house and to the various departments upon the estate; being those transactions in which no money passes. Also amount of corn, hay, or other fodder supplied to farm horses, cows, sheep, &c., corn sown, corn threshed, casualties, and any other item of intelligence which it is deemed important to chronicle.

The Cash-book is a simple debtor and creditor account-book, in which are entered all cash transactions; money received for cattle, sheep, corn, or other produce, and money paid for labour, food, manure, and other outgoings.

ESTATE MANAGEMENT.

Chap. XI.
Sect. 1.
Farm Accounts.

Labour-book.

The Labour-book is ruled in columns, the first column to contain the name of the labourer, the next twelve columns for the working days of the fortnight, and one for rate of pay, concluding with columns for money total and observations.

The register of labour is kept by making a stroke with a pen every night against each man's name, if he has been at work on the farm that day. It is made up at the end of the fortnight, and when paid, the total is carried to the expenditure side of the cash-book.

When taskwork is resorted to, a separate book may be kept ruled as follows: column for name of labourer, nature of task, cost per acre or piece, acreage, amount drawn, balance due, and total payment, with a space for observations.

Inspection of books by steward.

At certain fixed periods, say monthly or quarterly, these books are forwarded to the steward for inspection and posting. At the same time all vouchers relating to the farm are given in; these, however, are not numerous in farm transactions.

Examination and posting of farm-books.

When given in, the steward examines each book thoroughly, correcting the totals, carrying out and checking the calculations, and otherwise submitting them to close scrutiny.

Steward's farm-ledger.

This being done, the steward will proceed to post each book in his ledger. There are but few debtor and creditor accounts necessary in farm transactions, as most are conducted upon purely cash principles. The ledger is therefore used more as a book in which to summarise the various transactions. The various ledger headings may be somewhat as follows: Wheat sold, wheat bought, barley or other corn sold or bought, cattle or other live stock bought or sold, purchased foods, manures, incidental expenses, labour, rates and taxes, and any other which may from time to time seem necessary.

Each item then from the foregoing books is duly carried to its respective headings, and ticked off. The books are then signed by the steward and returned to the bailiff. If any entry is incorrect, or in the event of any omissions, notes must be made, with references to the page upon which they occur, and corrections or explanations be required.

At the end of the financial year, the ledger will thus contain all the necessary materials to form a balance-sheet, except of course the valuations which have been already explained both in the chapter relating to "Valuations" and in that upon the "Home Farm."

The valuation then having been made, the method of arriving at the "balance" is as follows: The expenses of the farm are taken from the ledger and placed in order on the debtor or left-hand side of the sheet, the receipts then are taken and placed upon the creditor or right-hand side of the sheet. Upon the debtor side, and generally as the first entry, is placed the total amount of the valuation of stock of the previous year, because for the purpose of the account the farmer is for the time being to be treated as an incoming tenant and as having purchased this stock. On the creditor side, as the last entry is placed the total amount of valuation of stock of the year in question, the farmer being in this case an outgoing tenant, the amount representing the sum which he supposes he would receive if immediately sold.

These two columns, then cast up, will show by abstracting one from the other, the balance for the year; whether a "profit" or a "loss" will depend of course upon which column is in excess of the other.

It must be borne in mind that all transactions relating to the consumption or use of home-grown produce should be entered upon both sides of the balance-sheet; for, if the farm uses corn which has been grown upon the farm, the farm is to be treated as having sold it on the one hand and bought it on the other; otherwise the balance sheet will not fairly represent the year's transactions.

Another important matter is the charging of interest (generally 5 per cent.) upon the capital employed, *i.e.*, the amount of the valuation of the preceding year. It is clear that, before a correct result can be arrived at, the interest which

CHAP. XI.
Sect. 1.
Farm
Accounts.

could be obtained by simple investment, or which a farmer would have to pay if he borrowed his capital, ought to be deducted before striking the balance. The result then shows the profit or loss obtained purely by agricultural pursuits.

We may conclude the subject of farm accounts by giving an example of a balance-sheet.

Dr.	1875. £ s. d.			Cr.	1876. £ s. d.		
To Valuation of Live and Dead Farming Stock and Tillages, March 25th, 1875	4236	0	0	By Cattle sold	717	3	10
				Sheep ,,	507	0	0
				Pigs ,,	105	0	0
Sheep purchased	293	0	0	Poultry	6	0	0
Rams ,,	30	15	0	Wool	166	15	0
Pigs ,,	32	6	0	Wheat ,,	457	2	6
Seeds ,,	125	4	3	Sundry receipts	14	1	8
Seed Wheat purchased	21	0	0	Hops	228	15	7
Manures purchased	181	5	0	Food grown and consumed (Hay and Corn) as per contra	687	0	9
Food grown and consumed (Hay & Corn)	687	0	9	Seed grown and used as per contra	103	6	0
Seed grown and used on Farm	103	6	0	HOUSE ACCOUNT.			
Oil and Cotton Cake, Wheat, Meal, &c., purchased	236	10	4	Dairy Account	111	8	7
				Sheep	195	13	3
				Bullocks	18	0	0
Blacksmith's and Foundry accounts	79	12	0	Pigs	92	7	6
Coal	8	0	0	PRIVATE STABLE ACCOUNT.			
Implements	11	0	0	Hay & Straw	237	10	0
Beer for Harvest and Hay-time	26	6	0	Oats & Bean	145	10	0
Harness Account	19	8	2	KEEPER'S ACCOUNT.			
Incidental Expenses, including Auction Expenses and carriage of Cattle	55	14	4	Barley, Wheat, &c.	106	4	0
				Straw sold, Keepers and Garden	15	0	0
Rates and Taxes	120	1	7	Corn for Poultry on outlying Farm	6	2	0
Tithe Rent Charge	200	0	0				
Bailiff's Wages	65	0	0	Hire of Farm Horses for House and Estate work	198	0	0
Labour	705	9	8				
Underwood	13	19	1	Valuation of Live and Dead Farming Stock and Tillages, March 25, 1876	4469	9	6
HOP EXPENDITURE.							
Labour 40 0 0							
Picking . 37 10 0							
Manure ... 16 0 0							
Sundries . 23 5 3	116	15	3				
Rent	500	0	0				
Interest charged on capital, 5 per cent	211	16	0				
Profit	507	0	9				
	£8587	10	2		£8587	10	2

SECTION II.

Estate Accounts.

OBSERVATIONS—CLERK OF WORKS' ACCOUNTS—FORESTER'S ACCOUNTS—STEWARD'S ESTATE ACCOUNTS.

ESTATE accounts proper are those which relate to woods and forests, building and repairs, and the income derived from the letting of land, quit and chief rents, &c., and the expenditure required for rates, taxes, and maintenance. We will first consider the accounts kept by the clerk of the works.

The clerk of the works has little to do with sales; his books, on most estates, relate to expenditure for labour and purchase of material. The plan we adopt is to require a statement each quarter of each man's work with a summary and total; for instance, the carpenter or bricklayer, when and at what work they have been employed; sawyers, what they have sawn, the measurement and price; brick makers, the number of bricks made and the price; bills paid for various items, for which vouchers must be given, and other details requisite for full information.

These particulars are rendered quarterly, and are duly examined and posted by the steward into his ledger. During the quarter, if necessary, an advance is made, which is deducted from the total at the end of the quarter. The posting should be so arranged that from the ledger every detail can be obtained; for example: if the men have been employed at any special work, building a cottage, stable, or other work of like nature, the cost of each class of labour should be ascertained from the ledger.

The accounts of the forester we also obtain quarterly. They consist of statements of labour, with the amount of timber, bavins, poles, &c., cut for use upon the estate; also timber, bark, underwood, thinnings of plantations, &c., sold or for sale; number of trees bought for nursery, number planted, where and when, and every other detail of this character.

CHAP. XI.
Sect. 2.
Estate
Accounts.

Steward's
estate-
accounts.

The foregoing books of the clerk of the works and forester are examined by the steward, and the results carried to his ledger, under such heads as the following: "Carpenters," "Bricklayers," "Brickmakers," "Woodmen," "Timber cut for use on estate," "Timber or bark sold," "Underwood sold." At the end of the year statements as follows are forwarded to the principal.

STATEMENT OF ESTATE LABOUR.

	£	s.	d.
Woodmen	237	14	11
Brickmakers, 99,000 bricks (1875)	67	10	0
Carpenters	109	10	0
Engineer	46	16	0
Bricklayers	108	7	0
Sundry Work	56	9	4
Sawyers	91	8	1
Estate petty Cash (Clerk of Works)	26	2	4
*Hire of Horses from Farm	198	0	0
Coal, Lime, Hair, &c.	19	16	6
	£961	14	2

STATEMENT OF TIMBER, BARK, AND COPSE SALES.
1876.

	£	s.	d.
140 Beech Trees sold	363	0	0
Smaller „	13	14	6
25 tons of Bark	112	19	0
Oak (40 loads)	153	0	0
Ash	6	0	0
Bavins sold to Labourers	47	2	0
7600 Oak Bavins	41	16	0
20 acres of Underwood	142	10	11
	£880	2	5

TIMBER, BAVINS, &C.
Used and in Use upon the Estate, Year ending 1876.

	£	s.	d.
20 loads of Oak	95	8	4
Larch Poles	127	16	0
Ash	11	17	2
Beech	82	10	0
13,000 Kiln Bavins	32	10	0
3250 Sale and House Bavins	17	17	6
Elm	8	0	0
	£375	19	0

---

* See Balance Sheet.

In his own special department the steward's accounts will consist of rents received, allowances for taxes to tenants, quit rents paid or received, fines, heriots, royalties, or other charges or receipts of similar nature, payment of material accounts, or of landlord's rates, taxes, or tithes; everything in fact paid or received should be carefully and systematically posted into the ledger from the various books under their respective headings, so that at a glance any particular can be at once obtained.

It will be seen from the foregoing remarks that our object has been, not to lay down a plan with a quantity of ruled pages as examples, and to encourage intricate systems of accounts in the various departments; such systems will make the subject wearisome at once to him who keeps them, and to him who peruses them. The object to be arrived at is, simplicity coupled with accuracy, so as to enable the various officials to account methodically, but without causing them needless labour.

CHAPTER XII.
USEFUL RULES OF ARITHMETIC AND MENSURATION.

CHAP. XII.
Rules of Arithmetic, &c.

ALTHOUGH we have already given some rules of calculation in the chapters upon Farm Valuations and upon Repairs and Material, it is possible that the student, whose memories of his school or college experience are not so fresh as they should be, may find it useful to have some rules of arithmetic and mensuration presented to him in a handy form. We have therefore selected the following rules from well-known works upon those subjects:—

DECIMALS.

Decimals.

Ciphers on the right-hand of decimals make no alteration in their value, for ·5 ·50 ·500 and so on, are decimals of the same value, being $\frac{5}{10}$ or $\frac{1}{2}$. But when ciphers are placed on the left hand of a decimal they decrease its value in a tenfold proportion, thus: ·5 is $\frac{5}{10}$, ·05 is $\frac{5}{100}$, ·005 is $\frac{5}{1000}$, and so on.

The first place of decimals, counted from the left hand towards the right, is tenths, the second hundredths, the third thousandths, the fourth ten-thousandth parts, and so on.

Addition of decimals.

Addition of Decimals—Write down the numbers in such a manner, that tenths may be under tenths, hundredths under hundredths, and so on, in which order the decimal points may stand directly under each other; then add as in

USEFUL RULES OF ARITHMETIC AND MENSURATION. 243

whole numbers, and put a point in the sum directly under the other points.

*Chap. XII.
Rules of Arithmetic, &c.*

Thus—

```
   ·253
   ·142
  6·72
   ·0061
   ·06
 149·8
 ───────
 156·9811
```

Subtraction of Decimals—Write the less number under the greater, according to the value of their places, as in addition, then subtract as in whole numbers, and place the decimal point in the remainder straight under the other points.

Subtraction of decimals.

Thus—

```
 67·53281
 24·0234
 ────────
 43·50941
```

Multiplication of Decimals—Multiply as in whole numbers, and point off in the product as many decimal places as there are in both multiplicand and multiplier; but if the product does not contain so many figures, supply the deficiency by ciphers on the left.

Multiplicati of decimals.

Thus—

```
  437·65
    ·317
 ────────
  3·06355
  4·3765
131·295
 ────────
138·73505
```

Division of Decimals—Divide as in whole numbers, and point off as many decimal places in the quotient as the dividend has more than the divisor; but if there be not as many places in the quotient, put ciphers on the left to supply the defect; and if the dividend has not as many places of decimals as the divisor, annex ciphers until they

Division of decimals.

R 2

Chap. XII.
Rules of Arithmetic, &c.

are equal, before commencing to divide. By annexing ciphers thereto the division may be prolonged, so that the quotient may be brought to any required degree of exactness.

Thus—Divide 63·2871 by 5·25.

```
5·25)63·28710(12·054
     525
     ―――
     1078
     1050
     ―――
      2871
      2625
      ――――
       2460
       2100
       ――――
        360
```

Reduction of decimals.

Reduction of Decimals—A Vulgar or Common Fraction is reduced to its equivalent decimal by dividing the numerator of the fraction by the denominator, and the quotient is the decimal required having its value decreased by as many ciphers, less one, prefixed as may have been annexed to the right hand to form a dividend. Thus $\frac{1}{2}$ is 1·0 divided by 2, or ·5; $\frac{1}{8}$ is 1·0 divided by 8 or ·125; $\frac{1}{12}$ is 1·00 divided by 12 or ·0833, &c.

Any number of moneys, weights, or measures of a lower denomination may be reduced to the decimal of a higher denomination by dividing the number of the lower denomination by the number of which it is contained in the higher; or a decimal of money weights, or measures, may be brought to its proper terms in a lower denomination, by multiplying the decimal by the number of the lower denomination contained in the higher, and pointing off the same number of places of decimals in the product; and the remaining decimal reduced to its proper terms in a still lower denomination by a similar process.

Thus, to reduce twelve shillings to the decimal of a pound sterling—

USEFUL RULES OF ARITHMETIC AND MENSURATION. 245

Divide 12·0 by 20, which is ·6.

Again, to reduce ·625 of a pound sterling to its proper terms, multiply ·625 by 20 and the product is 12·500 shillings; and ·500 or ·5 multiplied by 12 is 6 pence; viz., ·625 of a pound is 12s. 6d.

CHAP. XII.
Rules of Arithmetic, &c.

DUODECIMALS.

As decimals are tenths, so duodecimals are twelfths of an integer; and as each succeeding inferior place in a decimal decreases in value in tenfold proportion, so each succeeding inferior place of duodecimals are twelfths of unity, expressed by ', and called "primes;" the second are 144ths of unity, expressed by ", and called "seconds"; the third are 1728ths of unity, expressed by '", and called "thirds," and so on.

Duodecimals.

Multiplication of duodecimals is chiefly used by artificers in computing superficial and solid contents from dimensions taken in feet and inches. In the operation

Multiplication of duodecimals.

Feet multiplied by feet give feet.
Feet multiplied by primes or inches give primes or inches.
Feet multiplied by seconds give seconds.
Primes or inches multiplied by primes or inches give seconds.
Primes or inches multiplied by seconds give thirds.
Seconds multiplied by seconds give fourths.
Seconds multiplied by thirds give fifths, and so on.

Having placed like denominations or places in the multiplicand and multiplier under each other, multiply the lowest place in the multiplicand by the highest place in the multiplier, dividing the product, if above 12, by 12; setting down the remainder, and carrying the quotient to the result of the next lowest place in the multiplicand, multiplied by the highest place in the multiplier, proceeding, as before, to divide such result by 12, setting down the remainder, and carrying the quotient to the result of the next lower place of the multiplicand, multiplied by the highest place of the multiplier; and so proceed to multiply the places in the multiplicand in their increasing order, until the highest place in the multiplicand comes to be multiplied by the

CHAP. XII.
Rules of Arithmetic, &c.

highest place in the multiplier; after which proceed with the less places in the multiplier in the same manner; then add the like terms together, carrying all completed twelves from the lower to the higher denomination.

Thus—

	Ft.	′	″		Ft.	′	″	‴
	8	9	0		30	7	6	0
multiplied by	3	6	0		2	3	0	0
	26	3	0		61	3	0	0
	4	4	6		7	7	10	6
is	30	7	6		68	10	10	6

The result 30.7′.6″ of the first part of the foregoing example of the process of multiplication of duodecimals may be supposed to be the superficial area 8ft. 9in. long, by 3ft. 6in. wide; and the result 68ft. 10′.10″.6‴ of the other part of the example may be supposed to be the cubic content of the three dimensions of 8ft. 9in. long, 3ft. 6in. wide, and 2ft. 3in. deep. If in the last result the 68ft. be divided by 27 it will then be 2 cubic yards 14ft. 10′.10″.6‴.

FRACTIONS.

Fractions.

A fraction or broken number is an expression of a part, or some parts of an integer, or whole number. It is denoted by two numbers placed one below the other with a line between them—thus ¾. The number below the line is called the denominator, as showing how many parts the integer is divided into; and the upper number the numerator, as enumerating how many such equal parts it contains; and in this form it is called a vulgar fraction. Another form of fraction, called a decimal, is when the denominator is unity, with as many ciphers annexed to the right hand as there are figures in the numerator; and it is usually expressed by the numerator only, with a point prefixed: Thus, $\frac{3}{10}$ is written ·3 ; $\frac{23}{100}$ ·23, and so on.

The mode of reducing or converting vulgar fractions to their decimal form will be found upon p. 244.

To find the Area of Circles.

Rule 1. Multiply half the circumference by the radius (half the diameter), and the product will be the area. Or, divide the product of the whole circumference and diameter by 4, and the quotient will be the area.

Rule 2. Multiply the square of the diameter by ·7854, and the product will be the area.

Rule 3. Multiply the square of the circumference by ·07958, and the product will be the area.

Useful Rules relating to Circles.

(*See* Nesbit and Ewart.)

The diameter of a circle multiplied by ·8862269, or the circumference × by ·2821577, will give the side of a square of equal area.

The diameter of a circle × by ·7071068 will give the side of the inscribed square.

The side of a square × by 1·414214 will give the diameter of its circumscribing circle.

The side of a square × 4·442883 will give the circumference of its circumscribing circle.

The side of a square × by 1·128379 will give the diameter of a circle equal in area.

The side of a square × by 3·544908 will give the circumference of a circle equal in area.

When the diameter of a circle is 1 its circumference is 3·1416 (II.).

When the circumference is 1 its diameter is 1÷3·1416— that is, ·3183.

The areas of circles are to each other as the squares of their diameters or their radii.

The area of a circle is equal to the area of a triangle, the base being equal to the circumference, and the perpendicular equal to the radius.

CHAP. XII.
Rules of Arithmetic, &c.

Triangles and trapezoids.

DEFINITIONS AND RULES RELATING TO TRIANGLES AND TRAPEZOIDS.

An equilateral triangle has all its sides equal.

An isosceles triangle has only two sides equal.

A scalene triangle has all its sides unequal.

A trapezoid is a four-sided figure with two of its opposite sides parallel.

To find the Area of a Triangle.

Multiply the base by the perpendicular and divide by 2, and the product is the area required.

To find the Area of a Trapezoid.

Multiply the length by the sum of the two parallel sides and divide by 2, and the product will be the required area.

SUPPLEMENT

ON THE

LAW RELATING TO LANDOWNERS

AND LAND STEWARDS.

INTRODUCTORY NOTE.

IN the preparation of this supplement the writer has endeavoured to summarise such rules of the law as appear to have a direct bearing upon the subject-matter of the book. The intricacy of the laws of this country relating to land is, indeed, such that neither owner nor agent can be safely advised to attempt to act as his own lawyer in formal transactions respecting it. But the duties of a steward, especially in dealing with tenants, involve many informal acts in the performance of which a knowledge of some legal principles cannot be useless. Whilst the general nature of ownership in land is therefore only briefly alluded to, these principles are discussed with such detail as the space at command admits of.

F. G.

Lympstone,
   South Devon,
      March, 1879.

CONTENTS.

CHAPTER I.
THE GENERAL NATURE OF PROPERTY IN LAND.

	Page
Feudal origin of property in land	257
Legal meaning of an "estate"	257

CHAPTER II.
THE DIFFERENT KINDS OF ESTATES IN LAND.

Estate in fee simple	259
Estate tail	260
Estate for life	260
Estate for years	260

CHAPTER III.
FREEHOLD AND COPYHOLD PROPERTY.

The nature of a manor	262
Origin of copyhold tenure	262
Present difference between freeholder and copyholder	263
Copyhold resemble freehold interests in respect of their duration	264
Meaning of "the freehold"	265

CHAPTER IV.
THE NATURE OF A SETTLEMENT.

When land is said to be "settled"	266
The actual proprietor usually a tenant for life	267
Settlement only allowed within certain limits	267

CHAPTER V.
THE MANAGEMENT OF A LIFE ESTATE.

	Page
Voluntary waste	267
Cutting timber	267
What trees are timber	270
Exception to rule against cutting timber	270
Trees which tenant for life can cut	271
Property in timber which has been cut	271
Property in trees, not timber, which have been cut	272
Timber for repairs	272
Working minerals	272
Other acts of voluntary waste	273
Permissive waste—neglect to repair	273
Equitable waste	273
Leases	274
Sales	274
Works of improvement	275

CHAPTER VI.
LANDLORD AND TENANT.

SECTION 1.
Tenancy and the Mode of its Creation.

Tenancy at will	277
Tenancy from year to year	278
Notice to quit	278
Tenancies for longer periods	279
In what cases a deed is necessary	280
Unsealed writings or memoranda may be—	
(a) leases	281
(b) agreements to grant or accept leases	281
Stamps on leases	283
Costs of the lease	283

SECTION 2.
Rights incident to Tenancy by Law and Contract.

Payment of rent	284
Distress	284
What goods are distrainable	285
Mode of effecting a distress	285
Other remedies to enforce payment of rent	286
Covenant to pay	287
Proviso for re-entry or forfeiture clause	287
„ relief against forfeiture	287
„ waiver of forfeiture	287

CONTENTS.

	Page
Rates, taxes, and assessments	287
Repairs	289
Landlord's liability	289
Tenant's liability	290
Covenants to repair	290
Damage by fire and tempest	292
Insurance	292
Assignment and underletting	293
Cultivation	293
Consumption of hay, straw, and manure	294
Waste—	
in respect of minerals	294
in respect of trees and underwood	295
in respect of pasture or other land	296
in respect of fences	296
Property in fences	296
Game	297
Fixtures	298
What is a fixture	298
Tenant's fixtures	299
Agricultural fixtures (st. 14 & 15 Vict. c. 25)	300
Agricultural Holdings Act, 1875, s. 53	301

SECTION 3.
Tenant Right.

Right to emblements	304
Right to compensation according to custom of country	305
Right to compensation under Agricultural Holdings Act, 1875	306

CHAPTER VII.
THE AUTHORITY OF A LAND STEWARD.

Transactions with agents generally	310
General and special agents	311
In what sense a land steward is a general agent	312
Cases in which a special authority may be necessary	313
Leases	314
Notice to quit	314
Distress	314
Sales	314
Purchases	315
Appointment of sub-agents	316
Mode of signature by agent	316
Personal liability of agent	316
Ratification of unauthorised acts	317

CHAPTER I.
THE GENERAL NATURE OF PROPERTY IN LAND.

It is necessary at the outset for the student to understand that the English law knows of no such thing as absolute property in land. Under the feudal system, which we read of as prevailing in this country in the time of our Norman and Plantagenet kings, every possessor of land was considered to be the *tenant* (or "holder") of the land under some superior lord to whom he was bound to render military or other services in respect of the land he held. So that the possessor was not the *owner* of the land. Still less could the lord be called the owner; for not only was he generally powerless to interfere with the possession of the tenant, so long as the terms as to services or rent were duly observed, but he also was, in respect of the land over which his lordship extended, the tenant of some lord higher up in the scale than himself, to whom he in like manner was bound to render services, the chief part of such services consisting in bringing together at his lord's summons a certain number of his tenants, ready armed, to follow the lord to battle. It may be said, speaking generally, that every proprietor in the kingdom was a tenant, except the king, who was lord paramount over all.

Chap. I. The General Nature of Property in Land.

Feudal origin of property in land.

Thus it is that the law, which was framed by feudal lawyers, still regards land as the subject-matter of *tenure*. When speaking of a horse or any other chattel, it speaks

Legal meaning of an estate.

CHAP. I.
The General Nature of Property in Land.

of ownership. But technically it does not talk of the owner of land, because it does not conceive that any person can own it in the same way in which he owns a horse. Although in popular language a tenant is a man who obtains an interest in a house or farm by hiring it for a definite period, in legal phrase every proprietor is a tenant or holder of the land. He may be, however, and is, called in law the owner of that particular interest in it which he holds, that interest, whatever it may be, being called an *estate*. Thus the lessee for fourteen years of a farm clearly does not, in any sense, own the farm; but legally he owns an estate for years in the farm; and his landlord is considered in law not as owning the farm, but as being the owner of another estate or interest in it—an estate which, as we shall see, may vary considerably in its qualities and duration. The distinction between the legal meaning of an estate as an *interest in land*, and its popular use in which it signifies *an area of land*, is most important, as nothing can be understood of the land laws without attending to it.

CHAPTER II.
THE DIFFERENT KINDS OF ESTATES IN LAND.

THE following are the most important of the different kinds of interest which may be had in land :—

1. An *estate in fee simple* is the largest interest in land which can be had, and the man who has the fee simple has at the present time what practically amounts to absolute property. For his interest is one which lasts for ever; he can dispose of it by deed or will as he pleases; and, although the law still calls him a *tenant* in fee simple, it is but rarely that any of the burdens or symbols of tenure attach to his estate. He obtains such an estate by a grant of land to *him and his heirs* (the word grant being applicable whether he takes by purchase, or gift, or in any other way).

It is important to observe that some one or other is always the owner of an estate in fee simple in every piece of land, although the actual proprietors of the land may only have one of the smaller estates which are specified below. For instance, if A., the owner of the fee simple, grants an estate tail to B., B. would be called the proprietor. But although A. has thus parted with the present proprietorship, he has not parted with all his own estate, for an estate tail is smaller than an estate in fee simple. The fee simple remains in him, and will entitle him to take possession again so soon as the estate tail comes to an end.

CHAP. II.
The Different Kinds of Estates in Land.

Estate tail.

2. *An estate tail* is that which passes by a grant to a man and the heirs of his body. The owner is called a *tenant in tail*, and when land is so granted, it is said to be *entailed*. The estate lasts so long only as the tenant in tail has heirs of his body, in other words, so long as his children or the descendants of his children are living; and, so long as it remains as an estate tail, the owner of it has no power to dispose of it beyond his own lifetime. But the peculiarity of the estate is that the person who has got it, and is in possession of the land in right of it, may by a special process (the enrolling of a deed in Chancery) turn it into an estate in fee simple. This process is called disentailing the land. In the instance above given of a grant by A. of an estate tail to B., in the ordinary course of things, on B.'s death without children, the estate tail would come to an end, and A. would take possession again in right of his fee simple. But if B. in his lifetime had disentailed the land, he would thereby have acquired the fee simple, A.'s interest would have been destroyed, and the land would pass under B.'s will, or, if he died without a will, would go to his heir whoever he might be—for he might have an heir (for instance, a cousin), although not an heir of his body. We thus see that the prevalent idea that, when land is entailed, it must remain in the same family from generation to generation is entirely false.

Estate for life.

3. *An estate for life*, the name of which sufficiently describes it for the present purpose. But it may be noticed that a life estate is not always of the same duration as the life of the owner. For if A. have an estate granted to him for his life, he may grant the estate away to B., and then B.'s estate lasts as long as A. lives.

Estate for years.

4. *An estate for years*, under which term may be included all interests of lessees or persons who, in the popular sense of the word, are tenants; in other words, all *leasehold* property. An important practical difference between this kind of estate and any other lies in the fact that the law does not regard it as real or landed property at all; it

does not allow it to pass on the owner's death to his heir, but it goes to his executors in the same way as do his stock and money. Ordinary language adopts a similar distinction; for though a man is called a "landowner," if he holds for life, or in tail, or in fee simple, he is hardly so called if he is only a tenant under a lease.

CHAPTER III.
FREEHOLD AND COPYHOLD PROPERTY.

Chap. III. Freehold and Copyhold Property.

The nature of a manor.

THE leading division of landed property into freehold and copyhold property is specially illustrative of what has been already said with regard to the general nature of property in land. The *lord of a manor*, with whose rights and claims copyholders are familiar enough, has the lordship which belonged to the old feudal lord, although the course of civilisation has altered or abolished the feudal services. The manor over which the lordship extended seems in feudal times to have consisted of three parts. Firstly, there was the lord's *demesne*, which was that part of the manor which he reserved for his dwelling, or for his other private purposes—that part which, in modern phrase, he kept "in hand." Secondly, there was the portion of the manor which had been granted out to, or was held by, the lord's free tenants, who held upon the terms of rendering him some regular and certain services, and were called the *freeholders* of the manor. They held estates for life at the least, an estate for life being the smallest which it became the dignity of a freeman to accept. And lastly, there was the *waste* of the manor, which served as a grazing ground for the cattle of both lord and tenants.

Origin of copyhold tenure.

The copyholders probably had no place in the original manorial system, and appear to have originated in this way :—The villeins or slaves whom the lord kept to till his own demesne were rewarded for their services, or at least had granted to them as a means of subsistence, small plots of the demesne to cultivate on their own account, but upon the terms of their still giving to the lord either the amount of manual labour required upon the rest of the demesne, or a certain amount of produce. But the grants were only to hold "at the will of the lord," and were determinable at the lord's pleasure. Gradually, however, custom, or the general practice of the particular manor, was recognised as regulating the condition of these persons in respect both of the services required of them and of the duration of their interest. Their holding, instead of being at the will of the lord simply, was said to be at the will of the lord "according to the custom of the manor." As the grants made to them were made at a manor court, and were entered by the lord's steward upon the roll or record of the court's proceedings, and as a copy of this roll constituted their only title deed, they came to be called holders by copy of court roll, or copyholders. As such they acquired rights as secure as, though different in kind from, those of the freeholder.

CHAP. III. Freehold and Copyhold Property.

The most important difference between the freeholder and copyholder is that the lord has no *estate* in the freehold lands of his manor; for the lordship, or lord's claim to rent and services in respect of them does not amount to an estate in the land. But the lordship carries with it the fee simple in the copyholder's land, for even when the copyholder's interest became permanent, the law did not consider it as an interest in any way interfering with the existence of the fee simple. The copyholder only had a sort of customary right of enjoyment, and could not touch either timber or minerals (except within certain narrow limits) for these both belonged to the lord in right of his estate. This original distinction between the two kinds of property has been increased by the lapse of time. For, as the freeholder had the whole estate in his land, the relation of lord and tenant was gradually lost sight of when the progress of

Present difference between freeholders and copyholders.

CHAP. III.
Freehold and Copyhold Property.

order and civilisation made it of little importance to either party. Thus the greater number of freehold tenants became independent of their lords altogether. In many instances, however, the relation of dependence is still traceable in an annual payment of nominal value claimed by the lord and called a *quit* rent, or rent by which the tenant became quit of all other manorial claims upon him. The small amount of this rent, where it is claimed, is of course due to the difference in the value of money at the present time and its value several hundred years ago when the rent was fixed. On the other hand, this severance of the connection with the lord was impossible in the case of the copyholder; for the lord had got the fee simple. Moreover the copyholder could not dispose of his interest by deed or will alone (as could the freeholder), but only by a transfer upon the court rolls of the manor, and the lord is often allowed by the custom of the manor to impose a heavy fine upon every transfer; so that there existed both the means and the motive for keeping the copyholder in the inferior position which he still occupies.

Copyhold resemble freehold interests in respect of their duration.

There is, however, one particular in which the copyholder's interest resembles the freeholder's, and that is in respect of its duration. For the different estates in land which might be had by the freeholder, and which we have enumerated, served as the models for the interests which should be taken by his inferior neighbour; and the words of grant which were regarded as making the freeholder's estate an estate to last for life, or for years, or for ever, were held to create interests of similar duration in the case of the copyholder. Yet when a copyholder holds land to " him and his heirs according to the custom of the manor of X.," he does not, as we have seen, really hold the fee simple; he is sometimes said to have a copyhold fee simple. But it is clear from what we have said that there cannot be such a thing as a copyhold fee simple; and the term is only applied to the copyholder's interest because there is no other short term to make use of.

In conclusion, as has been already observed, freehold tenure was the tenure by which a free-man held, and he never held an estate less than a life estate. Hence it is that the immediate owner of a life estate, or of any greater estate in land of freehold tenure, is said to have the *freehold*.

Chap. III.
Freehold and Copyhold Property.

Meaning of the freehold.

CHAPTER IV.
THE NATURE OF A SETTLEMENT.

Chap. IV.
The Nature of a Settlement.

When land is said to be settled.

When a man has an estate in fee simple in a hundred acres of land, there is one mode of dividing his interest which is at once apparent—he may cut the land up into smaller plots and grant it away piecemeal. In other words, he may divide the area. But there is another way of dividing his interest which the law gives him, which is not so apparent. He may, without dividing the area, cut his estate or legal interest in it to pieces by granting a number of smaller estates or interests in the whole area to different persons in succession, or, as the law calls it, *in remainder*. For instance, he may execute a deed or will granting a life estate in the land to A., and after A.'s death, an estate tail to A.'s son B.; and when that estate comes to an end (by reason of B. and all his issue having died) another life estate to C., with another remainder to C.'s son D. in tail, and so on to any number of persons in succession, until he concludes by granting the fee simple, after which there is nothing left in him to grant. Each of the persons to whom an estate is thus given is called, until he comes into possession, a *remainderman*. When land is subject to a deed or will whereby estates in remainder are granted in this way, it is said to be *settled*. As the greater part of the land in this country is settled, it is important for the agent concerned with the management of it to understand the nature of a settlement, and what is the position of the proprietor for whom he acts.

It may be said, speaking roughly, that almost every large landed proprietor in this country is only a tenant for life, and the reason for this state of things is not very difficult to explain. If the proprietor held, as he is commonly supposed to hold, an estate tail, he would, as we have already seen, be practically at liberty to dispose of the land as he liked, for he could always disentail it. But it is to be observed that it is only when he is in actual possession of the land in right of his estate tail that he can thus disentail it, and defeat the rights of all the remaindermen that come after him. Until he is so in possession the disentailing process requires the concurrence of the person who has the possession. Referring to the example above given, B. alone cannot, during the lifetime of A. the tenant for life, disentail, so as to turn his estate, which is an estate tail in remainder, into an estate in fee simple in remainder. But A. and B. together can disentail at any time, and acquire the fee simple between them, or B. can disentail alone when he takes possession after A.'s death. Now it will generally be the object of A., who is in enjoyment of the family property, to keep it in the family, and to put it for ever out of his son B.'s power to acquire the fee simple and sell it; and B., as a young man imbued with the like ideas of preserving the family heritage, is scarcely likely to offer any obstacle. Accordingly, as soon as B. comes of age, A. and B. join in disentailing the land and acquiring the fee simple; and then having between them the power to dispose of the fee simple or whole interest in the land as they like, they at once execute a fresh settlement whereby a life estate is again given to A., then another life estate (instead of an estate tail) to B., and after that an estate tail to B.'s unborn son.

The actual proprietor usually a tenant for life.

It is nothing, therefore, in the law of entail which prevents land from being sold or disposed of. But the persons who have the power to dispose of it prefer to exercise their power by cutting down their own interests to life estates and vesting in an unborn person the estate which will carry

Settlement only allowed within certain limits.

a power of disposition with it; so that the land is tied up till that person comes into being and attains majority. The law, however, only allows estates to be given to the next unborn generation. If they could be given, not only to that generation, but to its unborn children, and so on indefinitely, it is clear that a landowner might, by giving successive life estates to coming generations, tie up the land till the millenium. As it is, it can be tied up for a great many years; for a settlement giving a life estate to a young child, with estates tail in remainder to his unborn issue, may prevent any one person from having a power of disposing of the land for nearly a hundred years. For the child might only have issue very late in life (perhaps sixty or seventy years after the date of the settlement), and it would not be till the eldest of such issue came of age that the land could be disentailed. It is usual, however, in every settlement to provide that the trustees of the settlement may sell the property if circumstances make it desirable, and in the event of such a sale the maintenance of the family dignity is provided for by a declaration that the purchase money shall be invested in other land, which shall be settled in precisely the same way, or shall be applied in paying off incumbrances on any part of the settled property not sold. Recent Acts of Parliament, called the Settled Estates Acts, have moreover given similar powers of sale to the High Court of Justice, which can accordingly be applied to if a sale is desired, and the settlement does not give the means of effecting it.

CHAPTER V.
THE MANAGEMENT OF A LIFE ESTATE.

IT is clear that the proprietor who is only interested for his life has not the same powers in respect of the land as has the owner of the estate in fee simple, and it is therefore necessary for his manager or agent to understand in what respect his employer's powers are limited. Firstly, he must neither do nor omit anything which will materially diminish the value of the land, so as to injure the interest of the person entitled in remainder after his death; and, secondly, he cannot by any act of his (except in so far as the power has been given to him by modern Acts of Parliament), bind the land beyond the period of his own life. If, for instance, he grants a lease for thirty years, and he dies before the thirty years have expired, the lessee cannot claim to hold the land against the remainderman.

CHAP. V.
The Management of a Life Estate.

With regard to the first point, the limited rights of the tenant for life are expressed in law by saying that he has no power to commit *waste*. And waste may be either by positive act of destruction, when it is called *voluntary* waste; or by mere omission to do what is requisite for the preservation of the property, when it is called *permissive* waste.

Voluntary waste.

The most important check which the law against voluntary waste imposes on the tenant for life, is in preventing him from felling timber. Timber trees whilst they are growing are considered as part of the land itself; so soon as they are felled they cease to be a part of the land, and

Cutting timber.

CHAP. V.
The Management of a Life Estate.

become a mere chattel. To allow a tenant for life, therefore, to cut down timber and appropriate it as his own chattel, would be as injurious to the remainderman as to allow him to sell a part of the land out-and-out and pocket the proceeds. If it be clear that the timber needs cutting, the courts will, on an application being made by the tenant for life, order it to be cut, taking care that the proceeds are invested so that he gets the benefit of the interest only. But it will never allow him to appropriate the timber. The law upon this subject is so admirably expressed in a recent judgment of the Master of the Rolls (Sir George Jessel) in a case of *Honywood* v. *Honywood* (L. Rep. 18 Eq. Cas. 309), that we shall do best by citing it at length.

As I understand the law, it is this: The tenant for life may not cut timber. The question of what timber is depends, first, on the general law, that is, the law of *England*; and, secondly, on the special custom of a locality.

What trees are timber.

By the general law of England, *oak*, *ash*, and *elm* are timber, provided they are of the age of twenty years and upwards; provided also, they are not so old as not to have a reasonable quantity of useable wood in them, sufficient, according to a text writer, to make a good post. Timber, that is, the kind of tree which may be called timber, may be varied by local custom. There is what is called the custom of the country, that is, of a particular county or division of a county, and it varies in two ways. First of all, you may have trees called timber by the custom of the country—beech in some counties, hornbeam in others, and even whitethorn and blackthorn, and many other trees, are considered timber in peculiar localities—in addition to the ordinary timber trees. Then again, in certain localities, arising probably from the nature of the soil, trees of even twenty years old are not necessarily timber, but may go to twenty-four years, or even to a later period, I suppose, if necessary; and in other places the test of when a tree becomes timber is not its age, but its girth. These, however, are special customs. Once arrive at the fact of what is timber, the tenant for life, impeachable for waste, cannot cut it down.

Exception to rule against cutting timber.

That I take to be the clear law, with one single exception, which has been established principally by modern authorities in favour of the owners of timber estates, that is, estates which are cultivated merely for the produce of saleable timber, and where the timber is cut periodically. The reason of the distinction is this, that as cutting the timber is the mode of cultivation, the timber is not to be kept as part of the inheritance, but to be considered as part, so to say, of the annual fruits of the land, and in these cases the same kind of cultivation may be carried on by the tenant for life that has been carried on by the settlor on the estate, and the timber so cut down periodically in due course is looked upon as the annual profits of the estate, and therefore goes to the tenant for life. With that exception, I take it, a tenant for life cannot cut timber; therefore, I hold in this case, it not being a timber estate, that the tenant for life cannot cut timber at all.

CHAP. V.
The Management of a Life Estate.

The next question to be decided is, what can the tenant for life cut? The tenant for life can cut all that is not timber, with certain exceptions. He cannot cut ornamental trees, and he cannot destroy "germins," as the old law calls them, or stools of underwood; and he cannot destroy trees planted for the protection of banks, and various exceptions of that kind; but, with those exceptions, which are waste, he may cut all trees which are not timber, with again an exception, that he must not cut those trees which, being under twenty years of age, are not timber, but which would be timber if they were over twenty years of age. If he cuts them down he commits waste, as he prevents the growth of the timber. Then, again, there is a qualification that he may cut down timber trees under twenty years of age, provided they are cut down for the purpose of allowing the proper development and growth of other timber that is in the same wood or plantation. That is not waste; in fact, it is for the improvement of the estate, and not the destruction of it, and therefore he is allowed to cut them down. If, therefore, in the course of the proper management of this estate, any oaks, ashes, and elms under twenty years old have been cut down for the purpose of allowing of the growth of the other timber in a proper manner, that would not be waste on the part of the tenant for life, though impeachable for waste.

Trees which tenant for life can cut.

Then, the only other question to be decided is, in whom is the property of the timber cut down vested? There, I think, the law is reasonably clear. If the timber is timber properly so called, that is, oak, ash, and elm over twenty years old (I am not saying anything about exceptional cases), the property in the timber cut down, either by the tenant for life or anybody else, or blown down by a storm, belongs at law to the owner of the first vested estate of inheritance (*i.e.*, estate in fee simple or tail). There is in equity an exception where the remainderman, the owner of the first vested estate of inheritance, has colluded with the tenant for life to induce the tenant for life to cut down timber, and then equity interferes and will not allow him to get the benefit of his own wrong. There is, again, a second equitable exception, and that is this: that where timber is decaying, or for any special reason it is proper to cut it down, and the tenant for life in a suit properly constituted, to which the remainderman or the owner of the vested estate of inheritance is a party, gets an order of the court to have it cut down, there the court disposes of the proceeds on equitable principles, and makes them follow the interests in the estate. In that

Property in timber which has been cut down.

CHAP. V.
The Management of a Life Estate.

Property in trees, not timber, which have been cut down.

case, therefore, the proceeds are invested, and the income given to the successive owners of the estate, until you get to the owner of the first absolute estate of inheritance, who can take away the money.

Then we come to the property in trees not timber, that is, those which are not timber either from their nature or because they are not old enough, or because they are too old. In all those cases, I take it, the property is in the tenant for life. If he cuts them down wrongfully, and commits waste, the property is still in him, though he has committed a wrong, and would be liable to an action in the nature of waste. I am not sure that would follow in equity. My impression is that equity would say that he should not be allowed to take the benefit of his own wrong, and that he should not be allowed to take the property in those trees he cuts down. This is not the case at common law, and I am not aware that the exact point has been decided in equity.

But the point upon which his Lordship expresses a doubt —the point, namely, whether where the tenant for life commits waste by cutting down young trees which would become timber, equity would interfere upon the application of a remainderman to prevent him from appropriating them—is a case scarcely likely to arise, as the mischief lies rather in destroying the prospect of valuable timber hereafter than in appropriating the value of the young trees.

Timber for repairs.

In alluding to the exceptions to the general rule which prohibits the tenant for life from cutting timber, the judge did not refer to one which may be of some practical importance, though it had no bearing upon the case before him— the exception, namely, which entitles the tenant for life to cut down timber trees for the purpose of repairing buildings on the property where the damage has occurred in the ordinary course of decay.

Working minerals.

The second important check which the law against voluntary waste imposes on the action of a tenant for life is in preventing him from working for minerals. He may not dig for gravel, brick, stone, or clay, except in such pits as were open and usually dug when he came into the property. Nor may he open mines of metal, coal, or any other substance. But as to pits or mines open before, it is not waste for him to continue to dig them, for it has become a part of the annual profit of the land. It is a question of degree to be established by evidence whether the working of a dormant or abandoned mine is waste or not. It seems that a mine, the working of which has been discontinued for twenty or thirty years in consequence of its having been unremunerative, may, after that time, be worked by a succeeding tenant for life; but a mine, the working of which has been abandoned by the owner of the inheritance for the advantage of the property, cannot be worked by a succeeding tenant for life. For the same reasons for which it forbids the working of minerals, the law forbids the tenant for life to cut turf for sale, except in bogs previously used for that purpose.

<small>Chap. V. The Management of a Life Estate.</small>

Converting arable land into wood, or wood into arable, or ploughing up ancient pasture, will likewise be waste; for such acts create a difficulty in the proof of the title. And the alteration of buildings is clearly waste; it has even been said that the building of a new house is waste; but this is a proposition which it is not necessary to discuss here.

<small>Other acts of voluntary waste.</small>

The liability of the tenant for life for permissive waste, as for allowing buildings to get out of repair, is not very clear. According to the old plan of procedure in this country, whereby one system called *law* was administered at Westminster Hall, and another system called *equity*, which had power to override the former, was administered at Lincoln's Inn, the tenant for life was clearly liable at law for permissive waste; but equity hesitated to enforce any obligation upon him in respect of it; and inasmuch as under the recent fusion of the two systems the rules of equity prevail it will probably be difficult to fix him with a liability for permissive waste.

<small>Permissive waste—neglect to repair.</small>

The above observations are, however, to be qualified by another, namely, that if, as is frequently the case, the deed or will which created the life estate declares that the tenant for life shall take *without impeachment of waste* or be *unimpeachable for waste*, he is not subject to these rigorous prohibitions, but may cut timber in a husbandlike manner for his own benefit, and open mines and commit other similar

<small>Equitable waste.</small>

T

CHAP. V.
The Management of a Life Estate.

acts with impunity. Yet even in that case he is not allowed absolute freedom, for the courts will restrain him from acts of wanton damage, such as the destruction of the mansion house or the felling of ornamental timber. As such acts would be clearly inequitable, the law with a curious perversity, calls them *equitable waste*, meaning probably, that acting in a spirit of equity, it will prohibit them.

Leases.

With regard to the inability of the tenant for life to bind the land beyond the period of his own life, two points are to be noticed. It is very usual for the deed or will by which the estate is settled to give him or the trustees of the settlement an express power of leasing for certain periods, and in that case the rights of the lessee will, of course, be good against the remainderman. Therefore, when any question of letting arises, the first point is to discover what, if any, powers of leasing are contained in the settlement. If it contains nothing which enables the tenant for life to effect the desired object, he will probably find by referring to the Settled Estates Act (40 & 41 Vict. c. 18) that Parliament has supplied the deficiency. Section 46 of that Act authorizes the tenant for life of a settled estate *without application to the court* to grant leases of any part of the property except the mansion house and the lands usually occupied therewith, for any term not exceeding twenty-one years. Other sections of the Act enable the court, on the application of any person entitled to any estate for life, or to any greater estate in settled property, to authorize leases for longer periods (including mining leases for forty years and building leases for ninety-nine years). The court may direct, in authorizing a particular lease, whether the tenant for life, or what other person shall act as lessor, or it may order general leasing powers to be vested in the trustees of the settlement. But application to the court must be made with the consent, generally speaking, of the persons in existence who are interested in the property.

Sales.

Whilst referring to this Act it is worth while to mention

that it enables the court, on such an application and with such consent as are above indicated, to order a *sale* of the whole or any part of any settled property. But the sale moneys will, of course, be applied by the court for the benefit of the persons entitled under the settlement, as, by redeeming land tax, or incumbrances on parts of the settled property not sold, or by purchasing other land to be settled in the same way, and until it can be so applied, it will be invested, and the interest paid to the tenant for life. But in well-drawn settlements, it is usual expressly to authorise the trustees with the consent of the tenant for life to sell when occasion requires, and apply the sale moneys as above pointed out; and when the settlement contains such a power it will not be necessary to have recourse to the Settled Estates Act.

CHAP. V.
The Management of a Life Estate.

But it is not only with regard to leasing and selling that the Legislature has come to the assistance of the tenant for life. The system of settlement is so prejudicial to the development of the land in the bar which it creates to the free expenditure of capital by the proprietor (for a proprietor is not likely to spend large sums of his own in the improvement of a property in which he has only a life interest) that efforts have been made at various times to encourage such expenditure by empowering him to borrow money for works of improvement, and to secure the repayment of the loan by a charge upon the whole fee simple. Of these Acts we may refer to the statute 8 & 9 Vict. c. 56, whereby persons having limited interests are empowered to apply to the court for leave to make any permanent improvement by draining the land with tiles, stones, or other durable materials, or by warping, irrigation, or embankment in a permanent manner, or by erecting thereon any buildings of a permanent kind incidental to or consequential on any such operations. In the event of the applicant proving that his project is likely to be a beneficial one to all parties interested, the court will authorise a loan to be secured by a mortgage of the fee simple or inheri-

Works of improvement.

T 2

Chap. V.
The Management of a Life Estate.

tance; but the principal money must be repaid by equal annual instalments extending over a period which is in no case to exceed 25 years. Other important Acts are the "Improvement of Land Act, 1864" (27 & 28 Vict. c. 114), and the "Limited Owners Residences Act, 1870, Amendment Act, 1871" (34 & 35 Vict. c. 34), whereby other permanent improvements of a similar nature are authorised, including the erection or improvement of a mansion house, the repayment of the money borrowed for the purpose with interest thereon being provided for by means of a rent-charge for a term not exceeding 25 years. But none of these Acts can be said to have had the generally beneficial result which was expected of them. The expense and delay of making and supporting by evidence the requisite applications, and the aversion of the proprietor to having works upon his property conducted under the eye of public officers—for it is, of course, necessary for the authorities to see that the money raised is spent in accordance with the object declared—sufficiently account for the comparatively small use which has been made of them.

Nevertheless, the powers given by such Acts may prove very useful. The proprietor or his agent desiring to further inform himself as to what facilities they offer for assisting in the accomplishment of any special work, may, instead of applying at once to his solicitor, address himself to the "Inclosure Commissioners for England and Wales, Whitehall, S.W.," who have the superintendence of these loans, and who will furnish him with information and forms to fill up. He may also, if he has any idea as to what are the particular Acts which are likely to aid him, obtain, for a few pence, copies of these Acts from the Queen's printers, Messrs. Eyre and Spottiswoode, East Harding-street, London, E.C., a plan which will enable him to read for himself the provisions applicable to his case.

CHAPTER VI.
LANDLORD AND TENANT.

In considering the landlord's relation with his tenants, or with persons about to become his tenants, it will be well for the steward or agent to be in some degree acquainted with (1) the formalities requisite to create a tenancy; (2) the rights which the *law* gives to the parties so soon as a tenancy of any kind is created; and (3) the way in which these rights are usually modified by *contract* when the letting is effected by a written instrument. After discussing the first point we shall briefly consider the two latter together; and we shall finally make some remarks upon the subject of tenant-right.

SECTION I.
Tenancy and the Mode of its Creation.

The lowest position which the occupier can hold is that of a mere *tenant at will*, in which case each party is free to determine the relation at pleasure. But the law always leans against a tenancy of this kind, and the practice of the parties with reference to the time of payment of rent, or the general custom with regard to letting such property as is the subject of the tenancy will generally furnish evidence of a letting for some period or other. If, for instance, it is a house, and rent is paid monthly, it will be regarded as a

_{Chap. VI. Sect. 1. *Tenancy and the Mode of its Creation.*}

_{Tenancy at will.}

CHAP. VI.
Sect. 1.
Tenancy and the Mode of its Creation.

Tenancy from year to year.

Notice to quit.

monthly tenancy; if a furnished lodging in a sea-side town, the occupier will be considered a weekly tenant, in the absence in each case of any evidence to the contrary. But if it appears that the property was held at an annual rent then he will be held to be a tenant from year to year.

For the latter kind of tenancy can not only be created by express contract, but it will be held to exist whenever the occupier has entered without any stipulation being made as to time, but on a verbal understanding that he is to pay a yearly rent, or where, although this understanding does not exist, he does in fact pay a rent which the court can presume to be yearly from the fact of its being paid quarterly or half-yearly. Such a tenancy can only be determined by either party on his giving six months notice to the other of a desire to determine it at the end of same year of the tenancy. If, for instance, the tenant entered at Michaelmas he can be compelled, by due notice, to give up possession the next or any following Michaelmas, but at no other time. So that if he remains in possession for more than six months without any notice to quit being served upon him he is secure of an occupation of at least two years duration. With regard to the length of notice necessary it seems that although six months is the period fixed by law, the custom of the district may avail to show that a notice of a different length is necessary. And the parties may, of course, override the law by agreeing what notice shall be requisite. It may be useful to observe that, although a notice is necessary to determine a tenancy from year to year, it does not follow that a person who is in for a year is such a tenant. If either party can show that the agreement was "for a year" or "for a year certain" the tenancy will expire with the expiration of that year without any notice being given, as is always the case when any certain period is agreed upon. But this will rarely happen, as it is generally intended in the case of a yearly letting that it shall be a letting from year to year. Care should, however, be taken when any writing passes to call it a letting *from year to year*; for if it is "for a year from the   day of   , and *so on from year to year*" it is a tenancy for two years at the least, for to make it determinable at the end of the first year would be to give no effect to the words in italics.

CHAP. VI.
Sect. 1.
Tenancy and the Mode of its Creation.

The safest method for an agent to adopt in giving notice to a tenant from year to year is to write it (though this is not essential) and to word it thus—

Form of notice to quit.

To X. Y.

of   I hereby give you notice to quit and deliver up possession   which you hold of C. D. as tenant, on the   day of   next [*or* at the expiration of the year of your tenancy, which shall expire next after the end of one half year from the service of this notice.]

Dated

(Signed)   A. B. (*the agent*) on behalf
of the above-named C. D.

The use of the words in brackets is to save the effect of the notice where there is any doubt about the commencement of the tenancy. If there is no doubt about it they are unnecessary.

The notice must extend to the whole of the property which was comprised in the letting. And the agent must have authority to give it prior to doing so, as subsequent ratification by the landlord of what he has done is not sufficient.

The forms of tenancy which we have been considering are the only ones likely to be created without any writing or deed. But although no prudent person will accept or become a tenant without the terms of the tenancy being reduced into writing, the law does not require writing of any kind if the term granted does not exceed three years, and if the rent reserved amounts to two-thirds at least of the full improved value of the land. But in every case

Tenancies for longer periods.

Chap. VI.
Sect. 1.
Tenancy and the Mode of its Creation.

In what cases a deed is necessary.

where the term is more than three years, and in every case (even in a tenancy from year to year) where the rent is less than the above amount, the effect of the Statute of Frauds*, and of a subsequent statute is that the tenancy

---

* Until the reign of Charles II. interests in land (including both freehold and leasehold interests) could be created or transferred, and agreements for the sale or letting of land could be made by word of mouth, without any writing passing between the parties. But the *Statute of Frauds* passed in that reign (29 Car. 2. c. 3) required transactions of this nature to be reduced into writing; and as to *leases* a recent statute (8 & 9 Vict. c. 106, s. 3) declares that such of them as the former statute required to be in writing should thenceforth be made by deed only; and all conveyances and assignments which the Statute of Frauds directs to be put into writing must now be made by deed to be effectual. But the Statute of Frauds remains the foundation of the law as to the necessity for leases and agreements for selling or letting land being in writing; and it may therefore be worth while to quote its leading provisions, as some of them will have to be referred to again :

By sect. 1 it is enacted that "all *leases*, estates, interests of freeholds, or terms of years, or any uncertain interest of, in, to, or out of any messuages, manors, lands, tenements, or hereditaments, made or created by living and seisin only [*i.e.*, by symbolical giving up of possession by one party and taking it by the other], or by parol, and *not put in writing and signed by the parties* so making or creating the same, *or their agents* thereunto lawfully *authorised by writing*, shall have the force and effect of leases or estates at will only; and shall not, either in law or equity, be deemed or taken to have any other or greater force or effect; any consideration for creating any such parol leases, or estates notwithstanding."

But sect. 2 excepts from the operation of the above enactment "all leases not exceeding the term of three years from the making thereof, whereupon the rent reserved to the landlord during such term shall amount unto two-third parts at the least of the full improved value of the thing demised."

Sect. 3 enacts that "no leases, estates, or interests, either of freehold or terms of years, or any uncertain interest not being copyhold or customary interest, of, in, to, or out of any messuages, manors, lands, &c., shall at any time be assigned, granted, or surrendered, unless it be by *deed* or *note in writing, signed by the party* so assigning, granting, or surrendering the same, *or their agents* thereunto lawfully *authorised by writing*, or by act or operation of law."

Sect. 4 enacts amongst other things that "no action shall be brought whereby to charge any person upon any *contract* or *sale* of lands, tenements, or hereditaments, or any interest in or concerning them, unless

must be created by a written instrument, and that instrument must be a *deed* or formal document sealed by the parties.

This deed is usually called a *lease*, but in law any valid grant of a term is a lease. Thus a grant of a term of three years at a rack rent is a lease whether it be made by word of mouth, or by simple writing, or by deed.

Inasmuch as a deed is necessary for the grant of a lease when word of mouth is insufficient, it is natural to inquire the object and effect of the numerous unsealed or simple writings generally called "Memoranda of Agreement" passing between parties on the creation of a tenancy. In the first place it is clear that, in cases where word of mouth is legally sufficient, a writing is practically the only safe way of preserving evidence of the terms of the tenancy; and according to the definition just given such a writing may properly be called a lease.

But, secondly, when the lease is one which cannot be granted without a deed, a writing may prove that the parties had agreed that one should be granted or accepted; and in cases of this nature the courts, holding that what

CHAP. VI.
Sect. 1.
Tenancy and the Mode of its Creation.

Unsealed writings or memoranda may be—
(a) leases.

(b) agreement to grant or accept leases.

---

the agreement upon which such action shall be brought, or some memorandum or note thereof be in *writing*, and *signed by the party to be charged therewith, or some other person thereunto by him lawfully authorised.*"

And by sect. 17 it is enacted that no contract for the sale of any *goods* for the *price of 10l. sterling or upwards* shall be allowed to be good except the buyer shall, first, *accept part of the goods* so sold and actually receive the same; or, secondly, shall give something in earnest to bind the bargain, or in part payment; or, thirdly, unless some *memorandum or note in writing* of the said bargain be made, and *signed by the parties* to be charged with such contract, *or their agents* thereunto *lawfully authorised.*

It is to be observed that although by sect. 2 certain leases may still be made without writing, the effect of sect. 4 is that when the intention of the parties is, not to make a present lease, but to agree that one shall be made at a future date, the agreement must be in writing, as a contract for an interest in land. Thus a present lease from year to year at a rack rent may be made by word of mouth (by sect. 2); but an agreement to grant at a future time a lease from year to year at a rack rent must be in writing (by sect. 4).

Chap. VI.
Sect. 1.
Tenancy and the Mode of its Creation.

the parties have agreed to do ought to be done, will come to their assistance. For it will compel either of them to carry out or " specifically perform " an agreement of which there exists a memorandum or note in writing signed by him or some other person thereunto by him lawfully authorised: (see sect. 4 of the Statute of Frauds, set-out *ante*, p. 281, note.) Nothing, indeed, is commoner than for an agreement of this kind so fully to embody the terms of the letting that the tenant takes and holds on the mere right which he thus has to compel his landlord to execute a lease framed on those terms. But the plan of allowing such an agreement to take the place of a lease is not to be encouraged. The Legislature, aware that it would offer an easy means for avoiding the stamp duties imposed upon leases, has made such agreement subject to the same duty as would be the lease itself, and remits the duty on a lease executed in a pursuance of it.

Popular phraseology calls the arrangement a lease, if it is contained in a deed; an agreement, if it is a mere memorandum. The true distinction is that it is a lease where it actually grants an interest, and an agreement when it only agrees that one shall be granted at a future time. Thus so-called " Memoranda of Agreement" (as example B., *ante* p. 14), where they relate to tenancies at a rack rent for three years or under, (being tenancies which can be created orally) are generally leases; for no special form of words is needful for the grant of a lease. The usual words are " doth demise, lease, and to farm let; " but if they be that " A. agrees to let and B. agrees to take," the effect of such a memorandum will be precisely the same, and an immediate interest will pass; and, on the other hand, just as a paper styled upon its back " a memorandum of agreement " may be, in fact, a lease, so may a document styling itself a lease be nothing more in law than an agreement; for if the term be one which can only be granted by deed, and the document is an unsealed writing (in other words a memorandum of agreement), the courts, instead of holding it to be merely a void lease, will construe it as an agreement to grant a lease, and will order specific performance accordingly.

The stamp duties upon leases are as follows :

If the rent, whether reserved as a yearly rent or otherwise, is at a rate or average rate—

	If the term is definite, and does not exceed 35 years, or is indefinite.	If the term being indefinite exceeds 35 years, but does not exceed 100 years.	If the term being definite, exceeds 100 years.
Not exceeding £5 per annum ...	0 0 6	0 3 0	0 6 0
Exceeding £5 and not exceeding £10	0 1 0	0 6 0	0 12 0
,, 10 ,, 15	0 1 6	0 9 0	0 18 0
,, 15 ,, 20	0 2 0	0 12 0	1 4 0
,, 20 ,, 25	0 2 6	0 15 0	1 10 0
,, 25 ,, 50	0 5 0	1 10 0	3 0 0
,, 50 ,, 75	0 7 6	2 5 0	4 10 0
,, 75 ,, 100	0 10 0	3 0 0	6 0 0
,, 100, for every full sum of £50, and also for any fractional part of £50 thereof	0 5 0	1 10 0	3 0 0

Of any other kind whatsoever not hereinbefore described 0 10 0

DUPLICATE or COUNTERPART of any instrument chargeable with any duty :—
Where such duty does not amount to 5s. ... ... { The same duty as the original instrument.
In any other case 0 5 0

In the absence of any agreement to the contrary, it seems that the lessee is bound to pay the costs incurred in the preparation of the lease, but that the expense of the counterpart falls upon the lessor. This is a useful rule to recollect when, as frequently happens, the lessor's solicitor acts for both parties. If the lessor means to pay none of the costs, he should make a stipulation to that effect. When the lessee intends to employ a separate solicitor to act for him, and settle and approve the lease on his behalf, it is always desirable for the lessor, whose solicitor should prepare and engross the lease, to have an express agreement about the payment of his (the lessor's) solicitor's bill, unless he intends to bear the cost of it himself; as he will, of course, be the person liable to his solicitor.

SECTION II.

Rights incident to Tenancy by Law and Contract.

Chap. VI. Sect. 2. Rights incident to Tenancy by Law and Contract.

Assuming now that the tenancy has been created at a certain rent payable at some fixed periods, and that nothing beyond this has been agreed upon by the parties (as may often happen in the case of a tenancy created orally), the law confers upon each of them certain rights and liabilities. Something must be known of these in order to apprehend the bearing of the stipulations which, whenever the letting is effected by a written document, are usually entered into between them in order to modify their legal position. Some of the stipulations expressed in such a document can indeed scarcely be said to have this object, for they do in effect merely confirm, by express agreement, what would be the legal obligations of the parties without them. But as a whole their effect is to modify these obligations. When the stipulations are contained in a deed they are called *covenants*. We shall contrast the rights conferred by such stipulations, whether contained in a deed or memorandum, by calling them the rights given by *contract*, as distinguished from the rights given by law.

Payment of rent. Distress.

In the first place the law gives to landlords a remedy for the recovery of rent in arrears, which is not available for debts generally. And this remedy they do not lose even if they take a bill of exchange or note of hand for the rent, for such a course does not constitute any alteration of the debt until payment. The right of *distress* to which we allude entitles the landlord, without taking any legal proceedings, to seize upon the goods found upon the premises in order to enforce payment. The right extends in theory to everything which can be moved from the premises and brought back without injury. This principle excludes the seizure of fixtures, and also of articles that would at once perish, such as milk or fruit; but it does not exclude crops, although they are not yet cut. There are, however, exceptions to the general principle. Beasts of the plough and sheep are not distrainable if there is, without them, sufficient distress on the premises other than growing corn, although it appears that other kinds of cattle are; and all the instruments of husbandry or of a man's trade are similarly privileged. But articles in actual use, such as a machine at work, or a horse on which a man is riding, can in no case be seized.

Chap. VI. Sect. 2. Rights incident to Tenancy by Law and Contract.

What goods are distrainable.

Distress may be made either during the currency of the term or six months after its duration if the tenant is remaining in possession. The proper mode of effecting a distress is for the landlord, or his agent authorised for the purpose, to sign and hand to a bailiff or broker (and for this purpose any private person may act as such) a "distress warrant," a document which requires no stamp, and which should run in terms like these:—

Mode of effecting a distress.

To Mr. M. N., my bailiff.

    I hereby authorize and require you to distrain the goods and chattels [and also the cattle and growing crops] in and upon the farm, lands, and premises of X. Y., situate in the parish of   in the county of   for £   being   quarters rent due to me for the same at Lady Day and Midsummer Day (or as the case may be); and to proceed thereon for the recovery of the said rent as the law directs. But you are hereby expressly prohibited from taking any property not legally liable to a distress for rent.

    Dated this   day of

                  (Signed)   A. B. (the landlord)
                            or A. B. by C. D.
                               his agent.

The bailiff must then, at some time in the day between sunrise and sunset, enter upon the premises and expressly declare that he distrains either certain articles or part in the name of the whole; but he must not break open the outer door of the house or force the gates or doors of outbuildings.

The next step is to *impound* the goods, which may be

CHAP. VI.
Sect. 2.
Rights incident to Tenancy by Law and Contract.

done by removing them to the pound, or, if they are left upon the premises, either by shutting them up together there, or by obtaining the tenant's written consent to their being considered as impounded where they stand. Indeed, a statement in the notice of distress, that they are impounded in the premises in such a place would seem to be sufficient. But if they are left on the premises, the safety of the landlord requires that a person be left in possession on his behalf.

An inventory of the goods seized must be taken, and a copy of this together with a written notice that the goods named have been distrained, must be served upon the tenant, by being put into his hands or left at his house. The notice should also state the amount of the arrears for which the distress is made, and the date when it became due, and that unless the amount and costs be paid within five days the goods will be appraised and sold according to law.

If no tender be made within the five days, within which the law allows the tenant to replevy (or recover) his goods, the landlord must have them appraised by two sworn appraisers, and may then proceed to sell them at the best price that can be got. The surplus (if any) of the sale moneys is to be left in the hands of the sheriff, undersheriff, or constable.

Other remedies to enforce payment of rent.

Distress is, therefore, the landlord's most efficacious remedy by reason of the priority which it gives him over other creditors; and some understanding of the process is useful, because there may be occasions in which it is necessary to commence proceedings before recourse can be had to legal advice. But the law gives the landlord other remedies; for he may bring an action of debt for rent, or, if the demise be not by deed, an action for use and occupation. And the position of the landlord is still further strengthened by the contract contained in every properly drawn lease.

For, firstly, the lessee is always made to *covenant* expressly for the payment of rent, a plan which makes him personally responsible for the payment throughout the whole time, even though he assign the lease to another.

And, secondly, the lease almost always empowers the landlord to *re-enter for non-payment of rent or breach of any covenant or stipulation*, and to take possession again as though no lease had been made. But this liability imposed upon the tenant of forfeiting his lease if he tenders his rent a day late, or forgets to pay an insurance premium in accordance with the agreement, has been considered by the courts an unfair burden upon him. Therefore, so far as regards the payment of rent, the courts consider the proviso as intended as a security only, and annul the forfeiture on the tenants paying all arrears and costs incurred. The courts have now also power to grant similar relief in the case of a breach of a covenant to insure, provided no damage by fire has happened. But as to the breach of other covenants, such as the contract to repair, no similar relief can be obtained, and the landlord may re-enter, if the terms of the covenant have been broken, although at the time of re-entry the repairs may have been effected. But such conduct would be discouraged by the courts by all the means in their power.

It is also to be observed with regard to forfeiture, that a landlord intending to avail himself of it must be cautious in accepting rent, after he has notice of the breach upon which he proposes to rely. For acceptance after notice is an implied waiver of the forfeiture. If, however, the breach is of a continuing kind, as allowing premises to remain out of repair, the waiver does not extend to the breach continuing after the acceptance.

Chap. VI. Sect. 2. Rights incident to Tenancy by Law and Contract.

Covenant to pay. Proviso for re-entry or forfeiture clause.

Relief against forfeiture.

Waiver of forfeiture.

If may be useful briefly to summarise the position of the parties with reference to rates and taxes, although something has been said in the text on the practical bearing of the question.

Property tax is a tenant's tax as between him and the

Rates, taxes, and assessments.

CHAP. VI.
Sect. 2.
Rights incident to Tenancy by Law and Contract.

public; but he is entitled, after actual payment, to deduct the amount from his next payment of rent (or from subsequent rent accruing due during the current year of the tenancy, or other the period, during which the tax was accruing due), and of this right he cannot deprive himself by contract, it being intended by the Legislature that the tax should fall upon the landlord's income.

Land tax is also a tenant's tax as between him and the public, though it is intended that the landlord should ultimately bear so much of it as equals his interest in the land. The tenant is therefore entitled to deduct from his rent such a proportion of the amount which he has paid, as the rent bears to the assessed annual value of the premises, so that if the rental is as high as, or exceeds the assessment, he is entitled to deduct the whole. But of this right the tenant can deprive himself by contract; even an agreement to pay rent "free of all outgoings" will be regarded as an agreement by him to pay the land tax.

Sewers rates are also collected from the tenant, but in the absence of any agreement to the contrary, they are intended to fall upon the landlord, and the tenant is entitled to deduct the amount of his payment from the rent.

The above appear to be the only three dues which are intended to take effect out of the landlord's interest.

House tax falls, like all the assessed taxes, upon the person using and enjoying the article taxed, who is in this case the tenant. He has no right to deduct it from his rent unless the landlord has agreed to pay it.

Poor rate is a personal charge upon the occupier or tenant, in respect of his possession—not upon the owner in respect of his ownership. But under some modern Acts of Parliament the owner of any small tenement may, in certain cases, be rated instead of the occupier.

County rates and *highway rates* are as between landlord and tenant in a similar position to the poor-rate, and all three of these rates are collected by the same machinery (referred to in the text, *ante.* p. 28). But the highway rates under the Highway Acts which are made by the surveyor of highways and collected after they have been certified by two justices of the peace, are to be distinguished from such rates for the purposes of highways as may be included in the

CHAP. VI.
Sect. 2.
Rights incident to Tenancy by Law and Contract.

District rates.—These are made by local boards of health for any purpose within their district (including the maintenance of highways), for which they are authorised to raise money by the statutes which regulate their proceedings. District rates are likewise charged on the occupier, who, in the absence of agreement has no right to recoup himself by deduction from his rent, except in certain cases provided for in the Acts, as in the case of improvement rates.

In the preparation of an agricultural lease, the most desirable form of stipulation on this subject is that the tenant shall pay "all taxes, rates, assessments, impositions, and outgoings whatsoever, whether parochial, parliamentary or otherwise, which now are, or shall at any time during the said term be taxed, assessed, or imposed upon the demised premises or upon the landlord or tenant in respect thereof, except property-tax and ——," any tax or rate, *e.g.*, land tax, or sewers rate, which it is intended the landlord shall pay. By imposing the whole liability in general terms upon the tenant who is usually intended to bear it, and thus excepting anything that he is not intended to bear, the position of the parties is put before them in a way that neither of them can easily misunderstand.

In the absence of contract, the fact of tenancy does not place the landlord under any liability in respect of repairs; for the law will not imply any promise on his part either to repair the premises, or that they are reasonably fit for habitation or cultivation, or other the purposes for which they are let. If they are burned down, the landlord need not rebuild them. The tenant cannot, unless in certain cases provided for by a statute (14 Geo. 3, c. 78), even compel him to expend

Repairs.
Landlord's liability.

U

CHAP. VI.
Sect. 2.
Rights incident to Tenancy by Law and Contract.

money which he has received from an insurance office in rebuilding, but must go on paying his rent during the rest of the term, though his house and farm buildings be gone. And it makes no difference that the landlord has covenanted for quiet enjoyment, for this covenant only relates to the landlord's title.

Tenants' liability.

On the other hand the law places every tenant under some obligation in this particular. A *tenant from year to year* is not bound to do substantial and lasting, or general repairs, such as new roofing when a roof is worn out. Nor is he liable to make good ordinary wear and tear. But he is said to be liable for fair tenantable repairs. This means that he must do such small acts as may at any time be necessary to keep the property from wasting and deteriorating, for it would be negligence if it were injured through the disregard of ordinary precautions to keep it wind and water tight, as for instance, for want of mending a broken window or door, or replacing a slate upon the roof; and for such negligence he is liable, it being a breach of the duty which the law imposes upon him to use the premises in a tenant-like manner. A *tenant for years*, on the other hand, is bound to execute all necessary general repairs, but this general legal liability is in almost every case rendered unimportant by the express contract to repair, contained in a lease for years.

Covenants to repair.

For the tenant should always, in agricultural leases, expressly covenant to keep the premises in repair. In a lease from year to year the covenant is usually qualified so as to make the tenant's liability in a great measure similar to that which would, without the covenant, be imposed by law. The terms of the covenant or agreement, for instance, may be "to keep the farmhouse, buildings, cottages, and premises with their respective fixtures and appurtenances, except external walls and roofs, and all gates, gate-posts, stiles, rails, and dead fences in good and tenantable repair and condition (ordinary wear and tear, and damage by extraordinary storm or tempest excepted)."

But in a lease for a term of years it is not usual so to qualify the covenant, but to impose a general liability to repair. The tenant is sufficiently protected by the construction with the courts put on such a covenant; for a jury, in deciding whether or not the covenant has been broken, are to regard the general condition of the property at the time he entered; for in the case of an old house he is not bound to give it up in an improved condition, or to avert the natural process of decay, but only to preserve the property in so far as this may be done by a timely expenditure of care and money. In leases of farm houses and buildings for terms of years, therefore, there seems no reason why the covenant required from the tenant should be in any way limited. He should satisfy himself that the property is in good and tenantable repair before he enters; and there is no hardship in requiring him to keep and deliver it up in this condition, in so far as it is reasonably possible by careful labour and expense, which is all the law appears to regard the covenant as implying. Words excepting "ordinary wear and tear," when a long term of years is in question, may only result in complicating and confusing an issue already sufficiently difficult. To simplify it, and make the tenant's obligation more definite and explicit, should always be the object of the landlord or his agent. It is for this purpose that we often find in the general covenant to repair an enumeration of particular objects—*e.g.*, walls, fences, gates, rails, stiles, drains, hedges, weather-boarding, racks, mangers, doors, windows, pumps, thatch slates, tiles, which, although they may be included in the general terms, it is thought useful to call the tenant's attention to. But this must be done in such phraseology as to make it clear that the enumeration is not intended to be a complete list of the things to which the tenant's liability is to extend—a difficulty always to be borne in mind when general language is followed by particular description. The general covenant should also be followed by special covenants to paint outside and inside,

CHAP. VI.
Sect. 2.
Rights incident to Tenancy by Law and Contract.

and to tar, limewash and the like at fixed periods during the term.

It is common in leases such as we are referring to, for the landlord to provide the necessary material, and when he agrees to do so there is no objection to making the tenant's liability conditional on the landlord's performing his part of the agreement.

Damage by fire and tempest.

Under a general covenant by a tenant to repair; or, still more obviously under a covenant to repair, maintain, and uphold (which terms are preferable as being more explicit), he will have to rebuild in case the premises are burned down, or thrown down. The tenant, therefore, usually and fairly claims to have damage by fire and tempest excepted from the operation of his covenant, although as to tempest a pecuniary limit is sometimes fixed for damage. To that amount he is liable, but not beyond it; for instance, it is declared that he shall not be liable to make good damage by fire, or damage by tempest exceeding 40s. It is also important for the tenant to obtain from the landlord a covenant to rebuild and make good in these excepted cases, because, as has been already stated, the latter is under no legal liability to do so. Some landlords, in addition to entering into such a covenant, allow a clause to be inserted, providing that the rent shall not be payable, or shall be reduced, so long as the destruction continues. Tenants, however, frequently sign leases whereby they undertake absolutely to pay rent for buildings for a long term of years, although no one is bound to rebuild them in case they are burnt down.

Insurance.

When the lease contains no stipulation about insurance, it is because the landlord intends to insure himself, and as the tenant has no guarantee that he will do so, it is in these cases that the tenant might find himself in the unfortunate position just alluded to. But where it is agreed that the tenant shall insure, he has less reason to concern himself about the possible destruction of the premises, as he has some security for their being rebuilt. The usual form of a covenant by a tenant to insure, is to insure the premises in a specified office for not less than a fixed amount, either in the name of the lessor or in the joint names of the lessee and lessor, and to keep the same insured during the term, and to produce the policy and the receipt for the premium for the current year when required to do so by the lessor or his agent.

Chap. VI. Sect. 2. Rights incident to Tenancy by Law and Contract.

In leases of farms it is usual for the lessor to desire that no one but the person whom he accepts as a tenant shall occupy that position; and as the law entitles the tenant in the absence of any agreement to the contrary to assign or underlet the premises to another, such an agreement is often made. The wording of the covenant must be carefully looked to; a covenant "not to assign, transfer, or set-over, or otherwise put away the lease or the premises hereby demised or any part thereof," was held not to be broken by an under-lease; therefore under-letting, as well as assigning, must be provided against. A covenant against assignment does not appear to be broken by a bequest of the premises (but this is doubtful), or by the plaintiff's depositing the lease with a banker as a security for a loan if no actual assignment by way of mortgage be made.

Assignment and underletting.

The operation of the bankruptcy laws upon such a covenant involves points which can scarcely be considered here; but as a general rule it is better when the lessor wishes to be protected against the assignment, which would be consequent on bankruptcy, that he should reserve *power to re-enter* in the case of the tenant becoming a bankrupt, or a liquidating or compounding debtor, as well as in case of breach of covenant,—as such a power of re-entry will enable him to avoid any contention with the trustee in bankruptcy or liquidation as to what is or is not an "assignment" within the meaning of the covenant.

CHAP. VI.
Sect. 2.
Rights incident to Tenancy by Law and Contract.
Cultivation.

The tenancy of a farm imposes an obligation on the tenant to farm the land in a husbandlike manner, according to the custom of the country where the same is situate. Therefore, in this, as in many other cases, the insertion of an express covenant by him to do so is only useful for the reason that an express covenant is legally more satisfactory than an implied one. But whether the covenant is express or only implied, it may be said that in the present state of agriculture it is not desirable to rely upon it as binding the tenant to anything except the avoidance of acts of manifestly bad farming. If it is desired to compel him to follow some exact course of cultivation it will certainly be safer not to rely upon the custom of the country, but to express in exact terms what is expected of him.

Consumption of hay, straw, and manure.

The last observation applies also to the tenant's duty in respect to straw, hay, and manure. Good husbandry requires that the dung and manure produced upon the farm be used upon the premises and not taken away or sold; so that it would be a breach of the express or implied covenant to observe the laws of good husbandry if the tenant were to remove or sell any of these things during the term or at its expiration, unless the act were justified by some special custom in the country where the farm is situate. The right at law (in the absence of custom regulating the matter) to remove hay and straw seems to be doubtful. But in a matter of such importance it is clearly best to have the understanding of the parties expressed in the lease, especially as it is now generally desirable for the tenant to have some limited right of selling his hay and straw.

Waste in respect of minerals.

Allusion has been made in a previous chapter to *waste* as between a tenant for life and the owner of the fee or inheritance. But waste is a matter of equal importance as between landlord and tenant, and the rules with regard to it are almost precisely the same. For the law forbids a tenant for years to do any act which will result in a permanent spoiling of the property, whether it be by positive act (in which case it is *voluntary waste*) or by negligence and omission (when it is *permissive waste*). Such acts are a breach of the covenant which is always implied when it is not expressed, to use the premises in a tenant-like manner. Thus it is waste for the tenant to open either mines or pits for gravel, clay, &c., not open at the time of his entry, except in so far as it may be necessary to dig for such materials as chalk and clay for the purposes of application on the holding. But as to pits or mines already open, it is said that he is at liberty to work them, for they constitute a visible part of the annual profit of the holding.

It is to be observed, however, that *waste* can only happen with reference to the thing actually demised. Therefore, where, as is frequently the case, the mines and minerals are excepted out of the demise, the abstraction of them would not be waste (except in so far as the surface might be injured) but an offence of a different nature.

So with regard to timber; the landlord's interest generally requires that all trees and underwood shall be excepted from the demise, and that the tenant shall expressly covenant not to injure them. But if the lease contains no such exception the law against waste will prevent the tenant from cutting down or destroying timber trees or anything that would become timber; but it will not prevent him from cutting hazels, hornbeams, or any bushes or underwood which would never become timber— for bushes are the property of the tenant in the absence of exception or agreement to the contrary. Moreover a tenant bound to repair and find material will not commit waste even by cutting such timber trees as are necessary for the purpose of the repairs. For every tenant has a right to wood for fuel to burn in the house, for the making and repairing all instruments of husbandry and for repairing the house, and the hedges and fences. But this right will of

CHAP. VI.
Sect. 2.
Rights incident to Tenancy by Law and Contract.

In respect of trees and underwood.

CHAP. VI.
Sect. 2.
Rights incident to Tenancy by Law and Contract.

In respect of pasture or other land.

In respect of fences.

Property in fences.

course be defeated by an exception of the nature above referred to.

Another form of waste is by ploughing up meadow or pasture land. This offence is usually provided against by reserving an additional penal rent of so much for every acre in respect of which it is committed. It has been said, in the old books, that changing the course of husbandry is waste; but this principle can only be applicable where the soil is applied to some purpose which will for some time materially affect or prevent the possibility of its use for ordinary agriculture.

In all the above cases the tenant breaking the law will be guilty of voluntary waste. An obvious instance of permissive waste will be the neglect to repair and maintain, in so far as a liability to do so is imposed on the tenant by law, and not by contract—breach of express covenant being an offence of a different nature to that now under consideration. The neglect to maintain fences, whether live or dead is permissive waste, for such maintenance is clearly a part of the general duty of a tenant for years, although the landlord may by the custom of the country be bound to find material. A tenant from year to year is not liable (except to the extent which was indicated in speaking of repairs) for permissive waste, and is therefore not under the same obligation to maintain fences. But fences are usually either the subject of express covenant, or if not expressly named are covered by a general covenant to repair.

Whilst alluding to the subject of fences—including in that term all artificial boundary lines—it may be well to point out the legal position with respect to ditches constituting the external boundary line of the demised property. Where there is a ditch and a bank planted with a hedge, the ditch, in the absence of evidence to the contrary, is a part of the property on which the hedge is situate, and it is therefore the duty of the tenant in occupation of that property to clean and maintain it. That this is so, will be clear if we consider that a man making a ditch must make it on his own property. But in doing so he will cut to the very extremity of his own land; and he must therefore throw the soil dug out not upon his neighbour's side of the ditch, but upon his own, for he has no right to pile the soil upon his neighbour's land. When, on the other hand, the boundary line is not of this double nature, but consists of a hedge, or a ditch, or a wall only, the adjoining owners are to be considered owners in common of the barrier and the soil on which it is situate, unless such ownership is disproved by facts as to origin or user indicating that the proprietorship is of a different kind.

<small>Chap. VI. Sect. 2. *Rights incident to Tenancy by Law and Contract.*</small>

With regard to game, the law gives to the possessor of land a qualified ownership in all the wild animals upon it, such ownership consisting in the right to kill and appropriate them whilst they are upon the land. This ownership will, on a lease of the land, pass to the tenant, unless, as is generally the case, they, or those of them which are called *game*, are excepted out of the property leased. Precisely the same observation applies to the fish in any stream upon the premises. When fish or game are thus excepted it is proper that the exception be accompanied by a reservation of the right of entry to the landlord for the purposes of sporting; and there is frequently added, in the case of game, a covenant by the tenant to use his endeavours to preserve the nests and eggs and young ones of partridges and pheasants.

<small>Game.</small>

The question so frequently discussed in conversation as to what birds and animals are "game" scarcely admits of an answer. The term may be said to signify those wild birds and animals in respect of which the Legislature has created certain special rights and remedies by the statutes classed together as "the Game Laws." But one statute has this operation in respect of one set of creatures, and then another statute is passed affecting a set partly, but not entirely, identical with the former. *Hares, pheasants, partridges, grouse, heath or moor*

CHAP. VI.
Sect. 2.
Rights incident to Tenancy by Law and Contract.

game, and *black game* appear to be the only species which are always and for every purpose to be considered game, whilst *woodcock, snipe, quail, landrail, rabbits* (or conies) are all within the scope of some of the provisions of the game laws. The Game Act (1 & 2 Will. 4, c. 32) defines game in one manner, excluding rabbits; the Act for the Prevention of Poaching (25 & 26 Vict. c. 114) defines it in a totally different manner, including rabbits; whilst an intermediate statute (23 & 24 Vict. c. 90) requires a license to be taken out for killing "any *game* whatever, or any woodcock, snipe, quail, or landrail, or any conies, or any deer." It is clear, therefore, that the term is too loose a one to rely upon for any purpose except as covering the species above stated to be invariably comprised in it. If it is desired to except woodcock, snipe, quail, landrail, rabbits, or wild fowl, they should be specially named in the exception.

Fixtures.

Considering the difficulty which attaches to the subject of *fixtures,* it is to be wondered that differences between landlord and tenant on the subject are not more frequent than they are. The fundamental principle of the law, which it is necessary that the landlord's agent should bear in mind, is, that any article affixed to the soil or to the fabric becomes part of the freehold, and consequently the property of the freeholder. The result of this principle is that what has once been so affixed by the tenant cannot be removed by him either during the lease or after its termination. Articles so affixed to the freehold should, according to this rule, all be called "*landlord's fixtures,*" as belonging to the landlord. But there are important exceptions to the generality of the rule about removal, and articles coming within these exceptions are generally called "*tenant's fixtures—*" a term meaning that the articles are parts of the freehold or fabric which the tenant has a right to remove.

What is a fixture.

But, before considering what these exceptions are, and whether an article is a landlord's or a tenant's fixture, it must be discovered whether the article in question is properly a *fixture* at all. For it may appear to be such, it may, indeed, be an actual erection on the premises, but yet not be in any way fastened to them. If, for instance, it be a barn or a mill set up by the tenant, and merely held by its own weight upon the ground, or upon a foundation of brick or stone, and if it can be removed without injury to the freehold, it never loses its character of being a mere loose chattel, and if the tenant does not take it away during his term he may remove it afterwards. Supposing that the landlord detains it, the tenant may, indeed, recover it by just the same remedy which he would use to recover a horse left behind in the stable. And this same rule will apply to an article, even although slightly fastened to the soil or to the fabric of the house, provided that the object of the fastening is merely to assist in the more convenient use of the thing as a chattel, and that it can be removed without injury to itself or to the freehold. For instance, screwing a stocking frame to the floor to keep it steady will not make it a fixture, and many similar cases might be cited of machinery slightly attached by screws or otherwise, never becoming a part of the freehold, but retaining its chattel character.

Assuming, however, that the article is so annexed as to be a fixture, the question arises whether it comes within the exceptions which we have alluded to, which make it a "tenant's fixture" as opposed to a "landlord's fixture." At an early period the inconvenience of confiscating the property of the tenant the moment it became attached to the soil or the fabric was apparent to the judges, and exceptions were made in favour of tenants putting up fixtures, either for purposes of trade, or for mere ornament and convenience to make a house habitable, such as looking glasses, cupboards, and the like. Whilst these are affixed, they are to be deemed a part of the freehold, and not as mere chattels (and consequently are not distrainable for rent), but they are nevertheless severable by the tenant and can be removed by him *during his term*. But if he allows

CHAP. VI.
Sect. 2.
Rights incident to Tenancy by Law and Contract.

Tenants' fixtures.

ESTATE MANAGEMENT.

Chap. VI. Sect. 2. Rights incident to Tenancy by Law and Contract.

them to remain fixtures till the term has come to an end, his right of removal is gone. He cannot claim to enter and sever them afterwards. Moreover, in ascertaining how far a tenant in any particular case has the right of removal, it is often necessary to refer to the words of the covenant to yield up the premises at the end of the term, for that covenant often provides for the delivery up of things which, but for it, the tenant might claim to remove as tenant's fixtures.

Agricultural fixtures.

But the curious feature of the question is that, although an exception of this kind was made in favour of traders, the exception was not extended to agricultural tenants. The latter, even to the present day, cannot claim the benefit of a similar privilege to sever and remove fixtures. The Legislature has endeavoured to protect them by two Acts of Parliament; but with what slight result will be seen by considering the statutes in question.

Statute 14 & 15 Vict. c. 25, s. 3.

By the statute 14 & 15 Vict. c. 25, s. 3, it is enacted as follows: "If any tenant of a farm or land shall, after the passing of this Act, *with the consent in writing of the landlord* for the time being, at his own cost and expense, erect any farm buildings, either detached or otherwise, or put up any other building, engine or machinery, either for agricultural purposes or for the purposes of trade and agriculture (which shall not have been erected or put up in pursuance of some obligation in that behalf), then all such buildings, engines, and machinery shall be the property of the tenant, and shall be removable by him, notwithstanding the same may consist of separate buildings, or that the same or any part thereof may be built in or permanently fixed to the soil; so as the tenant, making any such removal, do not in anywise injure the land or buildings belonging to the landlord, or otherwise do put the same in like plight and condition, or as good plight and condition, as the same were in before the erection of anything so removed; provided, nevertheless, that no tenant shall, under the provision last aforesaid, be entitled to remove any such matter or thing as aforesaid without first giving to the landlord or his agent one month's previous notice in writing of his intention so to do; and thereupon it shall be lawful for the landlord, or his agent on his authority, to elect to purchase the matters and things so proposed to be removed, or any of them, and the right to remove the same shall thereby cease, and the same shall belong to the landlord; and the value thereof shall be ascertained and determined by two referees, one to be chosen by each party, or by an umpire to be named by such referees, and shall be paid or allowed in account by the landlord, who shall have so elected to purchase the same."

Chap. VI. Sect. 2. Rights incident to Tenancy by Law and Contract.

The privilege here given to tenants depends upon their having obtained their landlord's written consent to the erection of the fixture. The 53rd section of the Agricultural Holdings Act, 1875 (statute 38 & 39 Vict. c. 92) does away with the necessity for this; but as it is customary for the parties to avail themselves of the right given by section 54 of that Act to exclude its operation, farmers cannot be said to have attained at present any large degree of protection. The 53rd section is as follows:

Agricultural Holdings Act, 1875, sects. 53 to 60.

Fixtures.

Where after the commencement of this Act a tenant affixes to his holding any engine, machinery, or other fixture for which he is not under this Act or otherwise entitled to compensation, and which is not so affixed in pursuance of some obligation in that behalf or instead of some fixture belonging to the landlord, then such fixture shall be the property of and be removable by the tenant:

Provided as follows:—
1. Before the removal of any fixture the tenant shall pay all rent owing to him, and shall perform or satisfy all other his obligations to the landlord in respect of the holding:
2. In the removal of any fixture the tenant shall not do any avoidable damage to any building or other part of the holding:
3. Immediately after the removal of any fixture the tenant shall make good all damage occasioned to any building or other part of the holding by the removal:
4. The tenant shall not remove any fixture without giving one month's previous notice in writing to the landlord of the intention of the tenant to remove it:

CHAP. VI.
Sect. 2.
Rights incident to Tenancy by Law and Contract.

5. At any time before the expiration of the notice of removal, the landlord, by notice in writing given by him to the tenant, may elect to purchase any fixture comprised in the notice of removal, and any fixture thus elected to be purchased shall be left by the tenant, and shall become the property of the landlord, who shall pay the tenant the fair value thereof to an incoming tenant of the holding; and any difference as to the value shall be settled by a reference under this Act, as in case of compensation (but without appeal):

But nothing in this section shall apply to a steam engine erected by the tenant if, before erecting it, the tenant has not given to the landlord notice in writing of his intention to do so, or if the landlord, by notice in writing given to the tenant, has objected to the erection thereof.

It will be worth while to cite here the concluding sections of this Act, as they bear as well upon the application of sect. 53 as upon the application of the other sections to be presently referred to.

General Application of Act.

54. Nothing in this Act shall prevent a landlord and tenant, or intending landlord and tenant, from entering into and carrying into effect any such agreement as they think fit, or shall interfere with the operation thereof.

55. A landlord and tenant, whether the landlord is absolute owner of the holding for his own benefit or not, may, in any agreement in writing relating to the holding, adopt by reference any of the provisions of this Act respecting procedure or any other matter, without adopting all the provisions of this Act; and any provision so adopted shall have effect in connexion with the agreement accordingly.

But where, at the time of the making of the agreement, the landlord is not absolute owner of the holding for his own benefit, no charge shall be made on the holding, under this Act, by virtue of the agreement, greater than or different in nature or duration from the charge which might have been made thereon, under this Act, in the absence of the agreement.

56. This Act shall apply to every contract of tenancy beginning after the commencement of this Act, unless, in any case, the landlord and tenant agree in writing, in the contract of tenancy, or otherwise, that this Act, or any part or provision of this Act, shall not apply to the contract; and, in that case, this Act, or the part or provision thereof to which that agreement refers (as the case may be), shall not apply to the contract.

57. In any case of a contract of tenancy from year to year or at will, current at the commencement of this Act, this Act shall not apply to the

contract, if within two months after the commencement of this Act the landlord or the tenant gives notice in writing to the other to the effect that he (the person giving the notice) desires that the existing contract of tenancy between them shall remain unaffected by this Act; but such a notice shall be revocable by writing; and in the absence of any such notice, or on revocation of every such notice, this Act shall apply to the contract.   CHAP. VI. Sect. 2. *Rights incident to Tenancy by Law and Contract.*

In every other case of a contract of tenancy current at the commencement of this Act, this Act shall not apply to the contract.

58. Nothing in this Act shall apply to a holding that is not either wholly agricultural or wholly pastoral, or in part agricultural and as to the residue pastoral, or that is of less extent than two acres.

59. A tenant shall not be entitled to claim compensation under this Act and under any custom of the country or contract in respect of the same work or thing.

60. Except as in this Act expressed, nothing in this Act shall take away, abridge, or prejudicially affect any power, right, or remedy of a landlord, tenant, or other person, vested in or exercisable by him by virtue of any other Act or law, or under any custom of the country, or otherwise, in respect of a contract of tenancy or other contract, or of any improvement, waste, emblements, tillages, away-going crops, fixtures, tax, rate, tithe-rentcharge, rent, or other thing.

SECTION III.

TENANT RIGHT.

By the phrase tenant right is to be understood here a right given by the law, independently of contract, to the tenant, entitling him after the determination of his tenancy to some continuing interest in the holding or some claim against the landlord or the succeeding tenant. It may be said, speaking generally, that tenant right is a thing scarcely known to the English law; the instances to the contrary being of so slight an importance as to prove, rather than contradict, the general rule. These exceptional instances may be summarised as follows: (1) The law gives to tenants in a few rare cases the right to *emblements* (to be defined presently; (2) where a tenant can show that, in the district wherein his holding was situate, it is customary for an outgoing tenant to be allowed right of entry to reap crops,

CHAP. VI.
Sect. 3.
Tenant Right.

&c., or to be compensated by the incoming tenant in respect of particular matters, it will enforce such a custom in his favour; and (3) the Legislation recently gave or purported to give the tenant certain rights by the Agricultural Holdings Act, 1875. The cases in which tenants holding crown or college leases have considered themselves to have a right of renewing their leases, may suggest itself as a further instance of a tenant, independently of contract, having an interest continuing after the end of his term; but these tenants have no power of compelling a renewal (in the absence of an express covenant), and some of them have lately found how little their supposed tenant right was worth. They need not therefore be here considered.

Rights to emblements.

It will be recollected that all growing crops or vegetation constitute at law a part of the soil until severance; and as a consequence of this principle, when the tenant's interest in the soil determines, his right in the growing crops determines with it, except in so far as the law makes some exception from this principle in his favour, by giving him what it calls *emblements*.

Emblements are those crops which are annually produced by the labour of the cultivator; and when a tenant (whether for life or years) has an estate of *uncertain duration* which determines suddenly without fault on his part, he is entitled to take the emblements, or in other words, to reap the crops which his labour has produced. But where the tenancy of a tenant at a rack-rent comes to an end by reason of the death or cessor of the interest of a landlord whose interest was only a life interest, or some other uncertain interest, a recent statute (14 & 15 Vict. c. 25, s. 1) has provided that the tenant, instead of claiming emblements, shall continue to hold the land until the expiration of the current year of his tenancy, paying rent to the succeeding owner. The majority of claims to emblements, as between landlord and tenant, are covered by this Act, for the uncertainty of duration on which the claim depends must generally be an uncertainty in the landlord's interest. A determination of the tenancy resulting from the act of the tenant will never entitle him to emblements. The principle is that a tenant sowing, in the natural expectation that his tenancy will last long enough to enable him to reap, shall not lose his crop if his tenancy suddenly determines through no fault of his own.

CHAP. VI.
Sect. 3.
Tenant Right.

The law of emblements, therefore, leaves the majority of tenants for years, or from year to year, whose interest is not determined through the estate of the lessor coming suddenly and unexpectedly to an end, without any rights at all. It is laid down in the books that a tenant sowing, knowing that he will have no time to reap, must suffer for his own folly—a statement which shows how little trouble has yet been taken to adapt the law to the interests of agriculture. But inasmuch as to leave an outgoing tenant in this position would be fatal to the interests of both landlords and tenants, there have grown up various customs in different districts, whereby the outgoing tenant, after his tenancy is over, either continues in occupation of a part of the farm and reaps his own crops, or receives compensation from the incoming tenant for these crops (generally called "away-going crops"), as well as for various other matters of which the incomer takes the benefit. And such a custom when the outgoer can prove its existence the law will enforce in his favour. When the tenant has a lease, the question of compensation will usually be provided for by its terms; but, notwithstanding the existence of a lease, compensation may be claimed according to the custom, unless the terms of the lease are utterly inconsistent with such a claim. It is not sufficient in pleading a custom to show a uniform practice upon a particular estate, however large that estate may be; but the custom must be proved by reference to the practice of the district generally, and the witnesses must speak to facts, and not to mere matters of opinion. Where the custom entitles the outgoer to compensation for away-going crops, tillages,

Right to compensation according to the custom of the country.

x

CHAP. VI.
Sect. 3.
Tenant Right.

&c., his claim will be primarily against the incoming tenant; but there is an implied contract by the landlord himself to compensate according to the custom if there be no incoming tenant.

The matters in respect of which compensation is generally given are alluded to in the text, the most important being the away-going crops, tillages, and unconsumed straw, hay, and manure. Where instead of the tenant quitting the whole farm at once and claiming compensation, the custom entitles him to partial occupation, it is usually, but not always, upon the terms of his paying the rent and taxes for the part which he continues to occupy.

Rights to compensation under the Agricultural Holdings Act, 1875.

It was in this state of the law upon the subject that the Legislature passed the Agricultural Holdings Act, 1875 (38 & 39 Vict. c. 92). But inasmuch as the 54th and 56th sections of that Act (cited *ante*, p. 301) enable the landlord and tenant to agree that it shall have no operation on the tenancy; and as such persons usually do so agree, supposing of course that they understand how to transact their own business better than Parliament can teach them, the Act is chiefly interesting as evidence of the views which prevailed in 1875 on the subject with which it deals. The clauses with regard to compensation are as follows:—

Compensation.

Tenant's title to compensation.

5. Where, after the commencement of this Act, a tenant executes on his holding an improvement comprised in either of the three classes following:

FIRST CLASS.

Drainage of land.	Making or improving of watercourses, ponds, wells, or reservoirs, or of works for supply of water for agricultural or domestic purposes.
Erection or enlargement of buildings.	
Laying down of permanent pasture.	
Making and planting of osier beds.	Making of fences.
Making of water meadows or works of irrigation.	Planting of hops.
	Planting of orchards.
Making of gardens.	Reclaiming of waste land.
Making or improving of roads or bridges.	Warping of land.

Second Class.

Boning of land with undissolved bones. Chalking of land. Clay-burning.	Claying of land. Liming of land. Marling of land.

*Chap. VI.
Sect. 3.
Tenant Right.*

Third Class.

Application to land of purchased artificial or other purchased manure.	Consumption on the holding by cattle, sheep, or pigs of cake or other feeding stuff not produced on the holding.

he shall be entitled, subject to the provisions of this Act, to obtain, on the determination of the tenancy, compensation in respect of the improvement.

6. An improvement shall not in any case be deemed, for the purposes of this Act, to continue unexhausted beyond the respective times following after the year of tenancy in which the outlay thereon is made: *Time in which improvement exhausted.*

Where the improvement is of the first class, the end of twenty years:

Where it is of the second class, the end of seven years:

Where it is of the third class, the end of two years.

7. The amount of the tenant's compensation in respect of an improvement of the first class shall, subject to the provisions of this Act, be the sum laid out by the tenant on the improvement, with a deduction of a proportionate part thereof for each year while the tenancy endures after the year of tenancy in which the outlay is made and while the improvement continues unexhausted; but so that where the landlord was not, at the time of the consent given to the execution of the improvement, absolute owner of the holding for his own benefit, the amount of the compensation shall not exceed a capital sum fairly representing the addition which the improvement, as far as it continues unexhausted at the determination of the tenancy, then makes to the letting value of the holding. *Amount of tenant's compensation in first class.*

8. The amount of the tenant's compensation in respect of an improvement of the second class shall, subject to the provisions of this Act, be the sum properly laid out by the tenant on the improvement, with a deduction of a proportionate part thereof for each year while the tenancy endures after the year of tenancy in which the outlay is made and while the improvement continues unexhausted. *Amount of tenant's compensation in second class.*

9. The amount of the tenant's compensation in respect of an improvement of the third class shall, subject to the provisions of this Act, be such proportion of the sum properly laid out by the tenant on the *Amount of tenant's compensation in third class.*

CHAP. VI.
Sect. 3.
Tenant Right.

Consent of landlord for first class.

Deduction in first class for want of repair, &c.

Notice to landlord for second class.

Exclusion of compensation in third class after exhausting crop.

Exclusion of compensation for consumption of cake, &c., in certain cases.

Restrictions as to third class.

improvement as fairly represents the value thereof at the determination of the tenancy to an incoming tenant.

10. The tenant shall not be entitled to compensation in respect of an improvement of the first class, unless he has executed it with the previous consent in writing of the landlord.

11. In the ascertainment of the amount of the tenant's compensation in respect of an improvement of the first class, there shall be taken into account, in reduction thereof, any sum reasonably necessary to be expended for the purpose of putting the same into tenantable repair or good condition.

12. The tenant shall not be entitled to compensation in respect of an improvement of the second class, unless not more than forty-two and not less than seven days before beginning to execute it, he has given to the landlord notice in writing of his intention to do so, nor where it is executed after the tenant has given or received notice to quit, unless it is executed with the previous consent in writing of the landlord.

13. The tenant shall not be entitled to compensation in respect of an improvement of the third class, where, after the execution thereof, there has been taken from the portion of the holding on which the same was executed, a crop of corn, potatoes, hay, or seed, or any other exhausting crop.

14. The tenant shall not be entitled to compensation in respect of an improvement of the third class, consisting in the consumption of cake or other feeding stuff, where, under the custom of the country or an agreement, he is entitled to and claims payment from the landlord or incoming tenant in respect of the additional value given by that consumption to the manure left on the holding at the determination of the tenancy.

15. In the ascertainment of the amount of compensation in respect of an improvement of the third class,—

(1.) There shall not be taken into account any larger outlay during the last year of the tenancy than the average amount of the tenant's outlay for like purposes during the three next preceding years of the tenancy, or other less number of years for which the tenancy has endured; and,

(2.) There shall be deducted the value of the manure that would have been produced by the consumption on the holding of any hay, straw, roots, or green crops sold off the holding within the last two years of the tenancy or other less time for which the tenancy has endured, except as far as a proper return of manure to the holding has been made in respect of such produce sold off.

Deductions from compensation for taxes, rent, &c.

16. The amount of the tenant's compensation shall be subject to the following deductions:

(1.) For taxes, rates, and tithe rent-charge due or becoming due in respect of the holding to which the tenant is liable as between him and the landlord: *CHAP. VI. Sect. 3. Tenant Right.*

(2.) For rent due or becoming due in respect of the holding:

(3.) For the landlord's compensation under this Act.

17. In the ascertainment of the amount of the tenant's compensation there shall be taken into account in reduction thereof any benefit which the landlord has given or allowed to the tenant in consideration of the tenant executing the improvement. *Set-off of benefit to tenant.*

18. Where a landlord commits a breach of covenant or other agreement connected with the contract of tenancy, and the tenant claims under this Act compensation in respect of an improvement, then the tenant shall be entitled to obtain, on the determination of the tenancy, compensation in respect of the breach, subject and according to the provisions of this Act. *Tenant's compensation for breach of covenant.*

19. Where a tenant commits or permits waste, or commits a breach of a covenant or other agreement connected with the contract of tenancy, and the tenant claims compensation under this Act in respect of an improvement, then the landlord shall be entitled, by counter-claim, but not otherwise, to obtain, on the determination of the tenancy, compensation in respect of the waste or breach, subject and according to the provisions of this Act. *Landlord's to compensation.*

But nothing in this section shall enable a landlord to obtain under this Act compensation in respect of waste or a breach committed or permitted in relation to a matter of husbandry more than four years before the determination of the tenancy.

The remainder of the Act (other than the part set out on pp. 301-3) is occupied in providing a mode of procedure for estimating the amount of compensation, for charging on the land the amount so payable by the landlord, and in altering the law about notice to quit (making a year's notice necessary to determine a tenancy from year to year, instead of a half year's notice). It also contains some special clauses as to its application to crown and to ecclesiastical and charity lands.

CHAPTER VII.
THE AUTHORITY OF A LAND STEWARD.

CHAP. VII.
The Authority of a Land Steward.

INASMUCH as this book is addressed to land stewards rather than to persons carrying on the business of estate and house agents and engaged in buying and selling property on commission, the only points which will present themselves for discussion in this chapter are the nature of the authority requisite for the performance by the steward of different acts of management, and the nature of his liability as an agent.

Transactions with agents generally.

The authority of an agent assuming to contract an engagement on behalf of a principal is very frequently not proved to or inquired into by the person with whom the contract is made; and as the question whether or not the contract is binding on the principal depends upon the nature of the agent's authority, it may at first sight seem remarkable that such proof or inquiry is so generally omitted. The reason is that the nature of the agent's authority often cannot in practice be decided by asking information of the principal, or by asking the agent for proof. If this were requisite all business which is done through the medium of agents, such as brokers or land agents, or clerks in an office, could not possibly be carried on. Therefore, although the agent may be liable in damages to the principal if he transgresses his instructions, the principal is nevertheless liable to the person with whom his agent makes a contract, if it is made under circumstances which entitle such person to assume that the agent is authorised to make it. If the agent is engaged in a particular occupation or business, and he makes on behalf of the person employing him a contract such as persons engaged in that business are in the habit of making on behalf of their employers, the contract will be binding on the employer or principal, although he may have expressly told the agent not to make it. For the law calls an agent of that kind a *general* agent, and says that it is not necessary for persons dealing with a general agent to ascertain whether his acts are warranted by the precise terms of his instructions.

"The liability of the principal mainly depends, not on the instructions which he may have given to the agent, but on the question whether the agent was a *general* or a *special* agent. Firstly, if a servant or agent be accredited and invested by his master with authority to act for him in all his business of a particular kind; or, secondly, if the agent, being himself engaged in a particular trade or business, be employed by the principal to do certain acts for him in that trade or business, he will in such case be held to be with reference to his employment a *general* agent; and—the public having no means of knowing what, in any particular case within the general scope of the agent's powers, are the wishes and directions of the principal—the latter will be liable, although his orders be violated. In such a case the principal having, for his own convenience, induced the public to consider that his agent was possessed of *general* powers, is bound by the exercise on the agent's part of the authority which he has thus allowed him to assume:" (Chitty on Contracts, p. 200, 8th Ed.)

A *special* agent, on the other hand, is a person whose authority in a particular transaction cannot be assumed to exist either because of his having a general authority to act for the principal in transactions of that kind, or because he is himself engaged in a trade or business, in the exercise of which it is usual for such authority to be given. Persons

CHAP. VII.
The Authority of a Land Steward.

dealing with a special agent are bound to ascertain what authority his principal has actually given him; for the principal or master will not be bound by any act of the agent not warranted by the terms of his instructions.

These principles have been illustrated in this way:—" If a man send his servant with ready money to buy goods, and the servant buy upon credit, the master is not chargeable. But if the servant *usually buy for the master upon tick*, and the servant buy some things without the master's order, yet, if the master were trusted by the trader, he is liable." That is to say (the servant not being by the nature of his employment a general agent to buy goods for his employer), if the master gives him money to go to a shop and buy them, he is a special agent, and can only bind the master by following his instructions, that is, by paying for the goods when he received them; but if the master has been in the habit of employing him to buy goods upon credit, then the shopkeeper is entitled to assume that he has a general authority to buy goods upon credit. The servant has become by the master's conduct a general agent to act for him in business of that kind, and the master is liable without reference to the terms of the orders which he gave to the servant in the particular case.

In what sense a land steward is a general agent.

This being the general principle of the law, it must be applied to the circumstances of each case as it arises; for although it is clear that every land steward acts within certain limits as a general agent, it is difficult to state generally what these limits are. It would seem that, as a land steward's function is primarily one of oversight, an authority to perform definite acts and make contracts is scarcely inherent in the nature of his office. The nature of the authority of a particular steward then, will not be easily found by endeavouring to define the office of a steward, but rather by ascertaining what particular kind of business the proprietor has, by his conduct, shown that the steward is authorised to act in; and this is a matter of evidence rather than of law. This is equivalent to saying that his general agency is of the first, rather than of the second kind referred to by Mr. Chitty.

Nevertheless there are certain acts which have been definitely decided not to be within the scope of a steward's employment as such. He has no authority, as a steward, to enter into agreements to grant leases. And as this is so, he would likewise have no authority to give a notice to quit. Nor has he any power to distrain.

The kind of business in which the steward is frequently authorised by the conduct of his employer to act as a general agent will readily suggest itself. If, for instance, he has been allowed in practice to pledge his employer's credit in making purchases, the latter will be bound to pay for any particular article which the steward may buy for him of a dealer aware of the practice, and giving credit to the employer on the faith of it; even though the steward may have been expressly forbidden to buy the particular article. So, although it cannot be said that it is inherent in the office of a steward that he should have a general authority to hire and dismiss bailiffs and servants; such an authority may no doubt be conferred upon him by his employer's conduct. Even with regard to rents, to receive which the agent will generally have an express and written authority; if he has been accustomed to take them, and sign receipts without such an authority, the courts would certainly regard him as a general agent in the matter, and his receipt would discharge a tenant who had no notice that the rent was not to be paid to him as theretofore. But it may be observed here, that an agent having an authority (whether general or special) to receive payments on behalf of the principal, cannot bind the latter by accepting anything but money—as by taking a bill of exchange—unless there is some direct evidence to show that his authority enabled him to do so, or that it is a customary mode of settling.

In these matters, therefore, in which the steward is not, either by the nature of his office, or by his employer's

CHAP. VII.
The Authority of a Land Steward.

conduct, authorised to act as a general agent, he will require an express authority to enable him to act as a special agent, and persons dealing with him must see that he has it, and abides by the terms of it, for if he does not his principal will not be bound.

Leases.

The express authority need not, as a general rule, be in writing, though in some cases this is requisite. In the case of leases not required by the Statute of Frauds to be in writing (*ante*, p. 279), the proprietor may verbally authorise an agent to make them, and the agent may then make them either verbally, or by a writing signed on behalf of his employer, according to the terms of his valuations. But as to leases required by the first section of that statute to be in writing (*ante*, p. 280), a reference to the section will show that it enacted that where such leases are made by an agent, he must be authorised in writing to make them. These leases are now, however, to be made by deed (*ante*, p. 281), and it is a rule of the law that an agent can only execute a deed on behalf of his principal if he is authorised *by deed* to do so.

Notice to quit.

An agent need not have a written authority in order to give a tenant notice to quit. But his authority, although only oral, must be express at the time when the notice is given, or at latest when it begins to operate. A subsequent recognition or adoption of the agent's act by the principal is not sufficient in this case, although we shall presently see that it is generally so in others.

Distress.

Nor does a steward need a written authority in order to distrain upon his employer's tenant. But as we have said he must be specially authorised to do so. An authority to receive rents, and discharge the tenants by his receipts, will not impower him to distrain.

Sales.

With regard to sales, even when a contract for sale is required to be in writing—as are contracts relating to land or any interest in or concerning it, and contracts in certain cases respecting chattels, the writing may be that of an agent appointed by word of mouth. For sects. 4 and 17 of the Statute of Frauds (*ante*, p. 280, note), which make it necessary that the contract be in writing, say that the writing may be signed by an agent "lawfully authorised," instead of by an agent "lawfully authorised in writing," which are the words of sect. 1.

CHAP. VII.
The Authority of a Land Steward.

With reference to the subject of sales, it may be well here to point out to the agent that, where he is authorised to make them, he must take care that the contract for sale is made binding on the purchasers. If, for instance, it is a sale of land or of an interest in or concerning it, the purchaser or his authorised agent must sign a written memorandum, otherwise, by sect. 4 of the Statute of Frauds, the purchaser will not be bound. If it is a sale of chattels of the value of 10*l*. or upwards, there must (by sect. 17) be part delivery and acceptance, or part payment, or a similar memorandum. In the case of some sales made by a steward, as, for instance, of timber and underwood, it will be difficult for him to know whether what he is selling is an interest in land or a chattel, because, as we have seen in a previous chapter (*ante*, p. 267), things growing upon the land are legally a part of the land until they are severed. But it has been decided that a sale of growing timber, to be felled at once, whether by the purchaser or the vendor, is not a sale of an interest in land requiring a written contract. Yet, regarding it as a sale of chattels, a memorandum signed by the purchaser or his agent will generally be necessary under sect. 17, unless there is part payment at the time the bargain is made. And it may be laid down as a general rule that an agent in all cases of this kind should procure the signature of the purchaser or his agent to the terms of the bargain.

It is scarcely necessary to make any remarks upon the subject of purchases. The question of purchasing goods upon credit has already been incidentally alluded to; and as to purchases of land or any interest therein, it is only necessary to refer again to sect. 4 of the Statute of Frauds (*ante*, p. 280, note), from which it appears that an agent

Purchases.

CHAP. VII.
The Authority of a Land Steward.

to purchase need not be authorised in writing. But when an agent produces a written authority, whether to purchase an estate or to do any other act, the principal will be bound to persons dealing with the agent upon the faith of the written authority, although he may have subsequently varied the terms of his instructions to his agent.

Appointment of sub-agents.

It is a maxim of the law that an agent cannot delegate his authority. Therefore, if a steward be authorised to do any act—as, for example, to make a valuation, he must perform the act himself, and cannot without a further express authority employ a third person or sub-agent to do it for him.

Mode of signature by agent.

When an agent has to execute a deed on behalf of his principal, he will execute it, not in his own name, but in that of the principal—thus "A. B. (seal) by E. F., his attorney"—the agent in this case being called an "attorney" because the instrument appointing him to execute the deed is called "a power of attorney." This instrument, or a copy of it, the party in whose favour the deed is made, will generally require to have handed over to him, as evidence that the execution of the deed was authorised by the principal. But a matter involving a deed will generally be transacted under the supervision of a lawyer; and it is more important to point out to the agent the proper mode of making ordinary written contracts on behalf of his employer. For he must take care that in appending his signature he signs expressly as an agent —thus "(Signed) A. B. by E. F., his agent," or "(Signed) by E. F., on behalf of and as agent for the above-named A. B." If he *signs* in his own name merely, he may make himself personally liable on the contract, although in the body of it he is referred to as acting as agent for somebody else.

Personal liability of agent.

For it is to be recollected that there is nothing to prevent an agent from contracting a private and personal liability on behalf of his principal; and if he does not expressly contract in the name of the principal, it is a question to be decided on the whole terms of the contract whether or not the parties intended that the agent should be personally responsible. And if the agent contracts in his own name he cannot relieve himself from personal liability by showing that the other contracting party knew that he was agent for some one else. If he conceals his principal and contracts as though he himself were the real contracting party, the person with whom he contracts is entitled to sue him on the contract, notwithstanding the subsequent discovery of the fact that he was in reality an agent. But, although he will be subject to the liabilities, he will not have all the rights of a principal in such a case; for the principal, on whose behalf the contract was really made, is at any time entitled to step in and require the contract to be fulfilled to himself personally.

An agent making a contract professedly on behalf of another is considered to promise by implication that he has the authority of that other to make it. If he has no such authority, or if he exceeds or misrepresents the authority which he actually has, the principal will not in a case of special agency, as we have seen, be bound. But the agent will be liable to the person with whom the contract is made for a breach of the implied promise that he has the authority which he represents himself to have.

In the above observations as to the personal liability of the agent, it will be observed that we have only touched upon the question of his liability to third parties. His liability to his employer is a totally different matter, as to which it is sufficient to state that he will be liable in damages for any breach of the instructions given to him.

In conclusion, where the agent performs an act on behalf of his principal which he has no authority for, he should take care to get the principal to ratify it at once. The effect of such a ratification is to place all the parties in precisely the same position as though the necessary authority

Chap. VII.
The Authority of a Land Steward.

had been given in the first instance; and, so far as regards the liability of the principal to third parties, his ratification and adoption of a contract made by his agent on his behalf without authority will be presumed from very slight evidence.

APPENDIX.

TENANT RIGHT

FROM A

LANDLORD'S POINT OF VIEW.

Mr. Bear has laid before us a most clear exposition of his views upon tenant right in his rejoinder to the Duke of Argyll.

The Duke of Argyll's Essay on "The Commercial Principles Applicable to Contracts for the Hire of Land," lays the same subject before us in a landlord's point of view, but it fails to give such a clear and concise exposition as the important case seems to require.

Both pamphlets are excellent in style and argument, and, emanating as they do from such high authorities, cannot fail to carry with them great weight.

It is of course highly important that tenant's capital should be secured to them, otherwise it is impossible for them to extract from the soil as much as the soil is capable of yielding. In a legal point of view this security does not exist. A farmer holding from year to year, with only six months notice to quit, is in a worse position than a man who invests his whole capital in a rotten concern at a high interest, because he not only has a similar risk, but in such times as the present, receives little or no interest. A farmer holding under a lease, is, to a certain extent, in the same position; his capital is secure only whilst his tenure holds good, but in the event of the earlier determination of the lease, through any circumstance over which he may have no control, the capital lying in the soil and which he cannot at once realise is lost to him.

It is, therefore, clear that leases do not confer that security, which, by casual observers, they are supposed to do.

This position of agricultural affairs is not denied by landlords, and they see the necessity of security.

The question is, how is this to be effected? Certainly not by compulsory legislation.

"Commercial principles" only can affect this question. Why then it may be asked, have they not done so already? The answer is they have, and are affecting the question more and more every day.

"Commercial principles" are even now exerting such an influence upon agriculture as to be rapidly bringing about the very object of this proposed legislation. The longer the discussion of the "Landlord and Tenants' Bill" is postponed, the less will it be required.

Until lately "Commercial principles" acted strongly in favour of the landlord. The demand for farms was so great that there was no difficulty in obtaining the rent asked, and no difficulty in avoiding unpleasant discussions upon the subject of compensation or security. Now, however, the position is changed; the same principles have placed the landlord in the unpleasant position of a canvasser; his wares are a drug in the market, and to let his farms he has to reduce ground game, allow free cultivation and sale of produce, and give security for capital, or, failing this, farm his land himself.

If the case is so readily influenced by " Commercial principles," or in other words, by "supply and demand," why desire legislation?

For many years past this influence has been silently doing its work. As a proof we find, in nearly every county, compensation now given for unexhausted improvements induced by consumption of cake and other feeding stuffs, similar, in fact, to Class III. of the Agricultural Holdings Act, 1875.

I would ask, can legislation compel a landlord to compensate a tenant for improvements to which he has refused his sanction? Surely not. And yet, if the permission of the landlord is requisite, does it not at once become "permissive" *in fact*, if "compulsory" *in theory*.

The Agricultural Holdings Act also very justly considers that all improvements are exhaustible, and places a limit of years upon each class. It, however, somewhat contradicts itself when it states further on that, "in improvements of the first class, the compensation is not to exceed a capital sum fairly representing the addition which the improvement at the determination of the tenancy makes to the letting value of the holding."

Looking at compensation from this point of view the effect of improvements may continue for ever.

What, then, is Mr. Bear's general principal? Why this: "The tenant who invests his capital in some act that constitutes an 'improvement' is to receive a sum of money when he quits representing the increment of value of the increased rental value of the farm due to his improvement," or in other words, "a capital value of the increased or improved rental."

Now, it is clear that if this principle is admitted, it will be attended with great difficulties, and bring about an immense amount of litigation.

First of all the "improved rental" has to be proved, and in justice to the landlord it must be based upon "actual fact." It would be obviously unfair to call in parties to arbitrate as to the *supposed* increased value. The landlord would naturally desire a tenant found who would be willing to pay this extra rental. Failing this, is the outgoing tenant to go away empty, or is the landlord to pay for what does not exist?

Or again, supposing the increased rental is obtained, does the landlord benefit by it? Certainly not, he pays the increased rental himself by having invested in the departing tenant a sum of money which, if invested, would bring him in a similar sum.

Or again, if he gives the outgoing tenant a renewed lease at the expiration of his term, he must do so either on the same rental as before, or charge him an increased rental and give him at the same time a capital sum which he may invest to meet it.

Admitting, however, for a moment, the justice of this, will not " supply and demand " still influence this question ? Certainly.

If this improved rental is obtained, how is it to be proved that it has been obtained on account of the improvement? Why not on the demand for farms existing at the time, or some other independent cause?

Drainage will afford a good example upon which to base the different principles.

A man takes a farm which requires draining. The landlord or the tenant must perform this. If the landlord, he will expect interest upon his outlay, either directly or in the shape of improved rental. This at once affords him a home investment as secure as the consols.

If, on the other hand, it is performed by the tenant, he will need security for his outlay. A lease, as already stated, does not fully secure him; therefore he needs one of the following securities:

" A proportionate amount of the outlay in accordance with the unexpired term of his lease, looking upon the operation as exhaustible as far as he is concerned; or, a capital sum representing the improved rental value due to the operation at the time of his quitting the farm."

In the first case, his investment is a safe one, for he knows that the low rental which we assume he pays for the undrained farm enables him to pay an interest on his capital, and the increased crops yield him a return of principal; and the landlord knows that in the event of the lease expiring naturally at maturity, he has nothing to pay, and recovers his farm in an improved state He immediately receives a return in an increased rental. The landlord, therefore, has borrowed money from the tenant, and the tenant has lent the money to the landlord, and has received back his principal and interest through two channels, viz., low rent and increased production. Truly a satisfactory arrangement.

How about the second arrangement? Who reaps the benefit here? To understand this we must consider how capital value is arrived at. Capital value implies a sum of money, which, if invested at 3, 4, or 5, or any other percentage, will yield a sum similar to that in question—*e.g.*: If the increased rental is 10*s.* per acre per annum on a 200-acre farm, we have a sum of 100*l.*, which at 5 per cent gives twenty years purchase, or 2000*l.* The tenant therefore does not only reap the whole benefit of his outlay during his occupation, but receives a large sum of money when he leaves, as a reward for his industry and foresight. But it may be said the landlord reaps the benefit by increased rental; he does nothing of the kind, for he has purchased it in hard cash.

Truly this is "landlord's-wrong" if it is "tenant's-right."

If a "full rent" for the whole term is coupled to an arrangement of this kind, the matter will, of course, bear a different aspect.

There are, however, other "improvements" that might cut the other way. For example: "Laying down of permanent pasture," or "planting of hops." These are improvements only so far as they are regarded so by individuals; unlike drainage, which, if done correctly, is practically an inexhaustible improvement.

One man might deem these two operations improvements, another might not. As a consequence of this an increased rental might not been obtainable, as already noticed. In this case the outgoing tenant would get nothing.

On p. 12 of Mr. Bear's pamphlet, he says, in the case of drainage, that the increment of value is not the capital value of the improvement, but the capital value of the improvement in so far as it is not exhausted. If this is really his standpoint, why not state it in his "principle?"

The Legislature or Mr. Bear may place a limit upon the effect of drainage, but practically there is none. The parties called in to arbitrate, therefore, may fail to recognise this exhaustion, and the Duke of Argyle, and not Mr. Bear, may be found to be correct after all.

The fact is that "compensation" and "security" are not synonymous terms, as I think Mr. Bear would lead us to suppose. "Security" can convey nothing but safety to the capital invested; "compensation" may convey a different meaning—reward or recompense certainly. Under the term "security," "outlay" must be the starting-point; but the term "compensation" may apply to "outlay," or "improved value," or reward for services, so that care is required in selecting the phrases.

Landlords do not object to giving fair security for capital invested, based upon a proportionate amount of "outlay," provided the improvements are carried out with their consent, but they object to the term "compensation" when interpreted as capital value of supposed or real increased rental value.

If the landlord invited the tenant to invest his capital for his own benefit there might be some reason in this; but when the tenant desires himself to invest his capital because he sees his way, or fancies he does, to benefit himself, I fail to see why he should expect more than fair security.

The tenant rents only such portion of the soil as he can carry away through the medium of his crops; he has, therefore, every inducement to put in what he supposes he can recover in a reasonable time.

It is seldom that he will do more than he is obliged to during the last few years of his lease, as long as he can fairly pass muster at the end. Therefore, if fair security is given in the case of less transient improvements, to induce him to keep the land in heart up to the end of the term, it ought to be sufficient.

Mr. Bear's principle might induce the tenant to carry out all kinds of improvements just before he left, because such improvements might tend to induce an improved rental. The landlord would therefore be burdened with a heavy expenditure, in addition to the possibility of having his farm for a while thrown upon his hands.

This opens another question. Suppose a lease or term expires, and the landlord is unable to re-let his farm, how then is the increased rental to be decided? Arbitration cannot do it, without it can point to a new tenant willing to give the required rent.

No! if Mr. Bear's principle is fairly tested by practice it will be found unworkable, without the increased values are assessed by presumption. In real *bonâ fide* practice his clients would be found wanting, and I will go further and say that if such ideas became law the landlord would, on the whole, benefit more than the tenant.

The present crisis in agriculture is not brought about by want of security of tenant's capital. It is fallacious to think so. It is brought about by foreign competition. The increased amount of produce that might arise from giving the tenants legal security for their capital, would not bring about a better state of things. The consumer is only too willing to encourage foreign importations; the quantities cannot be too large for him, whether it be bread or meat; and as long as foreign countries can produce more than their populations require, so long will they pour it into England, and, as a consequence, the more our English farmers produce, the less will be the cost to the consumer.

The only matters that can affect the importation of foreign produce are a re-animation of general trade, with a corresponding rise of freights, and an increased consumption abroad, brought about by increased population, and, finally, bad harvests abroad and good ones at home.

The interests of the landlords and tenants are identical; they cannot be separated without the two suffering; and there is no more reason to legislate now than there was years ago.

Less reason, in fact, as I have already explained, because the common woe is bringing about the desired principle of security.

There is, however, one more view of the matter to take, and that is: if the landlord gives security or compensation to the tenant, has he not a right to expect the same from the tenant in case of depreciation of the value of his land by unjust cropping or neglect? Certainly he has.

The Agricultural Holdings Act gives him this compensation for four years before the determination of the tenancy. A better plan, however, might be for the tenant to assign to his landlord his unrealisable capital—that is: his acts of husbandry and improvements,—pending complete settlement of matters between them.

Freedom of contract is as necessary to one party as to the other. As long as there are dishonest tenants and unjust landlords, so long will legislation be useless, as they will drive their coaches and waggons safely through any Act that may be passed.

When there are no dishonest tenants or unjust landlords, no legislation will be needed.

To summarise, then: The landlord's views are a freedom of contract, a willingness to give liberty to the tenant to cultivate freely and sell what produce he likes; security of his capital, invested with his landlord's consent, except for such ordinary acts as consumption of food and application of manures, in which previous consent is not required. And, as a "set-off" to these concessions, a security against waste, such security to consist of assignment of tillages and other property inseparable from the holding.

I have assumed in the foregoing remarks that Mr. Bear, in laying down his principle, considers no improvement as exhaustible, so long as there is an improved rental.

If, however, he intends to imply exhaustion, and bases the capital value of the improved rental upon the number of years short of exhaustion, then he reduces compensation to a very small limit. He does not, I think, express this, except upon page 12 of his pamphlet, in which he expresses his surprise at the Duke's supposed case of drainage, but for this his principles would be clearly stated.

In conclusion, it may be remarked that absolute owners, or "owners in fee," are free agents. They can invest their capital in buildings or other permanent improvements, and still look upon it as their own; or they may give whatever compensation they please. It is, however, otherwise with life-owners or "tenants for life." If they invest their capital in the same way, they merge it in the freehold, or, in other words, give it to the "remainder-man." They are also unable to give an unlimited amount of compensation.

The advocates, then, of legislation upon the subject of tenant right, say, and not perhaps without some reason,—as there are so many properties held by "tenants for life," the law ought to give such security to the tenant to enable him to invest his capital, where his landlord is unable to do so, to bring about a full production for the public good; or some measures should be taken by the Legislature to modify the law of "settlement."

INDEX.

A.
Accounts, 235
Advice to land stewards, 55
Agreements, supplemental, 19
Agreements to grant leases, 21
Agricultural Holdings Act not to apply, 12, 19, 42
Agricultural Holdings Act, Class II., 44
Agricultural Holdings Act, Class III., 45
Alder, the, 100
Allotments, 173
Arbitration Clause, 12, 19
Arithmetic, rules of, 242
Ash, the, 89, 145
Ash, the mountain, 108

B.
Bailiff, his duties, 170
Barley, after wheat, 37
Bearing-reins, 183
Beech, the, 91, 146, 161
Beer, 173
Birch, the, 99, 146
Blights of wheat and other cereals, 229
Bone, adulteration of dust, 51
Bone, applied to arable land, 51
Bone, compensation for, 50
Bone, effects of dressing with, 50
Bone, object of, 50
Bone, price of, 51
Bone, undissolved, 51
Breaking up of pastures, 8, 16
Brickmakers' tools, 221
Brickmaking, cost of, 223
Bricks, 220

C.
Cake, compensation for, 11, 54
Cake, consumption of, 53
Cake, effect of, 53
Cattle, ear-marking of, 194
Cattle, registration of, 193
Cattle, weight of, 72
Cecidomyia tritici, 230
Cement, Portland, 219
Cement, Roman, 218
Cements, 216, 218
Chalk, 214
Chalking of land, 48
Cherry, the wild, 108
Chestnut, the horse, 94
Chestnut, the Spanish, 95, 144
Circles, rules relating to, 249
Clamp, the, 223
Clay burning, 48
Claying of land, 48
Cleansing ditches, 9
Compensation, for acts of husbandry, 41
Compensation at the expiration of term, 39
Compensation for unexhausted improvements, 42
Compensation for tillages, 11
Concretes, 219
Consumption, hay and straw, 17, 38
Cottages, 201
Cottages, general remarks on, 201
Cottages, sanitary arrangements of, 200
Cultivation, husbandlike, 8, 16
Cultivation, restrictive clauses of, 37
Custom, as it affects purchased foods, 40

D.
Date and parties to lease, 5, 14
Decimals, 242
Deliver up premises, 9, 17
Demise of described farm, 6, 14

Description of farm, 15, 25
Destroy ant-hills, 9
Destroy weeds, 9
Dilapidations, survey of, 70
Duodecimals, 245
Duration of tenancy, 15

E.

Elder, the, 106
Elm, the, 87
Elm, the wych, 88
End of tenancy, to leave hay, straw, &c., at, 17
Enjoyment during term, 10
Entry to view, 7, 9
Equivalent for hay and straw sold, 39
Erection of buildings, 44
Ergot of rye, 234
Exception of game, 6, 15
Exception of timber, &c., 15
Expend dung produced on premises, 9
Experiments, 169, 195

F.

Farm, erection of buildings, 199
Farm, the home, 168
Fences, 148
Fences, dead, 153
Fences, live, 148
Fences, number of plants required, 158
Fences, plants suitable for, 159
Fir, the Scotch, 114
Fir, the silver, 117
Fir, the spruce, 117
Fixing the rent, 2
Fixtures, 71
Flints, 214
Foals, treatment of, 183
Footpaths, 17
Form of lease, 5
Four-course rotation, 27
Fractions, 246
Freestones, 212
Furze, 163

G.

Game, 17, 25
General duties of steward, 2
Geology, utility of knowledge of, 204
Good husbandry, implied by occupation, 38
Granite, 208
Grasses suitable for woods, 165
Grass land, top-dressings of, 195
Greenstone, 209
Gypsum, 215

H.

Habendum, defining the length of term, 6
Harness, repairing of, 183
Harvest, 192
Haulage of material, 16, 34
Hay, 190
Hay, money for sale of, to be used for manure, &c., 8
Hay, to be paid for by valuation, 10, 11
Hay, unconsumed, to be left on farm, 10
Hay, weight of, 71, 72
Hazel, the, 143
Holly, 147, 162
Hops, planting of, 47
Hornbeam, the, 162
Horses, 181
Horses, management of, 182
Horses, treatments of accidents and diseases, 182

I.

Implements of the farm, 193
Inspection of buildings, 34
Insurance, 18, 35

K.

Kilns, draught, 223
Kilns, filling of lime, 217

L.

Labourer, the, 172
Laburnum, the, 109
Landlords and farmers, 1
Larch, the, 109
Leases, date and parties to, 5, 14
Leases, subject matter of, 22
Leases, when deed is not necessary, 13
Liability, lessee's, in respect of repair, 8
Liability not to extend to fire or tempest, 8
Limewash, lessee's covenant to, 7
Lime, 51
Lime, the, 101
Lime, compensation for, 52
Lime, quantity required, 52
Lime, reasons for applying, 52
Lime, superficial application of, 52
Limestones, 211
Limestones, adhesive and absorbent powers of, 212
Limestones, dolomite or magnesian, 212
Limestones, freshwater, 215

Lime, cost of burning, 216
Lime kilns, 216
Lime keeping of, 217
Lime, object of burning, 217
Lime, quick or caustic, 216
London clay, 215

M.

Making terms with tenants, 4
Malm rock, 214
Manure, analysis of farmyard, 187
Manure, farmyard, 185
Manure, treatment of farmyard, 186
Manures, artificial, 54
Maple, the, 108, 146
Marbles, 211
Marbles, Petworth and Purbeck, 213
Marl, testing of, 49
Marling, 49
Material, landlord's covenants as to, 18
Middlemen, 171
Mildew, 231
Minerals; 27
Mortar, 218
Mortar, use of sand in, 217

O.

Oak, the, 83, 146
Oolites, 212
Osier-beds (see also willow), 46

P.

Paint, lessee's covenant to, 7, 16
Permanent pasture, laying down, 45
Pigs, 184
Plane, the, 103
Planting, power of lessor to resume for, 12
Plaster of Paris, 219
Plastic clay, 215
Poachers, lessee's covenant as to, 9
Poultry, 184
Preserve trees and underwood, lessee's covenant to, 9, 17
Puccinia graminis, 231
Pug-mill, 221

R.

Rabbits, lessee to destroy, 11
Rams, breeding of, 178
Rates and taxes, lessee's covenants to pay, 7, 16
Rates and taxes, 28
Rebuild in case of fire, 10
Reddendum or reservation of certain rents, 6
Red gum, 231

Rent, additional, 16
Rent, annual, 15
Rent, fictitious, 3
Rent, lessee's covenants to pay, 7, 16
Rent, non-payment of, 12, 18
Rent, payment of, 28
Rent, penal, 6, 15
Rent, proportionate part of, 7
Repair, landlord's covenant to, 18
Repairs, 34, 198
Repairs, lessee's covenant to perform, 7, 16
Repairs, rules and examples for estimating areas, &c., 225
Repairs, supply of materials for, 11

S.

Sainfoin, 64, 69
Sand, 217
Sand, moulding, 221
Sandstones, 210
Sandstones, testing of, 210
Schedule, the, 13
Secale cornutum, 234
Seeds, 189
Septaria, 215
Sheep, 177
Sheep, selection of, for exhibition, 178
Sheep, lambing of, 179
Sheep, washing and shearing of, 180
Sienite, 209
Slate, 209
Sliding rule, description of, 127
Sloe, the, 109, 147
Smut, 231
Stock, live, 174
Straw, various matters relating to, 8—11
Sycamore, the, 103, 147

T

Tanks, 200
Tarring wood work, 7
Task work, 173
Tertiary formations, 215
Thorn, the common, 159
Threshing by 6th May, 10
Tiles, 224
Tillages, half, 67
Timber, conditions of sale of, 132
Timber, instruments used in measurement, 125
Timber, measurement of, 120
Timber, measurement of sawn, 122
Timber, private sale of, 136
Timber, sale of, 129
Timber, sale of, by auction, 128
Timber, sale of, by tender, 134

Tithe-rent charges, and various matters relating to, 30, 33
Trap rock, 209
Trapezoids, 248
Trees, 25
Triangles, 248

U.

Underwood, 25, 137
Underwood, number of plants required in planting, 142
Underwood, plants suitable for, 143
Underwood, sale of, 138
Underwood, tables of values of, 140
Uredo caries, 231
Uredo rubigo, 231
Uredo segetum, 230

V.

Valuations, 516
   Allowance of rates, 61
   Annual, 173
   Award, 58
   Of clover leys, 64
   Of clover seeds, 64, 68
   Custom of country, 57
   Failure of crops, 61
   Fallows, 63
   Farm yard dung, 65

Valuations:
   Feeding value of hay, 65
      ,,   of roots, 63
      ,,   of straw, 65
   Forms of, 76, 82
   Of growing crops, 62
   Of half tillages, 67
   Lady-day, 66
   Method of procedure, 61
   Michaelmas, 62
   Of preparation for wheat, 63, 68
   Of sainfoin, 64, 69
   Stamp duties, 58
   Of straw and hay, 65
   Of tillage, 59
Valuers, appointment of, 57
Valuer's charges, 59
Valuer's umpire, 59
Vibrio tritici, 229

W.

Walnut, the, 96
Waste-land, reclamation of, 47
Wealden, the, 213
Wheat midge, 230
Wheat, preparation for, by out-going tenant, 17
Willow, the, 104, 146

www.ingramcontent.com/pod-product-compliance
Lightning Source LLC
Chambersburg PA
CBHW030318240426
43673CB00040B/1202